Walking Home

A Woman's Pilgrimage on the Appalachian Trail

KELLY WINTERS

alyson books
los angeles | new york

Although the events described in this book are true, in order to protect the privacy of the people involved, names and identifying characteristics have been changed. The Trail names used in the book are typical, but they are not those of actual hikers encountered by the author. Any resemblance between names and identifying characteristics used in this book and those of actual people—on or off the Trail—is unintentional and purely coincidental.

Manufactured in the United States of America.

This trade paperback original is published by Alyson Publications, P.O. Box 4371, Los Angeles, CA 90078-4371.
Distribution in the United Kingdom by
Turnaround Publisher Services Ltd.,
Unit 3, Olympia Trading Estate, Coburg Road, Wood Green,
London N22 6TZ England.

First edition: September 2001

01 02 03 04 05 a 10 9 8 7 6 5 4 3 2 1

ISBN 1-55583-658-5

Library of Congress Cataloging-in-Publication Data
Winters, Kelly.
Walking home : a woman's pilgrimage on the Appalachian Trail / Kelly Winters.—1st ed.
Includes bibliographical references.
1. Hiking—Appalachian Trail. 2. Backpacking—Appalachian Trail. 3. Winters, Kelly—Journeys—Appalachian Trail. 4. Appalachian Trail—Description and travel. I. Title.
GV199.42.A68 W566 2001
796.51'092—dc21
[B]2001022801

Credits
A portion of this work appeared in "A Woman's Path: Women's Best Spiritual Travel Writing," edited by Lucy McCauley, Amy G. Carlson, and Jennifer Leo, Travelers' Tales Inc., 2000.
Cover design by Matt Sams.
Cover photography by Isabelle Summer.

This book is dedicated to my father, Gerard T. Scanlon, who gave me adventure, joy in living, self-confidence, and a sense of trust and peace in nature. Dad, I could not have done this walk, or learned anything from it, without your teaching.

For Lollie Winans and Julianne Williams: You are not forgotten. We still remember you and hope that someday justice will be done.

And to my beloved partner, Gladys, whose deep soul, warmth, humor, and constant love never cease to amaze me: *Ana bahibik ala toul, habibti*. This book is for you.

Acknowledgments

There's no way I could thank everyone who helped on this journey or with this book; a complete list would probably be as long as the book itself. First of all, many thanks to the administrators and volunteers of the Appalachian Trail Conference, who oversee and maintain the Trail. Without them it would not exist, and none of us could be out there on that crazy journey, walking north with spring.

Many kind strangers helped along the way: townspeople, folks in cars who gave a tired, dirty hiker a ride to town; people who offered food, advice, a place to sleep, or a smile; post office workers who willingly held mail and packages; hostel owners, shopkeepers; and all the other Trail folks, not least everyone who walks the Trail, for an hour or for a season. To all of those people I offer my heartfelt thanks.

To Lisa (BB) Groshong, fellow storyteller and incredible Trail buddy, whose humor, good nature, and entertaining talk got us through a lot of tough uphills and long days, and whose adventurous spirit made the trip what it was: Thanks. A thousand-mile friend is a rare and wonderful thing. Thanks for being there.

Bootah, Noodle, and BB: You might not have known it at the time, but you saved my life that night on Kinsman Mountain. I still owe you.

Michael Schwenk, thanks for suggesting a very special hike. You're a true Trail Angel, and you're directly responsible for more happiness than could ever be measured.

Special thanks to Irene and Drew Zerfas and Liz Davidson for their generosity. Thanks also to Jacqueline (Wanda), John (Traveler), and Hannah (Lion King) Bredar; Helen (Earth Teacher) Smathers; Veronica (Tree), Scott (Mountain), and Ellen (Flower) George; Jet and Mike Lakey; and to Rob (QE) Winters and Troy (Angelfish) Dassler, whose homes were a refuge for this migratory bird. Also, thanks to Pat Moran of EEI for the extra work that helped to pay the way.

Thanks to all the friends and family who wrote letters, sent cookies, and helped along the way.

I had no idea how social the Trail would be until I was on it; I had no idea I was joining a nomadic community. To everyone in that community, especially those who offered advice before the journey or became fellow wanderers during it: Thank you.

Thanks to my wonderful agent, Priscilla Palmer, for being so fast, resourceful, and full of energy and belief in this project. Thanks also to the great people at Alyson, especially my editor, Angela Brown, whose fine-tuning skill, good advice, and enthusiasm about the book is everything a writer could ask for; Dan Cullinane, marketing manager; Matt Sams, art designer; and Tiffany Watson, copy editor. And thanks also to Isabelle and Jane Summer for friendship and photographs.

Those who walk the Trail often come to feel that there's a guiding spirit out there, someone behind all those mysterious coincidences and gifts. Thanks to that spirit: to the birds and animals and plants who taught me more than I could ever put into words; and to the Path itself, the greatest teacher there is.

Beginnings

The wild requires that we learn the terrain, nod to all the plants and animals and birds, ford the streams and cross the ridges, and tell a good story when we get back home.

—Gary Snyder, *The Practice of the Wild*

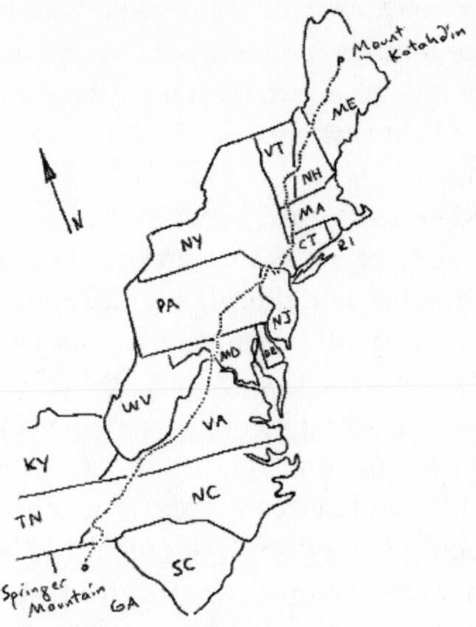

The Appalachian Trail

CHAPTER ONE

As soon as I'm old enough to walk, my father teaches me how to ski. We stand on the hillside, facing the same direction, my short blue plastic skis between his long black ones, his hands under my armpits. I'm carrying a bottle in one hand and a blanket in the other, because I refused to leave them at home. The snow is soft and clean, the air so sharp it tickles the inside of my nose. My mother stands nearby, tightening the straps on her ski poles, next to my brother, who's also learning to ski.

"OK," Dad says. "Ready?"

I nod and we begin moving, surrendering to gravity. My father shows me how we go back and forth down the mountain, long smooth curves across the snowy slope, how we dig in with the edges of our skis and lean from side to side, how we turn. I lean into his hands, feeling safe, testing how far I can lean without falling over. My mother and brother follow us.

He shows me how to do the snowplow to stop, the toes of the skis pointing together, heels out. I trust him, so I trust the mountain. I make my skis do what his do; it's a game. When I fall, I'm so small and light that nothing hurts; the snow is a friend, it just wants to play.

My brother gets a turn between Dad's skis. We all ski until my brother and I get tired, then go into the lodge and sit in front of a fire, drinking hot chocolate and eating hard-boiled eggs, triangular wedges of Laughing Cow cheese, and ham sandwiches we've brought from home. We ski almost every weekend, until we can all ski on our own, moving together down the hillside, waiting for one another to catch up, watching Mom turn to look behind her before she crosses the slope. Years ago on their honeymoon, when Dad taught her how to ski, she fell and broke her leg. Although she was back on the slopes as soon as it healed, she's still more cautious than the rest of us.

Be careful, she says. *Have fun, but be careful.*

I ski, reveling in the smooth speed, the almost-flight my father has taught me, and never look back before crossing the hill.

I'm five years old. I wake up and know something's wrong. The house is filled with a fog of pain, a mist of fear. I jump out of bed and run into my parents' bedroom, where my father is in the bathroom, vomiting uncontrollably all over the pink tile, moaning. My mother hustles me out of the room. An ambulance comes and takes them both away.

My father has cancer. Doctors operate, and the cancer is removed, supposedly forever. But my father is also a doctor, and he knows better than most people what his chances are. He can't count on living until retirement. He has always lived fully; now our life is even fuller.

He teaches my brother and me to fish and hunt, and to run river rapids in a canoe, kayak, or rubber raft. We drive thousands of miles across America to see what we can see. We go camping often, eating fish we've caught, listening to whippoorwills and owls as we fall asleep in our tents. We spend a summer living on a houseboat in a clear lake in northern Minnesota: When you need water for cooking, you dip a pot over the side into the lake; when you want to swim, you jump off the roof. We drive across Kansas in a covered wagon, dressed like pioneers, following the original settlers' still-visible wagon ruts toward the Oregon Territory. On clear nights we watch meteor showers and stars.

During all this time, my father's tests have come back clean. But when I'm 15 the cancer returns, and the next few years are a turmoil of morbid worry and visits to hospitals. My father, like a cat, seems to have nine lives: Too many times he almost dies, only to be resurrected at the last minute and given back to us. It pains me to see the look on my friends' faces when they come over and see him resting in the den. Always thin, now he looks like a skeleton, his face as stark as a skull's. They've never seen anyone so close to death, and they're afraid of him, my father, who wants nothing more than to be free of this, skiing down a slope, paddling on a river, walking in the woods.

He has another surgery and recovers yet again.

When I'm 19 we go to Florida on vacation. He smiles and tries to act as if nothing's wrong, but when he thinks no one notices he goes back to the condo alone and lies on the couch in the dark. He's tired. He's only 53 but walks like an old man.

One day I convince him to come out on the beach and walk in the sunlight, and we spot a seaplane flying over the water, with a person attached to a parachute floating behind it. Parasailing. It looks incredible. I smile, looking up at the sky. What would it be like to do that?

He looks at me, I look at him, and before I know what's happening he's talking to the pilot. They hook up the harnesses and check the lines, and the pilot takes off.

I'm standing on the beach in shallow water, and when the

plane takes off, it lifts me straight out of the water and into the sky. I glance down and see the look on my father's face.

"Go, go, go!" he yells, his head thrown back, arms raised in an athlete's salute.

I laugh uncontrollably. The ocean tilts crazily, and I see little kids running, pointing up at me, dogs jumping at their heels, the long parallel lines of surf moving in slow motion to the shore, a confetti of swimmers' heads and bodies in the water, the sun glittering off resort windows. A gull flies past and tilts its head to look at me with one dark and knowing eye, then flies on. My father waves, points me out to some people, and I know he's saying, "That's my daughter."

I wish my father could feel this: what it's like to fly.

The pilot turns and gives me a thumbs-up, and we bank, circle, and the plane comes down on the water softly, like a gull settling in. I float down and land gently on the beach, exactly where I was standing when we took off.

"Dad! You gotta try it!"

"I don't feel like it today. But don't you want to do it again?"

He insists. I fly again, and again. My father is a speck on the beach, waving, urging me on. Fly higher. Stay up longer. Longer. Come on. Fly.

Just let me see you fly free, once, before I die.

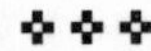

Three months later he's dead. We take a plane back to upstate New York with his body, and I watch as he's buried in the green hillside of his hometown cemetery. This land used to be a ski hill. He learned to ski here, and he probably skied over this exact spot more times than he could count. This is why we chose to have him buried here, instead of in the Catholic cemetery where my grandmother says he belongs. This hillside is the Protestant cemetery, and my grandmother insists that we call in a priest to bless the tiny rectangle of land he lies in. I know it's already blessed; he loved this place.

I miss him with every cell of my body.

He's gone, but what he has taught me—to live fully and live now, to take risks, and to feel completely at home outside in the woods—remains.

This lesson has stuck much better than the one about "Get a job and keep it," probably because my father once told me that no one on his deathbed has ever wished he spent more time at the office.

For most of my 20s I wander around, going from city to city, taking temp jobs because they allow me the freedom I need. Want a vacation? Take one. Want a day off? It's yours. I can type fast and can use every word processor and copy machine ever made, so I can move anywhere and get work the same day. It's low-level, boring, and leads nowhere, but at least it allows more freedom than a regular job, and often I luck into an assignment where, in between bouts of secretarial work, I can write several hours a day. I don't envy my friends with real jobs, despite their benefits—they've been brainwashed into thinking two weeks off a year is generous. Most women I know are on the husband/baby/house track, which is not for me.

What is for me? I'm looking for something, but I don't know what. If I wander enough, maybe I'll run into it.

My personal life is, to say the least, confusing. I don't fit in. I've had women lovers, alternating with men, as if I can't make up my mind. This disturbs me. It makes sense that if you're able to be partners with a man, why put up with all the discrimination you get if people see you with a woman? Give it a try.

I try, but my heart isn't really in it. I go back to women but feel uneasy there too. It all seems so political. The lesbians I know all seem to drink soy milk, save the whales, shave their heads, and have no use for men. This is fine with me, but the fact that I drink milk from cows, eat meat, have long hair, and have a lot of male friends is not fine with them.

I give up on it for the time being, decide to just wait and see.

Maybe I'll meet someone; if not, I'll be happy alone.

Certainty grows in me that there's a "place" I need to get to: not a physical place but an emotional, psychological, spiritual one. And although the place is not physical, somehow the only way to get there is to physically walk—a long, slow, arduous process. A pilgrimage. I don't know what the place is or what I'll find there, but I trust that it exists, that it's reachable, that it's as necessary as blood or breath.

It's 1994. I'm 31 years old. I'm working in a huge bookstore, running the travel books department. I love these books: "road books." They make you feel alive, as if adventure is as close as a wrong turn on the way home from work. Take a new road. Look around. Live fully and see clearly, with the new, wide-open eyes of a stranger. The books remind me of my father. He would love them too.

One day, shelving, I find a book about the Appalachian Trail stuck in between a batch of travel guides to India. A customer has left it here by mistake; it belongs in the sports/outdoor section on the other side of the store. The blurb on the back of the book describes the Trail: "Over 2,000 miles through the mountains from Georgia to Maine."

It's like being struck by lightning. This is the Long Walk I need. I know, in that instant, that it's not a wish or a dream. It's definite, as concrete as my bones, as real as the fact that I have brown hair: I'm going to do that. I look around the store. Nothing has changed. Customers are still browsing; the other workers are calmly shelving or running the cash register. No one knows I've suddenly become enlightened.

I take the book home and start planning. The Trail, I know, will take me where I need to go.

I read every book I can find about the Trail. I learn that it's a continuous footpath, built and still maintained by volunteers, running more than 2,150 miles through the mountains from Springer Mountain in northern Georgia to Mount Katahdin in central Maine. The actual length constantly changes, because each year parts of the Trail are rerouted to make it more scenic, to comply with nearby land disputes and negotiations, or for safety reasons involving factors like mudslides, fires, or floods. Most of it runs through dense forest—hikers call it "the green tunnel"—and most of it is surprisingly difficult. The Pacific Crest Trail, which runs from Mexico to Canada through the Sierras and Cascades, goes over mountains that are almost twice as high, but it's wide, graded for horse travel, and is never steep. The AT, like some old-time religion, heads straight for the top of every mountain, as steeply and narrowly as possible. No compromises. The two ends of the Trail, in the South and in New England, have the steepest and most difficult terrain and are the most remote, so no matter which end you start at, you're faced with extremely harsh terrain and sparse resupply opportunities.

The books say most hikers begin in Georgia, rather than face the hazards of Maine in spring: blackflies, snow, and the 100-Mile Wilderness, a stretch of about 100 miles at the northern end of the Trail in Maine, where there are no resupply stops and almost no roads, and where signs advise you to carry 10 days' worth of food and warn that you're venturing out at your own risk. Carrying the weight of 10 days' worth of food is difficult even for a seasoned hiker; doing this when you've just come from civilized life and are not yet in shape can be torture at best and impossible at worst. In addition, if you begin in Maine you're likely to enter the remote mountains of the South just as hunting season gets underway—not a comforting thought.

I decide to begin the trip in Georgia. I want to walk "north with spring," as Earl Shaffer, the first person to hike the Trail in one continuous journey, said. Mr. Shaffer made his trip in 1948, as a way to refresh his spirit after the disillusionment and soul-sickness he had felt as a soldier in the Pacific during World War II. He was the first "thruhiker"—or "end-to-ender"—and his motive for the journey—a personal transformation and rejuvenation—is shared by most thruhikers. Even for those who don't articulate it and would never admit it, the Trail is a pilgrimage.

I plan to hike next year in 1995. Things intervene. I meet a man. Wade is an artist, in town for a summerlong conference. He's talented, kind, funny, and so wholesome it's hard to believe. He goes to church, respects his parents, gets straight A's in his graduate art program, and is kind to old ladies, dogs, and small children. Everyone, including me, thinks he's wonderful. If I'm ever going to make it with a man, I think, he's the one. We fall in love, we spend the winter visiting back and forth and calling each other every day, and the next spring I spend the money I've saved for the Trail to move to Mississippi, where he's from, to be with him. Maybe I can put aside my confusion and have a normal life. I believe this will work, and for a little while it does.

A few months later, Wade and I are in a tent in the Shenandoahs. We're car camping, since he's afraid to go far into the woods and not strong enough to carry a backpack. I've never been with anyone who knows how to camp or likes the woods. I wonder: Are such people so rare? I've come to put up with this lack, since it seems so prevalent. My childhood of adventure and outdoor competence seems to be one of a kind. Like people I've been involved with in the past, he has consented to come on this trip, as I consent sometimes to go with him to events sponsored by his graduate art program: some guy reading a paper about deconstructionism and postmodernism, a woman discussing the history of the use of shading in soup-label art. Maybe the woods are just as boring to him as those events are to me. Nevertheless, we're here.

We lie in the tent. The wind moves the very tips of the trees, a faint hush. We're at the far end of the campground, in a place just for tents; our car is up at the top of a hill, and we're 50 yards below it. We have the illusion of backpacking, the illusion of privacy. There's one other tent space near us, with a strip of woods in between, but it's empty. I pretend we're somewhere very far away, not near a road at all. It's very dark. An owl calls. Momentarily my longing for wilderness and wildness is stilled, and I'm happy.

A car slides by on the campground road at the top of the hill, slows, then stops. We hear the *chunk!* of doors opening, voices, the sound of people gathering gear, doors closing, feet coming down the trail in the woods.

The people, a man and a woman, go to the tent site near us. They're competent campers; 10 minutes and they're all set up. Their hushed voices float through the thin woods between their tent and ours. They talk about what a long drive it was and where they'll hike tomorrow. Their voices are dreamy, contented. They've each found someone else who loves the woods.

I listen to the owls. Beside me, I can feel Wade is awake, tensed. Without looking at him, I know his eyes are wide open.

I fall asleep. Later I wake up. He's gone. I figure he's out peeing, and I lie half-asleep for a long time, until it dawns on me that something must be wrong; it's been too long.

I go outside. Something moves in the underbrush between our tent site and the other people's. An animal? I spotlight it with my flashlight.

It's Wade, and he's crouching outside their tent, masturbating. He turns an agonized face toward me. Behind him, the people in the tent talk on, peacefully. They're not having sex; they're still making hiking plans. They have a flashlight in there, and I can see the outlines of their bodies humped beneath their sleeping bags like crumpled mountain ranges.

"We could go up Old Rag Mountain," the man says.

"Yeah, but that's pretty far, at the other end of the park. We'd have to drive all the way up to the trailhead and back. How about Dark Hollow Falls? That sounds nice," the woman says.

Wade is unable to stop. His hand keeps moving, repetitively, like a machine. I spotlight his hand, then move up to his face. He turns his face away from my flashlight and hunches one shoulder up, like a celebrity caught in the glare of paparazzi.

I feel like vomiting. I had no idea. I don't know what to do. It's as if he's in the middle of some magic circle, caught in a spell like someone in a fairy tale. I don't understand. I can't talk to him, and he can't stop and talk to me. I snap my flashlight off and walk in the pure dark up the hill. The *whicker* of his hand against the cloth of his pants fades behind me, and so do the peaceful, unwary voices of the people in the tent.

I walk and walk, in the dark. My heart stops beating when a grouse, resting on the path in front of me, thunders up from under my feet. I reel sideways and fall against the hard and comforting bark of a tree. It's like a person, only better, solid and unchanging and trustworthy. If trees could talk, they would never lie: They'd be just who you thought they were.

I'm crowded with confusion and sickness and sadness and anger. My eyes adjust to the dark and I see by starlight. I walk across the campground, past the RVs and other tents and parked cars, find another trail and walk on it for a mile, moving down the mountain, then up another one, finding the trail more with my feet than with my eyes. It's very peaceful here, in the dark.

I wonder if his hand is still moving.

I wonder what's wrong with him.

I wonder what I'll do, where I'll go.

(*You can always leave, and walk on the Trail like you intended*, a little voice whispers, and jubilation flares up in me like a match on a windy night. *But I love him. But I care. Wait and see.* The little jubilant voice fades. The match blows out. I'm back in the relationship, committed to love.)

I go back. He's still in the same spot, his hand still moving. I spotlight him again, cruelly, and watch him cringe.

I go into the tent and lie down.

Whicker whicker whicker.

Finally, he comes in. He collapses on his sleeping bag, weeping.

"I'm a terrible person," he sobs. He's trembling all over; his nose is running and tears are pouring down his face.

"I can't stop it," he weeps. "Something just comes over me and I go...do that...and...I can't *stop*. I have no...control... I'm so...*scared...*"

His voice catches in his throat like a little kid's. His misery is thick enough to touch; it's real. This is something genuinely frightening, something that—he's right—he can't control.

"Does this happen often?" I ask.

He nods, his hands over his face. "I look through windows," he says. "At night. I walk around town. I—you know."

I look into the dark and think. I have little experience with men; for all I know this is normal, although I don't think it is. I have gay friends, straight friends, bisexual friends, friends who dress up and play games with their lovers. I'm accepting; whatever you do is fine as long as you're happy and don't hurt anyone. I feel like I should be accepting of him now, even if he does this, even if he uses nonconsenting strangers. I shouldn't leave him just because he has a problem. God knows I've had enough sexual confusion of my own.

"Look," I say, "everyone has problems. Some are worse than others. If you really hate this, if it really makes you unhappy, you can change it. You'll have to go to therapy. You'll have to work at it. I can't really help. But if you truly want it, I'll stand by you and believe in you, while you talk to someone about it and decide what you want to do."

He starts crying again, then falls asleep, exhausted. I can't fall asleep. I'm loyal, not the kind of person to back out of a commitment once I've made it. I think of his artwork, which is so beautiful: a portrait of a sharecropper, sitting on his porch in the light of a kerosene lantern, his lined face full of care, his hands resting on the head of his sleeping child. A drawing of a white-haired couple holding hands; they've been together so long that they resemble each other. A mountain woman singing, her face radiant, ethereal. His artwork is warm, rich, and loving. It's part of what made me fall in love with him; it's what makes me believe in him. I love him, I'm his friend, and I can't leave him now. He needs me.

We travel deep into Mississippi to visit his parents on their farm. They fascinate me: His family has lived in the same place forever, ever since Wade's ancestors came over in the 18th century.

I make friends with Wade's father, who loves to tell old family stories. Now he has an audience. My own father, whose unspoken motto was "Never look back" and who preferred the present and future to the past, never said much about his family, and my mother's family doesn't have any storytellers either. So I listen avidly to these tales about ancestors and farmers, about people clearing land, about events in the 1850s, all told in a Southern accent so rich and slow that at first I only understand half of what's being said. While I listen, Wade's retarded sister comes up and puts her hand in mine. She's usually shy, but she likes me, and I like her back. Wade's younger brother, who's known for having a temper and "hating everybody," gives me his seal of approval too.

We go to church, and the dressed-up ladies flutter around and fuss over us. "Such a sweet couple! You come on back now. Don't be shy."

Wade's hometown is small, slow, comforting. At night I lie in bed under quilts and listen to train whistles moaning and distant hounds baying, and in the morning, roosters wake me. I wish I could be part of this: belonging to a place, a people, a culture.

I'm in love with his family, with what they represent. Hometowns. Good food. Comfort. Belonging. A normal life.

Wade and I drive home, eating boiled peanuts and drinking locally made ginger ale. We talk about his painting and my writing, about our dedication to it, about the next projects we plan to do. It's nice being with someone else who's creative. It's a bond, and I think it's drawing us together as the summer goes on.

The house is full of fog. Something bad is happening. I can feel it. When the mail comes he grabs it and turns away so I can't see. Nothing there but bills. He relaxes. I ask what he's expecting.

"Nothing," he says.

The phone rings. I pick it up, and the other person hangs up.

We go to his office, and he gets the mail that is left in his box there. One of the letters makes him jump; he shifts it to the bottom of the pile.

"What is it?" I ask.

"Just a letter from an old friend."

He talks about going to therapy, but it stops with talk. His obsession has apparently returned: The crumpled Kleenexes and stiff paper towels in the wastebasket near his computer at home are evidence. I wonder what chat rooms and Web sites he has found. I wonder if he still walks around the neighborhood, looking into windows. I don't ask; everyone's entitled to some privacy, and also maybe I don't want to know. I want to think I'm in love, I want to think it will last. I want to think I respect him, admire him, that we can have a normal life together.

I read books about the Trail and dream my old dreams. Someday. I don't think about what this means: I'll have to leave him if I'm going to walk.

The fog of something wrong, of lies, fills the house. Because the lies are never spoken, they can't be challenged, but I know they're there. I can feel them.

It's a basement apartment, and in the hot Southern summer, with the air conditioner on, the windows are covered with condensation, beads of water sweating down. The apartment smells of mold, mildew, and old paper, since he can never throw anything away. When I moved in, there were cans in the cupboards that were so old that they predated the law that required all food to have printed expiration dates. One can had exploded, and several others were bulging at both ends, probably filled with botulin. We could have killed everyone in Mississippi, maybe even the whole United States, with the food in those cans. I threw them away, but he wouldn't let me touch the piles of paper.

In every corner, spilling across a whole wall of the bedroom, stuffing the storeroom, are sagging boxes full of old receipts, letters, phone bills from 10 years ago, yellow legal pads with eight-year-old phone messages painstakingly transcribed in his knotted, secretive handwriting: *Joe called. Jill called, she misses me. Debbie says she can't wait to see me. Dr. Little says call back, nice job on the presentation. Susan, 555-2947.* Under the couch is a scented letter from a high-school student in a week-long summer enrichment art class he once taught: *Dear Wade, I had such a nice time in your class. Maybe you and me and my friend Kate and her boyfriend, we could all go out to the movies sometime. You are so smart and funny, I really enjoyed your class. Love, Sue.*

Most people would laugh and throw it away, but he saves every mention of his name, every hint that anyone has ever thought of him, no matter how briefly. Especially women.

His habits grow stranger as the summer goes on, as I get to know him. The person he seemed to be—the well-adjusted, well-loved, down-to-earth regular guy who happens to be incredibly talented—is not the person he is. He can't keep up the pretense 24 hours a day. I'm too close, I see him too often. He begins to crack. Like the plants my fifth-grade science class subjected to darkness, cold, too much light, or other stresses, he seems to be growing into a funny shape. He's terrified of knives and fire, so he's afraid to cook or to let me cook, though I do anyway. Once I do cut myself, a surface wound, and by the time I yell "Shit!" and run to the sink, he has fainted. He has phobias of blood and open spaces. He's unable to take showers because the water cascading onto his head makes him feel like he's drowning, so he washes his hair in the tub. He shaves the inside portions of his eyebrows off with an electric shaver because he fears they will grow together over his nose. This gives him a permanently surprised look. For lunch he eats the same thing at the same time at the same restaurant, every day. He is terrified to use any toilet but his own.

Everyone is entitled to a little strangeness, I think, as long as it doesn't hurt anyone. His habits are odd but not pernicious.

But among all this, it's harder to detect the hurtful habits, sort them out from the strange-but-harmless ones.

I ask what's going on. I tell him I sense he's involved with someone else, and I want to know. He denies it, says he loves only me, how could I think such a thing? He is utterly devoted.

The piles of paper grow as the summer wears on. He's working on his thesis, an exhibit of his paintings and a critical study of Southern artists he's learned from. When he finishes it, we'll have a party.

He's a talented artist and speaker, that is true. I admire his talent. His paintings are so beautiful. It's hard to believe that someone who can create such clear portraits of love and faithfulness may be unable to live them in real life. He's gifted, funny, and kind, and he means well. He loves me, as well as he's able to. He's sick, and I can't leave him. Maybe in time I can help him. If he can paint love so clearly, he must have it in him somewhere.

He has told his parents, strict Southern Baptists who are disturbed about us living together, that we will marry.

"I love you," he tells me. I try to picture us married, growing old together like the people in one of his paintings. I try to believe it. I want to believe it. I have to believe it.

He has finished his thesis, and I'm decorating his cubicle at school to celebrate his exhibition. I tie yellow and purple streamers up, tack the balloons to his bulletin board, in between poems someone has copied by hand, flyers from various conferences, and smug cartoons about art. I'm careful to put the tacks through just the edge of the ring you blow through, so the balloons won't pop. I run out of tacks.

I open the top drawer of his desk hoping to find some more, and I do, but on top of them is a stack of letters addressed to Wade, the return address in round, girlish handwriting. The postmarks are recent.

Finally, proof. This is the source of the fog in the house, the unspoken lies, the mail he was waiting for that was sent to his office because sending it to the apartment was too dangerous, the caller who hangs up whenever I answer. This is the thing I've been sensing, which has been denied. The letters make me angry, but they're also like breathing clean air, the air of truth: a cold winter air that burns the lungs but makes you feel more alive.

My hands shake so much I can barely pick up the letters. I drop them on the floor, and the sheaf of letters scatters, making a noise like the whisper of a woman's skirt. In one minute I've gone from confident and jaunty, greeting passersby, telling them I'm decorating the cubicle and inviting them to the exhibit, to being a thief, praying no one will catch me looking in the desk, trying to act nonchalant when more people pass and look at me curiously.

I wonder what I have to hide. After all, *I've* done nothing wrong. I'm not the one cheating, lying, writing and receiving love letters from someone else. I'm up here doing something nice, and then I find this, like a cockroach in the middle of a freshly baked cake. I read.

There are descriptions of sunsets, the moon, the lover's arms. The writer talks about her "little house" and how empty it is without him, of dates they've had, how she longs for him. There's a lengthy passage about a recent cold; you can see her swooning on a chaise lounge, with the back of one pale wrist across her forehead. The copied-out poems on the cubicle wall are from her. She's in a graduate writing program, and she talks about the suffering of poets, how she looks in the mirror and sees her aging face and withering body and thinks of her own mortality. She's 28 years old.

It's clear from the letters that they went to college together, and she has seen his good side: the talented man, the gifted and sensitive artist, the man who paints such love and beauty, the funny man, the man who attends church and loves his parents, the man I met when he was in my town for the summer conference. Since then she's met him for brief romantic trysts behind my back, when he was on his best behavior. She has not seen the nightwalker, the one who looks in strangers' windows, the one who cannot help himself. She loves him, and believes in him; she believes he loves her, that he will marry her.

I stuff the letters back into the desk haphazardly. He'll know someone was in here looking at them, and sweat over it. I won't say anything. I'll let him wonder if I saw, how much I saw, whether I read them, what I'll do. Or he'll wonder if someone else, a student or a professor, was looking for a pen and saw them. I'll let him ride on it for a while. He'll be up in the night, gulping with indigestion, chewing cherry Rolaids, unable to tell me what's bothering him, consumed by guilt. He runs on guilt, like a car runs on gas. Let him run until his motor burns out. I'll turn over in the bed and smile. Sure, I'm evil, but not half as evil as I could be. I think briefly of posting the letters all over the bulletin boards scattered around this floor of offices, so that students and professors will see them. But I don't. I'm trying to keep my dignity.

Some acquaintances pass by and wave. They don't know what I've seen. They're in the world of normal people, where people mean what they say and say what they mean, where people are who they seem to be. They go home to people who don't lie, they sleep soundly at night, they trust.

One day soon after, I'm homesick. The phone rings repeatedly. I pick it up and say hello, and each time there's a short frightened intake of breath, and then she hangs up. There are more crumpled Kleenexes and stiff wads of paper towels than ever in the wastebasket, so many they're spilling out onto the floor, trampled by his jiggling feet as he sits there scanning the screen. He has been checking his E-mail too much lately, three or four or five or more times a day. Today he won't be home until late at night. I have all day, and I know how to hack into his computer and his E-mail. I've asked repeatedly what's going on; I've asked for truth, but he won't give it to me.

The truth is good. It cuts cleanly, like the knives he's so terrified of. I sit at his computer and cut myself repeatedly with the entries in his E-mail. I want to know everything, everything he has ever said or thought or done, so that I know what I'm dealing with.

With obsessive thoroughness, he has recorded every session he has ever had via E-mail and on the Internet. I follow the desperate wandering track of his mind from site to site. I read more E-mails from the woman, and his to her. He tells her everything he has told me, all the I love yous, all the lines stolen from books and old movies. She writes about how she calls him and I answer and it makes her heart sink, about how she's desperate to speak to him and cannot, about how they're star-crossed lovers and it's *so* hard.

I flip over to the Internet entries and see his chat-room conversations with a host of other Peeping Toms, with strangers who share their sexual experiences, who talk about me as if they know me, but I don't know them. He has conveniently marked the most erotic comments, like someone folding down the page of a book where there's a particularly spicy scene. I wonder what he's told these people about me. I feel violated: No one but your lover should know what you're like in bed. Most of these people are apparently married or in committed relationships, and they talk disdainfully about their wives or husbands, about how stupid they are not to know what's going on, how tiresome it is to see their pathetic, loving gaze every day. They talk about how their wife doesn't know they're doing it with the boss, or about how they may have to sign off soon because they can hear the garage door going up and their husband is home. There's an air of nasty thrill to this typed-out chatter, and I come to realize that this is the point: They *like* this betrayal, they get off on it.

I skim around. The web of people on the various porn chat lists seems endless, and I begin to think everyone in the world but me—every married person, everyone who's supposedly faithful, everyone who looks so honest and committed and normal—signs in here and writes about what they'd like to do to the baby-sitter, or what they saw through their neighbor's window and what kind of high-powered binoculars work best, or what they did without telling their wife, who knows nothing, or what they would do if they were only in the same room with each other. Like the letters from the girlfriend, I don't have to read much to get the idea.

I buy hiking boots and maps of every inch of the Trail. I call U-Haul. Wade begs me to stay. He weeps and moans. He tells me he's confused, he needs me, he loves me.

It's one thing to support a friend who's sick or has a problem and is working on it, but another to stay with someone who has no intention of changing. I've been here long enough already, nine months, long enough to have a baby. I don't want to have a baby, but maybe I've given birth to something else: my journey. What a fool I was to get sidetracked so easily, to confuse art with life.

It's December; I plan to start walking in April. I need a place to go in the meantime, and I can't spend a lot of money on it: Any money I make between now and April must be saved for the Trail hike. Two thousand dollars is the minimum. People who have completed the trek say the cost averages out to about a dollar a mile, mostly for food. I need to earn it fast—I only have four months to go, and I have no money now.

I spend all day on the phone, calling friends for advice, running up Wade's phone bill. When I moved here he said I didn't need to worry about the phone bill—he would pay it all each month, because I had spent my money moving to be with him, had a low-paying job, and hadn't yet built up a reserve. Trusting, I didn't realize at the time that this was not a favor, but simply a way for him to hide his long-distance calls from me. For nine months, grateful for this supposed kindness, not wanting to abuse it and run up the bill, I've kept my calls short or haven't called friends at all.

I call them now. I call in sick to work and pack, and spend all day on the phone. I call friends in faraway places early in the morning, tell them what's going on, and ask them to leave their phone off the hook all day. I leave the line open, running up Wade's bill, until they come home from work at night and we talk some more. By the time Wade gets the bill, I'll be gone. Sometimes, in between packing boxes, I pick up the receiver and listen to the daytime hum of my friends' faraway houses: peace, tranquillity, a refrigerator running, a distant bird flying past their window, calling.

I cry. My friends listen. "Get the hell out of there," they say.

My friend Wanda and her husband John offer me shelter: an apartment in D.C., rent-free. It's in the basement of their house, all fixed up, with its own bathroom and separate entrance. "Come here," Wanda says. "You can stay here a few months, make a bunch of money working in D.C., and then walk the Trail."

The U-Haul is parked outside, an orange trailer attached to my tiny blue car. It's night, the night before I'm due to leave. I can't sleep. I want to be gone. Wade snores; he's the kind of guy who escapes ugly situations by sleeping. He sleeps a lot.

I go into the bedroom and watch him sleep. His mouth is open, and a thin crust of saliva edges his lips. The stubble between his eyebrows is showing. I put my hands on his shoulders, one on each side, and press him down. My grip is so strong and my hatred so fierce that I think I could kill him.

I push him against the mattress; if it were a stone wall, he'd crack his skull on it. His eyes fly open, wide with surprise and fear. "What?" he says. He shrinks back. He's afraid of me. *Good,* I think.

"Get up," I say. "We're packing now."

"I thought you wanted to do it in the morning."

"Now!" There's a photo of us in a frame on the dresser next to the end of the bed. I throw it against the wall over his head. Splinters of glass shower down.

He gets up, and we pack the trailer. Each time I go in or out, I let the screen door slam.

"The neighbors—" he says. Ever the Southerner, he's

embarrassed suddenly, afraid they'll see me making a scene. These are the same neighbors he's spent hours watching, hiding behind the drawn shade in the darkened bathroom and peering out at them when they kiss on their porch, wishing he could see through their curtains when they go inside. Now he suddenly cares about their opinion.

"—can go to hell," I finish. Slam! The dog next door starts barking, and I see the neighbors peering out through a crack in their curtains at us, a nice change. I walk past Wade with a box of books and up the gravel driveway to the U-Haul.

I step in something soft on the curb as I load the box. Dog shit. I'm wearing my new hiking boots, and when I go back inside I grind my feet into the carpet, twisting and stomping with every step. *Here's your shit!* I think. *Right here at home where you can't avoid it!* It seems symbolic, and cruelly beautiful. The house fills with the smell of shit, and I wonder if he'll ever clean it.

We get everything packed. I slam the door of the trailer and get into the car. It's almost morning; the sky is slightly light, I can no longer see the stars.

He stands outside the car, looking in, crying.

I cry too.

"I love you," he says.

"I love you too," I say. I'm exhausted. A faint whiff of dog shit rises from my boots. I'm sick of the whole thing, the anger, the violence, the stupidity and pettiness. Where did everything go so wrong? Why was I so gullible? I wipe my nose, put the car in gear, and drive. His tiny figure gets smaller behind me as I drive away, then disappears as I turn the corner and head north, toward D.C.

Thank God for friends. The little apartment is a sanctuary. Warm, wood-paneled, it feels like a cabin in the woods. The house itself is in a part of D.C. where the people are so wealthy they even have yards. My friend tells me of a place that's hiring. They need proofreaders.

I've never done this before, at least not as an official job, although for years I've done it for writer friends for free. I make up a fake résumé, say I've been doing it for years, take a test, and get the job. It's a pleasure and a relief: ferreting out inaccuracies, everything neat and tight and smooth by the time I'm done, everything so sane and logical.

I still need more money. I get a second job in the sub-sub-basement of the Smithsonian, answering phone calls. The darkness gets to me. Being chained to the desk, a slave of the phone, gets to me. For sanity breaks, I tell my coworkers I have to pee and then run up three flights of stairs, out onto the snowy Mall, and run as fast and as far as possible for a minute—brief views of the Capitol, the Washington Monument, and the Air and Space Museum—then go back down into the dungeon. At the end of the day I take the train across the Potomac to Virginia and proofread. The sun? What's that? I never see it. Sleep? Who needs it.

I get up at 5 A.M. in the winter dark before work to train for the hike. I run five miles down Connecticut Avenue, then take the subway the rest of the way to the job. I'd run farther, but the neighborhoods I'd have to go through scare me. At lunchtime I run some more on the Mall, dodging tourists and people selling souvenirs.

On weekends I load up my big pack with D.C. phone books and bricks and hike through Rock Creek Park in the northern part of the city. With the pack on, I go into the subway station and climb up the down escalators and down the up ones until I'm exhausted. People shy away from eye contact with me. They probably think I'm homeless and will ask them for money.

Another friend, Elizabeth, who's done long-distance hikes and lives just outside D.C., keeps me company. A blizzard shuts down the city, and we snowshoe for hours through the drifts around the National Institutes of Health. We winter camp in the backcountry of Shenandoah National Park and hike all day with our packs fully loaded. These weekends, exhausting and exhilarating, in the company of a real and trustworthy friend, seem more important than food. Emotionally I still feel raw, vulnerable, as if all my skin has been removed.

At my jobs, coworkers ask about the trip. They ask if I'm going alone. If I'm taking a gun, a cellular phone to call the police, a laptop so I can tap into the Internet or send E-mail to friends.

I say I'm going alone. I'm not taking any of these things.

They look outside, at the D.C. streets. The city is bad enough, but no way would they even walk a mile in the woods alone. There's a madman who lives in the woods, with an ax, they say, and he's waiting to kill you.

At 11 at night I come home. The nearest subway stop is a mile from the house where I'm staying.

The road is usually deserted, lined with tall bushes and vast pools of darkness that in daytime are the playing fields of two schools. Every night I run this mile, jogging down the well-lit yellow line in the middle of the road, turning aside only for the occasional car, glancing warily into the bushes and the dark, crossing the street when a lone pedestrian ahead of me seems to be walking erratically. People have been attacked here; Wanda and her husband casually warn me to stay on the side of the street where cars are not allowed to park, because muggers like to hide on the other side behind the cars.

If I can survive a winter of this without getting mugged, raped, or killed, I think, *I can surely walk 2,000 miles in the woods.*

Fear is reasonable and useful, but I don't want to let it restrict me. My father's death from cancer has taught me that danger is everywhere, not just in the streets or in the woods: That feeling of security you may have, sitting at home in a comfortable chair behind locked doors and windows, is probably false. You could be dying from the inside out and never know it.

I don't want to go with anyone else. I don't want to take a gun. I don't want to take a laptop or a cell phone. I don't like what they represent. Carrying a gun is carrying fear. Carrying a phone is the same, and also seems silly. If you can't let go of civilization long enough to get off the phone, maybe you shouldn't be in the woods. Carrying a computer is too cumbersome; a paper notebook is lighter, requires no power, and allows you to tear off sheets and mail them home to lessen your load. And I've seen enough of the Internet and E-mail recently to last for a very long time.

I want to relearn trust, in other people, in the world, in myself. I'll go without weapons. I'll travel as lightly as possible. I'll go alone.

A week before beginning the Trail, I drive 1,000 miles in one day, from Washington, D.C., to my mother's house in Wisconsin, to leave my things in storage with her. In this obsessive, single-minded drive, hemmed in by rain and seemingly pursued by the U-Haul trailer full of stuff (*Who is that bastard tailgating me? Oh, it's me.*), I hardly see the land I'm traveling through, except for occasional startling glimpses of things like a hawk diving on a mouse in the median, or odd bits of Americana like the "Dutch-American-Owned Howard Hughes Motel" somewhere in Indiana. On this drive, encased in steel, plastic, glass, and speed, I'm disconnected from the natural world. In a week I'll begin walking more than twice as far, encased in nothing, out there in the wind and rain, sleeping outside, at the mercy of the mountains and any strangers I might meet. It's a daunting prospect. How much more awake will I be? How much more will I see, feel, do, be?

I load up my pack with simple gear and some food—enough candy bars, noodle suppers, and oatmeal to get me to the first resupply stop—then tie my sleeping bag and thin foam sleeping mat to the outside. I have a hiking stick, a bamboo staff I got when I was with Wade, which I cut in the yard of one of his friends. It's a good stick, but symbolic of my old life, of all the things I want to change. I plan to carry it all the way up the Trail, then toss it off the top of Mount Katahdin in Maine.

I put my boots on, hoist my pack, say goodbye to my mom, and get on the train, headed to Georgia and the Trail.

Heading Out

Pilgrims are persons in motion—passing through territories not their own—seeking something we might call completion, or perhaps the word clarity will do as well, a goal to which only the spirit's compass points the way.

—Richard R. Niebuhr, "Pilgrims and Pioneers"

April 8
Springer Mountain, Ga.

Chapter Two

In early April, my friend Heather, a schoolteacher in a nearby small town, drives me along Georgia back roads, past places with names like Nimblewill Gap, Big Stair Gap, and Winding Stair Gap, to a wide spot in a rough dirt road on the side of Springer Mountain. The Trail crosses the road here, and it's my first sight of the white blazes—2-by-6-inch white paint marks on trees—that mark the Trail and will lead me to Maine. My heart beats faster. We're a mile from the starting point. Without Heather's help, I would have had to hike here on an eight-mile approach trail, so steep that some hikers quit the trip before ever setting foot on the actual AT.

Other friends have come too—Heather's friends, now mine, who want to be part of the journey and who will walk the first mile with me. One is a teacher at Heather's school and another is her niece, Garnet, who's my age and tells me of her recent spiritual awakening as we drive. *Everyone's on a pilgrimage*, I think, watching a squirrel run along a branch. *Everyone's moving, looking for something, even if they don't know it.*

Another of Heather's friends, Joe, is a Sioux teacher. "This is what we call a vision quest," he says. "You're doing a holy thing. If you don't mind, I'd like to do a little ceremony for you before you start."

He's brought sage and a bundle of feathers, and we stand in a circle holding hands while Joe lights the sage, smudges us with the smoke, and chants prayers, blessing the journey. I'm deeply touched by his willingness to give, by his good wishes and those of all these other people who don't even know me. I pray, standing there, that I'll be worthy of their kindness.

Joe gives me another bundle of sage, and the feathers, to carry with me, as well as a necklace he has made. "Burn a little of the sage every morning," he says. "It's also a great tea for respiratory illnesses, if you get a cold."

We hike uphill, south, toward the starting point on the summit of Springer Mountain. It's cold, deep gray clouds hanging low, drizzling slightly. As we reach the top of the mountain, the rain briefly turns to snow, then back to rain.

At the summit, a rock slab decorated with a bronze plaque that shows a hiker setting out and the words APPALACHIAN TRAIL: A FOOTPATH FOR THOSE WHO SEEK FELLOWSHIP WITH THE WILDERNESS marks the beginning of the Trail. Next to it is a white blaze.

The Trail register, a notebook encased in a tattered plastic bag, sits inside a metal mailbox set into the rock. I sign in with my Trail name, Amazin' Grace, and note that I will be traveling the whole distance, from Georgia to Maine.

No one else has signed in today, though many have come and gone in the past few days.

I touch the plaque with the hiker, and the very first blaze. In my pocket is a scrap from a shirt I made for Wade before things went bad. Inside the shirt, beneath the pocket where no one but Wade would ever know it was there, I had embroidered our initials, intertwined inside a heart.

I ask everyone to give me a little time alone. They step back, and I walk a few paces away, kneel, and dig up the half-frozen, rocky ground with my bare hands. The wind whips at my cheap red poncho; wet hair sticks to my face. I can't tell the difference between the rain and my tears.

I bury the embroidered piece of cloth face down, put a stone over it, and pray. "Let only goodness come from this change, from this trip," I say. "Help me to forgive. Let me walk on. Let him walk on too."

I stand up, scuff leaves over the place with my foot, and begin walking north, toward Maine, without looking back. It's gone. I could never find it again, even if I tried.

My new friends walk with me for a mile, until we reach their car. We stand next to it, making small talk a lot longer than we need to, until the conversation fades. Around us, the woods are filled with the hushed tapping of the rain.

The Trail winds down the mountain, into the fog. I adjust my poncho, hug everyone one last time, and walk into the woods, my home for the next six months.

In the rain, everything looks polished, the burnished copper of last year's leaves mingled with mica sparkling in wet stones. The air smells wet and clean, of earth and rocks and water. I smile and wonder whether my father, wherever he is, is watching.

I'm here, I'm really here, I'm finally doing it. On my way.

I've heard that some hikers pick up a stone on Springer and carry it all the way to Maine, where they leave it on Mount Katahdin. I pick up a nondescript quartz pebble and put it in my pocket.

At Stover Creek, virgin hemlocks tower over a dense maze of green rhododendron thickets. In contrast to the wintry mountainsides, everything near the creek is green, hushed by the rain, filled with the sound of running water. I can't believe I'm finally here, after two years of dreaming and planning this trip, after so many wrong turns. I touch a blaze on a tree to remind myself it's real. The cold rain feels like a blessing.

I'm headed for Hawk Mountain Shelter, seven-and-a-half miles from the summit of Springer. There are shelters all along the Trail, generally rough three-sided lean-tos just big enough for six to eight hikers to sleep side by side. They're open to the wind and weather but are better than no shelter at all, and most are conveniently located at springs or other water sources.

Because I'm traveling alone, I've decided to stay at shelters whenever possible for two reasons: Hikers tend to cluster there at night, so even if I'm alone all day I might have companionship at night; and tents are heavy. I have an 8-by-10-foot nylon tarp, which I can use for emergency shelter if necessary.

It rains all day, making travel difficult. The footpath is muddy and slick, and the trail is steep. I pull out my map. The profile of the Trail in Georgia looks like the back of a stegosaurus: You walk up a steep mountain, take two paces across the sharp summit, and walk down an equally steep slope.

The woods are deeply quiet, all the animals and birds lying low, all the views shrouded by clouds. I stop twice, once to get water at a waterfall, another time to eat a snack, and rest often on fallen logs. Even though I've spent the winter running, there's no way you can prepare your body to carry 50 pounds all day up and down steep mountains.

By the time I reach Hawk Mountain, it's nearly dark.

Several hikers are already at the shelter, and they turn and smile as I walk up and take off my pack.

"You thruhiking?" a lean, gray-haired woman asks.

"Yes. Are you?"

"I sure am. I'm gonna go all the way to Maine. All of us are thruhikers, except Hal over there."

Hal is a middle-aged man with a strange gleam in his eye. The others have already laid out their sleeping bags in the shelter, but apparently no one wants to sleep next to Hal. I duck under a pair of muddy boots and a cluster of food bags hanging from the rafters and take a space next to the gray-haired woman's bag.

"I'm Aunt Bee," she says. "Welcome to the Trail."

"I'm Jenny," says another woman, who's about my age. She's

hanging up wet clothes. The shelter is festooned with them; she has about six separate outfits, and they're all wet.

"Every time I got wet I stopped and changed," Jenny says. "By the time I got here, I'd gone through everything."

The other hikers, all men, introduce themselves: Jesse, Speedbump, Tom, Army Jack, and GI Joe. Aunt Bee, who's retired, used to be a guard at a women's prison in Arkansas. Jenny is an accountant from Texas. GI Joe is a retired Army colonel, like his buddy, Army Jack. The others are in their 20s and have either just finished school or, like me, have bummed around through a series of low-paying jobs.

Hal has crawled forward and is looking me over. "Well, little girl, you look too small to be carrying such a big pack such a long way!"

Aunt Bee shoots him a poisonous glance. "Hal here likes to hike in the nude. We've heard *all* about it."

"That's right—I like to enjoy nature as nature intended me to be. 'Course, it's too cold right now." He chuckles. "Have you ever thought of doing that?"

I get out my water bottles and filter. "Where's the spring?"

"Behind the shelter," Aunt Bee says. "I'll show you."

"I'll come too," says Jenny.

"I'm ready for this trip," Aunt Bee confides, as we fuss with our filters and bottles. "I've got lipstick, I've got condoms. If you need them, you let me know."

The water is so cold it makes my teeth hurt. I splash some on my face and gasp. One thing I've vowed about this trip: no relationships. I need time off, to think and heal. That's another reason I want to hike alone: Even having a hiking buddy who's just a friend will distract me from my purpose. I won't be needing Aunt Bee's equipment, although it's nice of her to offer. "Don't tell Hal you have that stuff," I say. "He'll be all over you."

"He's not a thruhiker, thank God. He's just hiking a little section from Springer to Neels Gap. He says he's hiked naked all over the country."

"Let's hear it for freezing rain."

"You said it."

When we get back to the shelter I get out my stove, which burns wood, and scrounge around for dry twigs and chunks of bark. The shelter is raised about a foot off the ground, and underneath it's relatively dry. I poke around and come up with a handful of damp sticks. Hal the Nudist watches with too much interest.

"You need help there, little lady?"

"No, thanks."

"That wood's wet. You'll have to use some of my fire starter."

"Thanks anyway, but I don't need it."

"I don't know how you think you can start a fire with that wet wood. Have you been camping before?"

"Many times."

"You hiking alone?"

"Yes."

"Don't you want some company?"

"No, thanks."

The wood is wet, and difficult to start, but I'm not about to let him see me struggling to light it.

Jenny rummages in her pack for yet another set of clothes, and Hal turns to watch, evidently hoping she'll change where he can see her. While he's not looking I slip a chunk of my own fire starter into the stove. The fire blazes up. Hal swings back around, startled.

"My! You *are* a real little camper, aren't you?"

"Yep."

As I cook macaroni and cheese and make instant chocolate pudding, Tom comes over and sits on a rock next to me. He's limping and looks exhausted.

"What made you decide to thruhike?" I ask him.

"I don't even know. I'm not sure I should be. I'm thinking of bailing out at Suches. I saw a thing about the Trail on TV last year and thought it looked cool, but I had no idea it would be like this."

Suches is a tiny hamlet 20 miles down the Trail. It got its name when the residents were trying to decide what to call it and someone said, "It's small, but it's our town, such as it is."

Tom pulls off his boots. Both socks are soaked with blood. "My feet look like raw hamburger from blisters. My pack is killing me. I thought it would be, like, you know, a *walk* in the *woods*. They didn't say how fucking steep it was. I've been soaking wet and freezing all day. My stove doesn't work right, I miss my girlfriend, my knees hurt, and I have the runs. And to tell you the truth, it freaks me out to be alone out here."

He looks moodily out at the trees. "I saw some big animal today. I don't know what it was, but I think it was a bear."

"They usually don't bother people."

"Yeah, *usually*. How far is it to Suches? I hope I can make it there."

"You could go back to Springer and hitch out to Gainesville."

"Then I'd have to walk down that damn approach trail. I swore when I was walking up it that I'd never do it again."

"Do you need some blister stuff? I have some in my pack."

"Thanks, yeah."

Inside the shelter, Jenny is sitting at the center of a pile of gear. "This weighs too much," she says. "I have to get rid of something."

In the back corner of the shelter is a neat stack of things people have already divested themselves of: an ax, two full fuel bottles, a pyramid of cans of pork and beans, an iron skillet, a pound of spaghetti in a zip-lock bag, and a very heavy rubber and plastic poncho. If someone wanted to, they could tour all the shelters at the beginning of the Trail and collect quite a pile of free, though heavy, gear.

We get into our sleeping bags. No one talks for long. We're all too tired. I write in my journal until it's too dark to see, until I'm writing by feel rather than sight and the lines of print tangle on the page.

A mouse squeaks and scratches in the corner, but no one else seems to hear it. An owl hoots, and the mouse is still. I'm really here, really on the Appalachian Trail. *I'm doing it.* On my way. Walking to Maine.

The next day it's even colder. The mountains roar as wind pours through the leafless trees. I huddle in my sleeping bag, shivering. Icy mist swirls between our food bags and partly frozen rain gear. I get up, take a deep breath as if I'm diving into cold water, then, after a quick glance at Hal (he's awake) go behind the shelter and stand in the windy woods and change into yesterday's still wet hiking clothes. Fortunately, I last night put them between my sleeping bag and mat, where they've stayed cold and wet but at least are unfrozen.

I visit the privy and discover that like the shelter, it only has three walls. It has an expansive view, and so will anyone else if they walk past while I'm in it. Fortunately, no one does.

I scrounge some more wood, filter some water, shiver as I eat a quick breakfast of oatmeal and candy bars, and start hiking. As soon as I put on my pack and start up the first mountain, I have to stop to peel off a few layers of clothes. I feel great—not tired, not sore, still thrilled to be here.

The mountains are steep and difficult, and I stop to rest on nearly every fallen tree or rock, looking out at the vast views of mountains rolling away to the horizon. When the trees leaf out, all these views will be gone, hidden behind the green curtain.

The top of Justus Mountain is a jackstraw heap of immense blowdowns and leaning, creaking, talking trees, the result of a hurricane last year. I wonder what it sounded like when all those giant trees were torn up by the roots and snapped in half, whether any hikers were here that day, and if so, where they went for shelter from the storm.

Trail maintainers have cut a path through the maze of wrecked trees, for which I'm grateful. I sit on a sawed stump, check my map and guidebook, and eat some dried apricots and chocolate. The sun comes out; warm thermals alternate with bursts of winter air, as if I'm sitting on the edge of the great divide between winter and spring. On the other side of the mountain, turkey vultures whirl up on the air currents. According to the sun, it's noon.

Jenny comes up the Trail, panting, and sits on the log next to me. She looks wiped out.

"Take your pack off and rest a while," I say.

"Can't. This thing's so heavy, once I get it off my back I don't have the strength to pick it up again. Ugh. I have a terrible cold. Or the flu."

She takes out a bag of gorp—Good Old Raisins and Peanuts—and starts munching. "I can't even taste this," she says. "I'm just eating because I know I have to. Have you hiked a lot before? You seem to know what you're doing, unlike the rest of us."

"We camped a lot when I was a kid. My dad loved the woods."

"Nice. My family never took me anywhere except the mall. I've learned it all since college. Are you headed for Gooch Gap?"

"Yeah, are you?"

"I think I'll have to stop and camp somewhere before that. I'm feeling so awful, I don't think I can make it there."

"I hope you do. Once you get rid of some of your pack weight, it'll be easier."

"I hope so...I hope I can get rid of stuff. I just hope the whole trip isn't like this." She looks moodily out over the snarl of broken trees. "Hey, what do you think of this: I don't have a Trail name yet, and I'm thinking of calling myself Happy, because maybe it'll make me that way."

"That sounds like a good idea."

Hikers all take "Trail names" to use for the duration of the trip, and a week before beginning the Trail, I dreamed that I was in a gospel-preaching church, with an African-American congregation. I was standing in the choir, and the ladies around me, massive women with voices like organs, were singing "Amazing Grace." The song, full-throated and rich with harmony, resonated through my body, vibrating in my chest:

Through many dangers, toils, and snares
I have already come.
'Twas grace that brought me safe thus far
And grace will lead me home.

When the song ended, the woman next to me looked deep into my eyes and said, in a tone that would allow no argument, "Girl, your name has got to be Amazin' Grace." I knew she meant this should be my name for the Trail.

I don't go to church, and the idea of calling myself Amazin' anything is embarrassing; it seems egotistical. But I'm doing the Trail because I trust in dreams, and I also believe in the notion some tribal people have, that in a way you *are* your name: You live up to it, or down to it. On this pilgrimage, if I call myself Grace, it will have to bring a change into my life. Maybe it's a sign that I will complete the Trail safely and find what I'm looking for: some sense of home.

If so, I'll take it.

In the logbook at the shelter last night, I saw entries signed with Trail names like Slow and Accident-Prone and Sick Kid, and, mysteriously, Day-Glo Orange Baboon Butt. Jenny, with her wistful manner and too heavy load, could do worse than call herself Happy for the duration of her hike.

"Nice to meet you, Happy," I say.

We shake hands, and she smiles.

"I'm ready to move," I say. "Are you OK?"

"I'm just going to rest a while more."

"Well, I'll see you soon enough. Lose some pack weight and catch up—it's nice to see another woman out here alone."

"Yeah."

I leave her sitting on the stump, contemplating the wrecked trees. I hope she'll make it. Why is she unhappy? Maybe someday she'll tell me. Maybe by then all her burdens, both seen and unseen, will be lighter.

The shelter at Gooch Gap is festooned with "mouse-hangers," devices hikers have made to keep mice from eating all their food. These are miniature versions of the antisquirrel devices you often see on bird feeders: a cord hanging from the rafters, with an empty upside-down tuna can on the end, suspended over a horizontal stick. Hikers hang their food bags from the stick. A mouse, running down the cord from the rafters toward the food, will be stopped by the can. Theoretically, that is.

Three other hikers eventually show up: Aunt Bee, Jesse, and a big blond guy named Steelbone. No one has seen Bloodyfoot Tom, who was still at Hawk Mountain Shelter when everyone else left. Aunt Bee says Jenny stopped and camped on Justus Mountain, near where I saw her. GI Joe and Army Jack are also somewhere behind.

Aunt Bee and I go down to the spring. Now that I'm not hiking, it's cold. The little thermometer zipper pull on my jacket says it's 38 degrees. I wet my bandanna, stand with my bare feet in the icy runoff, and do a quick under-the-clothes wash. The water feels simultaneously painful and wonderful on my feet, which throb as if someone is driving nails into them. I don't have any blisters yet, just this bone-deep excruciating pain. All of my muscles are stiff, so I walk like an old woman. Aunt Bee, in fact, is more spry.

Aunt Bee says she's heard about Steelbone, who started hiking last year, broke his arm, and left after the first 50 miles of Trail. Now he's back. His pack is huge; supposedly it weighs 95 pounds, and he's proud of the weight. As we come back up the hill with our water, Steelbone takes three mousetraps out of his pack.

"Why don't you just use the mouse-hangers?" Jesse asks. He's a gentle man, in his mid 20s, with soft brown eyes.

"I don't bother with those. I have my own system. You can't let these rodents get out of hand." Steelbone snaps one of the traps to make his point. "I once killed eight mice in three minutes." He shows us the traps; each has a row of tiny notches along the edge. "This is my body count. I'm up to 36."

"Ooh, a Great White Hunter," Aunt Bee rasps from the shadows, where she's laying out her sleeping bag. "What do you do then, eat them?"

"I could. They have a lot of protein, you know. I'm planning to do a lot of living off the land on this hike. Hunting and so forth."

"Hunting is illegal on the Trail," Aunt Bee says. "And the mice are part of the ecosystem of the shelters. They clean all the crap and crumbs hikers drop."

"They're a nuisance and they need to be controlled. Man is meant to conquer nature."

I say, "Someone should just put a pair of black snakes at each shelter. That would take care of the mice. There would still be enough mice to clean the shelters, but not so many that they're out of control."

Steelbone flinches. Evidently he doesn't care for snakes.

"What other stuff do you have in your 95-pound pack?" Jesse asks.

"A Colt .45."

"Why, dude? You don't need it. It's too heavy. And it's dangerous."

"A man should carry protection."

Aunt Bee pauses in the middle of inflating her Thermarest mattress. "If it's protection you want, boy, I have it. Mint, cherry, ridged, regular, and lubricated."

"Oh, I have that too. I've always been popular with the ladies."

Jesse shoots me a glance that says, *Yeah, right*, takes a small wooden flute out of his pack, and sits at the edge of the shelter, looking out at the evening mountains, playing softly. I fire up my stove and put water on for mac and cheese. Aunt Bee takes some ibuprofen and rests on her back with her feet propped up on the wall.

Steelbone polishes his gun, rubbing it lovingly, glancing around to see if anyone is looking. No one is, and he puts it away.

Jesse plays his flute, point and counterpoint with the wind. It's beautiful, and we all tell him so. I wonder what it's like to play an instrument, carrying all those songs inside yourself. A person playing, alone in the woods, seems more a part of the woods than someone who's silent.

Steelbone fidgets. "You know," he says loudly, "I was pretty much born with an instrument in my hands. I can play anything. Duke Ellington once told me I was one of a select few."

"Why don't you play for us now?" Aunt Bee says. "Jesse, lend him your flute. I'd like to hear a master musician play."

Jesse hands over the flute.

"Well, I'm a little out of practice."

"We don't care."

"Hey, how about if I go back behind the shelter and practice a while? Get reacquainted with the instrument? You know, instruments are like women: You have to play each one a little differently, and it takes time to get to know them."

"Yeah, whatever."

Steelbone disappears into the woods. I stir my macaroni. After a while we hear little blurts of soft, disjointed tootling:

Tootle toot "Shit."

Tooo—tooOOOotle to— "Damn it."

Toot

Tootle

TooOO— "Shit."

Jesse says, "That guy was up on Springer the other night. I got the impression he'd been up there a while. He was eating the extra food. You know, the heavy cans of stuff people leave in the shelters? If you believe him, he's a world-class marathoner, a computer hacker wanted by the government, a boxer, a Pulitzer Prize winner, a pilot, and about 10 other things."

I eat my mac and cheese, candy bars, and some dried fruit, drink a couple of quarts of water, scrub out my cooking pot with a leaf and a little water, then stretch out in my sleeping bag.

I light my candle lantern and read the shelter logbook, a spiral notebook in a tattered plastic bag. The entries in this shelter's journal are a mix of exuberance, from the hikers who are feeling good, and despair, from those who aren't. It's strange to read journal entries from the hikers ahead of us: They can talk to us, but we can't answer unless we hike like hell and catch up to them or they get tired and stop for a day. In the same way, people coming along behind me will read what I write, but I may never see them. It's like a science-fiction story: We inhabit different, though parallel, universes.

I write a brief note across the time barrier encouraging Jenny and the others behind us to lose some of the weight in their packs and catch up. Then I get out my map and look over the terrain I plan to cover tomorrow. Just by glancing at the map, I can tell this is tough terrain. My map is already as smudged and worn as I am.

It's fully dark when Steelbone comes crunching back through the dead leaves.

"Hey, man, how about that concert?" Jesse asks.

"Not tonight—I'm rather tired, and you know a true musician really needs to put all his energy and heart and soul into it. Maybe tomorrow. I'm working on some material. I want to give you a really fine recital."

"Just give me back the flute, OK?"

Steelbone hands it over, then gets into his bag and turns over with his face away from us. Apparently he's too tired to set his mousetraps. I wonder how much his gun weighs, how much the traps weigh, how much his ax weighs. His arm is still crooked from the break last year. I wonder how far he'll make it. My guess is not far. My guess is that he'll leave the Trail soon and come back next year to Springer and sit in the shelter there, telling tall tales to green hikers, displaying his gun and bragging about his 95 pounds and survival in the wilderness. Like the mice, he has some kind of place in the Trail ecosystem, though who knows what it is. Maybe his job is to give everyone else some confidence: You're not as green as you think you are, and you could in fact be worse. Steelbone.

After what feels like a long sleep, I wake rested and happy. My feet still hurt, and all my muscles are stiff and sore, but that's to be expected.

I'm doing it, I think again. *Really here. I'm in the middle of nowhere in the mountains, on a path that leads for thousands of miles. The ultimate camping trip; six months of it. I don't have to go back to work after a few days of freedom.*

Slowly the shelter fills with white light. It's the moon, so bright I can read last night's journal entry and see the graffiti scratched into the wall: MOUSE WAS HERE. WILDFLOWER I LOVE YOU. The woods are all illuminated; even the blue blazes marking the shelter side trail are clearly visible, leading downhill toward the AT. The path is clear, crisscrossed by inky black shadows of leafless trees. I lean over and look at Jesse's watch: 3:30 A.M.

Quickly I pack, eat a quick cold breakfast of gorp, stuff more snacks in my pockets, grab my gear, and leave. Despite the bright moonlight, the stars are incredible. The woods are mysterious, silent except for an occasional rustle as an animal goes about its business. Owls call.

When I reach the AT, the white blazes shine on the trees like scraps cut from the moon.

I'm in love with the blazes. They seem to be more than just marks on trees showing the way to Maine or the way back to Springer. They're a symbol to me, a sign of the Journey, the Pilgrimage. *You're on the right path*, they seem to say. *You're going the right way. You're doing what you're supposed to do. Walk on.*

I come to a spot overlooking a valley, where the lights of a small town shine. I stand on the ridge thinking of the people snug in their warm beds, sleeping behind doors and walls, while I wander the dark mountains, shivering and hungry but thoroughly awake and alive. I wouldn't trade places with those people. I have 12 miles to go today and will do half of them before sunrise.

That night I sleep in a stone hut on top of Blood Mountain, named after a terrible slaughter between Creeks and Cherokees. The hut, once a fire warden's cabin, was abandoned for years and was home to a bear until the humans repossessed it and made it into a shelter. It's said to be one of the nicest on the Trail. Not only is it made of stone, but it actually has two rooms, four walls, a door that closes, and windows with heavy wooden shutters but no glass.

I'm almost asleep, trying to ignore the nails driving into my feet and my parched throat (there's no water on Blood Mountain, and my tongue feels like a stone), when a low scrabbling and scratching wakes me. Assuming it's one of the other hikers repacking his food, I ignore it until it occurs to me that not only is it pitch dark, but no normal human could ever be so obsessive. I sit up, light my candle lantern, and hold it high.

A beautiful little spotted skunk is busy attacking some candy-bar wrappers dayhikers have left in a wastebasket in the corner. The other hikers, disturbed by my lantern, sit up. Steelbone and Aunt Bee haven't made it here. Jesse has, and Army Jack and GI Joe from the first night have caught up with us. Like Bloodyfoot Tom, GI Joe has terrible blisters; unlike Tom, he's hiking anyway, either inspired or victimized by his military training.

The skunk comes over to our sleeping platform and tries to jump up. I don't mind it scrabbling in the corner, but I draw the line at letting it sleep with me. It puts its front paws on the platform at the end of my spot, and eyes my sleeping bag the way a cat does: hmmm, warm and cushy, a nice place to curl up for a nap.

"What should we do?" Jesse asks.

GI Joe rolls over and resumes snoring. The skunk isn't lusting after *his* sleeping bag. I'm not quite tired enough to be so blasé.

"Let's chase it out," I say. "I don't want it walking on me."

"I'm not doing it!"

"I'll do it."

I get up. Skunks evidently don't care for loud noises. I pick up the metal wastebasket and slam it on the floor. The skunk, disturbed, backs up. It's a dainty little animal, clearly offended by my unseemly behavior and bad manners. *Oh, really! Must you?* it seems to be saying. *Really, I'll never dine here again!* Clunk! I step forward and the skunk steps back. Clunk! I back it out into the other room, then out the door: a careful, respectful minuet. When the skunk's outside, I close the door and block it shut with a handy rock. It's freezing outside.

As soon as I blow out my lantern, we hear the scrabbling in the corner again.

"He's back!" Jesse says.

The skunk and I repeat our dance. This time I leave the wastebasket full of candy-bar wrappers outside, block the door with rocks so heavy I can hardly lift them, then use some rope to tie the shutters closed across the windows. We're sleeping in the same room a bear once used for a den; I wonder if the skunk was so persistent about visiting the bear.

Army Jack gives me a snappy salute and blows out the light.

We're not bothered again, but just as I drift off to sleep I hear some weekenders, camping in tents nearby, yell "SKUNK!" A familiar odor wafts in through the closed shutters. Jesse giggles. I grin, pull my sleeping bag up over my head, and fall asleep immediately.

Pizza! Soda! Ice cream! Apples! Orange juice! Milk! I almost shout as I hobble down the steep back side of Blood Mountain toward Neels Gap, the first civilized stop on the Trail. There's no town here, just a hiker hostel and store. The building is impossible to miss: The Trail goes right through it, and the building itself is marked with a white blaze.

I buy two pizzas, a liter of Coke, two apples, and a pint of Ben and Jerry's peanut butter cup ice cream, and eat them all for breakfast. I'm still hungry, still thirsty. It's strange to see cars on the road and to see people who look clean and rested. I check into the hostel, take a shower, and call my mother to let her know I'm alive and well. I'm actually sore, achy, and seriously dehydrated. My hands, for some reason, are so swollen that a ring is cutting off the circulation. Except for my fingers, I'm already thinner. I'll have to eat more. And drink more.

I go through my pack, sorting the supplies I've bought, getting rid of extra weight. There's not much to get rid of: a cup, a guidebook, a shirt. And the ring, which I have to soap my finger to remove.

People share news and gossip: Bloodyfoot Tom hiked out on a dirt road and hitched a ride with an Army Ranger toward civilization; Aunt Bee is talking about leaving too; GI Joe's blisters blossomed to the point where he had to be taken to a hospital; Steelbone is "back there somewhere," and so is Hal the Nudist. Speedbump is hiking slowly but steadily and is only a day behind. So is Happy, previously known as Jenny, who rumor says is still sick.

The hostel fills up with hikers. It's simple—beds and bunk beds in a single room, enough for 13 hikers—but the beds are soft, and it's warm inside. We've all walked almost 31 miles to get here. Only 2,125 to go.

I've caught Happy's cold, which is more like the flu. The next day my lungs feel like they're filled with molten lead. I cough up chunks of slime, and some British dayhikers who sit with me on Cowrock Mountain admiring the view down into Tesnatee Gap touch my forehead and declare that I have a fever.

On the way down the steep mountainside I catch up with Brightside and Little Cat, a young couple I met at the hostel.

"You look like shit," Brightside says. "What's the matter with you?"

"Flu," I say. "Fever. Do you have any water?"

"No. Sorry. There's supposed to be some in the Gap."

We go on down. My joints feel like someone is pounding railway spikes through them. My tongue is swollen. My feet are killing me, but that's nothing new. At least I don't have any blisters.

Down in the Gap there's a road and a tiny hiker parking lot. Off to one side, in a deep ditch, a thin stream of water trickles from a corrugated drainage pipe. Yum. I run down there and take off my boots, soak my pained feet in the cold water, then throw my filter intake hose upstream from my feet and start pumping. Ahhhh. As I pump, I note a deodorant cap and a cigarette butt next to the water, and an old Styrofoam cup in it. Thank God for filters. I take a big swig of the filtered water, which tastes wonderful, and gulp down a few ibuprofens.

Brightside and Little Cat join me, and we have a nice picnic, there in the drainage ditch.

"This can't be the water on the map," Little Cat says.

"I don't care," I say. "I'm dying of thirst and it tastes OK."

We mix lemonade and each drink a quart. Up in the parking lot cars crunch on the gravel, and a short time later an entire troop of Boy Scouts leans over the edge, looking down at us as we picnic in our welter of trash, soaking our feet in ditch water.

I raise my Nalgene bottle of Kool-Aid and toast them. "Want an M&M? Don't mind me—I'm feverish."

We resume hiking. I stagger along in a haze, dimly aware of the beauty of the terrain we're passing through and the tender blossoms of the first spring flowers, bloodroot and hepatica and trillium.

It's only about five more miles to the shelter, but it feels like 20. My pack seems to accumulate mass and weight as I walk, as if I'm moving toward the center of a black hole. It's a relief to see the blue blazes marking the turnoff to the shelter.

If the number of mouse-hangers in a shelter is an indication of the severity of the mouse problem there, we're in for a long night in the shelter at Low Gap. At least 20 of them hang from the rafters. Like wind chimes, they swing in the breeze, giving the place a festive air. Some are decorated with strings of acorns, others have intricately carved sticks to hang the food bags from, and a few have poems or initials scratched into the rusty tuna cans. Evidently a posse of hikers has spent a rainy day beautifying the place with their Swiss Army knives. The rain must have ended suddenly, though, because a checkerboard carved into the wooden floor is only half-finished.

Jesse, Army Jack, Speedbump, and a hiker named Too Much are there, along with a couple of other hikers I don't know.

"Who wants to play checkers?" Army Jack asks.

"We don't have any men," Jesse says.

"I'll be acorns, you be sticks."

"I'd rather be pebbles."

"Whatever you want. Let's play."

Mouse, whoever he is, has carved his name in the ceiling here too. He's everywhere. As soon as we put out our lights, mice boil up out of the floor, gnaw their way out of the walls, and drop from the rafters. The shelter resounds with squeaking and the patter of tiny running feet. We cinch the hoods of our sleeping bags tight over our heads and giggle nervously.

Too Much screams, "It's over by me!" His sleeping bag swishes as he jerks his feet away from the wall. His flashlight beam swings wildly.

"There's one over here!" Brightside yells. His breathing is quick, almost panicked. "Jesus, would you look at that bastard?"

We all turn on our flashlights. The mouse jumps off his sleeping bag and disappears into a crack in the floor. It's actually kind of cute, with shell-like ears, a white belly, and lively dark eyes. I decide that unless the mice are on my head, in my food, or in my pack, I'll ignore them. I'm too tired and sick to care. I cough, and fall asleep to the sound of squeaking.

The next day, still feeling awful, I leave the shelter long after everyone else. A layer of high, thin clouds has rolled in, and it looks like it will rain by afternoon. The Trail is very quiet, the walk peaceful. Juncos fly out from under my feet as I pass their nests, dug into the bank at the side of the Trail. Once, I look to see where a bird has come from, part the long grass, and find a neat cup-shaped nest with four tiny eggs inside.

On the long, relatively flat stretch between Poplar Stomp Gap and Cold Spring Gap, it begins to rain, and I feel spooked, as if someone or something is watching me. A cop friend of mine once said that if you get this feeling, it's generally for a reason. "The victims who say, 'I felt like something wasn't right, but I just kept going' turn out to be just that—victims," he told me. "The smart people know something is wrong and take precautions."

There are few precautions I can take out here, miles from anything or anyone. Standing still is probably not a good idea. I assess the feeling and decide it feels more like an animal watching me than a person. There's no basis for this, but then there's no basis for my feeling spooked in the first place. I walk faster, singing at the top of my lungs: "Amazing Grace," "Wayfaring Stranger," and other songs I make up as I walk, long rambling poems about the Trail. After a couple of miles the terrain grows steep again and the spooky feeling abates.

The rain slacks off but doesn't stop. I come to a long traverse of slippery, unstable rocks on a hillside, with water running underneath them. I step carefully from rock to rock, using my hiking stick for balance. Where's the shelter? Have I passed it? I check the map. If I don't find it after another mile, I'll camp wherever I am, as long as it's near water.

Just as I'm about to give up on finding the shelter, I come to the blue-blazed trail that leads to it. It's so foggy that the shelter is invisible until I'm right in front of it. It's packed with everyone who was at Low Gap, plus a couple of women and a family with four children. Everyone is silent and introverted, as if the fog is a blanket that has hushed them all. Eventually, driven out by the combined thruhiker silence, as well as the combined thruhiker reek, the family puts up a tent behind the shelter, and so do the two women.

I read the log. Someone saw a mountain lion the day before, in the same place where I felt spooked. He knew it was a mountain lion and not a bobcat because of its tawny color and long tail, which bobcats don't have. Also, it was very large. Officially there are no mountain lions in the Appalachians, but people keep seeing them and their tracks.

I decide to stay in this shelter for an extra day, eat constantly to fill up my calorie reserve, and try to get over the flu. I'm so weak and tired that going to the spring, even without my pack, is exhausting. On the way down I stagger and almost fall.

The rain returns, pouring, and paradoxically everyone in the shelter cheers up, beginning a lively game of cards, carving their hiking sticks, firing up their stoves and cooking huge dinners. I eat, then rest in my sleeping bag and look out at the rain, glad to have food, warm dry clothes, and a roof to keep the rain off. The cracks in the roof and the spaces between the roof and the rafters are stuffed with acorns, obviously the work of mice. There are probably about 20 pounds of M&Ms in there too.

That night, blissfully asleep, I slowly become aware of a weight on my head. A warm, not-too-heavy weight, like a cat curled up against my hair. Is it Brightside's feet? The shelter is so crowded that we're all sleeping head to feet, like sardines in a can. I nudge him with my foot.

"Hey, Brightside, move your feet."

He moves his feet over. The thing, whatever it is, shifts its weight and resettles against my head. I put up my hand and touch fur.

“What the—” I sit up and switch on my flashlight. A skunk, curled up where my head was, sleepily opens its eyes and yawns, showing a pink mouth and sharp little teeth.

“Get out of here!” I yell. The skunk picks itself up, stretches, gives itself a good shake, then saunters to the edge of the shelter and jumps down gracefully. It’s still pouring outside; I see the skunk’s tail disappear into the dry space under the shelter before I turn off my light.

The other thruhikers, the family, and the two women pack up and disappear down the Trail, urging me to get better soon and catch up. It’s my first taste of the “survival of the fittest” mentality of the Trail. Nice to see you, but we aren’t waiting for you. We have an appointment to keep in Maine.

I make some tea from Joe’s sage, then sleep until some Boy Scouts, who are on the last day of a five-day trip, stop at the shelter for lunch and give me their leftover food: a whole bag of Oreos, half a pound of summer sausage, cheese, crackers, Pop Tarts, half a loaf of bread, and an orange. I eat it all and answer all of their questions:

“Where are you going?”

“How far is it?”

“How much does your pack weigh?”

“How many miles a day do you hike?”

“Seen any bears?”

“How about snakes?”

“What else can you eat?”

After they leave, I rest some more. The shelter is at the edge of a deep valley, and all afternoon turkey vultures ride the thermals over it. Watching them is hypnotic, slow, soothing. Birds call, the wind moves the trees, and clouds drift past. It’s much more pleasant than being sick in civilization, and I start to feel better. Maybe walking all day through rain and sleeping outside in 30-degree weather is actually good for you.

By late afternoon, just as it seems that no one else is coming to the shelter (Where are all the hikers? Has everyone else quit at Neels Gap?), a lone hiker, Ronsonol Man, shows up. He tells me he got his name because he loves building campfires at night, and starts them with lighter fluid.

He builds one now, and we make supper and talk.

He's planning to hike half the Trail, 1,000 miles to Harpers Ferry in West Virginia, or until he gets bored. He's not bored yet. He works at a TV station in San Francisco but dislikes it and wants to do something else. Just what, he doesn't know, but maybe walking out here, he'll find it. He mentions his girlfriend back home often and lovingly. His message is very clear: We may be out here camped together in the middle of nowhere and sleeping in the same shelter, but that's it. Nothing more than friendship. I'm grateful for his clarity; it's reassuring. I'm still paranoid after the mess with Wade, still closed, and plan to stay that way until I get everything sorted out.

Ronsonol Man is stocky, with straight black hair, dark eyes, and tan skin. He looks like he could be Native American, Tibetan, or South American. He tells me his grandmother was involved with a Chinese man, a brief adventure; then he disappeared and left her pregnant with a daughter, Ronsonol Man's mother. They lived in a small town in Tennessee, and the locals, who hadn't seen many Asians, called her "nigger" and shunned her. The few African Americans in the area didn't want to have anything to do with her either. As soon as she grew up, she moved to San Francisco, where she fit right in. Ronsonol Man inherited her looks and says people often think he's Polynesian, Navajo, or Inuit. He enjoys their confusion.

We talk more about rednecks, and inevitably get into spooky stories about people who got lost or killed in the woods. In the mountains. On the Trail. There are places on the Trail where the locals are said to be hostile to hikers. A few hikers have been killed on the Trail, usually couples who were alone in a shelter...

It's nearly dark. We look at each other, but it's too late to take back the stories. We're spooked. Never again, I resolve, will I tell scary stories in the woods when night is near. In the morning, sure. But not at night.

From far away, echoing through the trees, we hear a loud, disjointed shouting. It sounds like a man, walking through the woods, raving at the top of his lungs. Getting closer.

I look at my spread-out gear and assess the amount of time it will take to grab it, shove it into my pack, run into the woods, and hide. Ronsonol Man does the same. We look at each other: It's iffy.

"Now I'm all edgy," Ronsonol Man says. "And it was so peaceful before."

"Can he hear us?"

"When I was at the spring before, I could hear you coughing just like you were next to me."

I raise my eyebrows.

"But that was a controlled burst. I don't think he could hear us just packing. He's pretty far away."

"It sounds close to me, like just past the spring."

The shouting continues. Hikers don't shout in the woods. They walk, quietly, and they talk if they're with someone, but they don't *yell.* This yelling is so garbled we can't understand a word. I imagine this lunatic, this crazed axman, wandering through the woods full of random anger, ready to hack apart the first hikers he sees, so freaked out that he doesn't even bother to sneak up on you. It's the city person's bogeyman, the thing people warned me about back in D.C.: A madman lurks in the woods, waiting to kill you.

We edge closer to our gear. Nervously I shove my food bag and journal into my pack. My stove is still hot, too hot to carry. I'll have to leave it. Ronsonol Man shifts from foot to foot, head cocked, leaning toward the woods, ready to run.

"I found it!" the maniac yells. A confused babble of other male voices echoes back. Ronsonol Man looks at me. Is there a whole *group* of madmen? That seems unlikely. We both relax a little.

The voices are clearer now: guys laughing, cursing, obviously town boys out in the woods, covering up their anxiety by being more boisterous than usual.

They come down the blue-blaze to the shelter and stop dead when they see us. They obviously didn't expect to see anyone, and Ronsonol Man and I, standing immobile in the middle of a dark camp, spook them as much as they spooked us.

A leader separates himself from the group and starts ordering people around. "Ty, you get more water. Dave, Jose, and Brian, set up the tents. Manny, get some wood."

"Hoods in the Woods," Ronsonol Man says.

"What?"

"You know, those programs where they take delinquent boys out on these wilderness trips and fill them with the clean manliness and wholesome rigor of the woods."

"Oh, yeah."

The boys all look exhausted and tense. It's obvious that they've never been in the woods before. An owl hoots, and Manny, who's collecting sticks near the shelter, jumps.

"What the fuck was that?!"

"An owl," I say. "It won't do anything to you."

He looks at us, at our gear. "How long are you guys out here for?"

"Six months. Two thousand miles to Maine."

"Six months! Two thousand miles! Jesus, I'd rather be in jail. You *want* to be out here that long?"

"Yeah, we do."

"Unbelievable." He looks us over again, with new respect. "Are you, like, Daniel Boone or something?"

We tell him about the trip and answer his questions. His face opens up as we talk. He looks at all our gear, at the maps, at our food, at our boots.

"How did you learn to live in the woods and not be scared?" he asks.

"Manny!" the leader yells, even though he's only 15 feet away. "I'm looking for that wood!"

Manny goes back to their campsite with his wood. They take a long time and a lot of shouting to get their fire going. The owl hoots again, its mate answers, and the two begin a long, quavering screaming match. The mice, who have come out of the walls of the shelter and begun their nightly raid on our packs and gear, temporarily retreat.

"It's only an owl," Manny tells the others with authority. "You pussies don't need to be afraid of it. See that girl over there? She's walking 2,000 miles. To Maine."

The others express their disbelief. A girl! No way.

"I believe it," Manny says. He pauses, looking out over their heads into the dark woods. "And you know what? Someday I'm gonna go there too."

The first mountain in North Carolina is called Sharp Top, and it's aptly named, though most hikers call it "That Bastard."

I struggle up this rocky needle, sweating and crying, exhausted. My water filter is acting up, and I'm seriously dehydrated. Earlier today I drank directly out of a stream, hoping my iron stomach will hold.

At the apex of Sharp Top is a huge cat track in the mud of the Trail. I have a bandanna that has animal tracks printed on it, with identifying features, and I take it off and compare it to this print. Sure enough, the track is cat, not dog. And it's huge. A mountain lion? Maybe it's the one someone saw back near Blue Mountain.

Finally, I reach the shelter. Ronsonol Man is there, along with hikers named Bearbait, Homer, and Steamroller Boy. Bearbait was in the Army and as a civilian most recently worked at a nuclear plant. He regales us with stories of mistakes, leaks, and near-disasters that the public never heard about because they were covered up. Homer is a retired journalist who was in the Navy. Steamroller Boy was in the Marines. Another hiker, Mosquito, is in his early 20s and has let his blond hair turn into dreadlocks. He sits apart from the others, wearing a tie-dyed shirt, evidently uninterested in their military reminiscences. Ronsonol Man is similarly bored.

I feel like I'm in a barracks. The three military men talk about drills, about combats and exercises, about shore leave and being absent without leave, about guns and ammo and heavy machinery. And women. And for some reason, gay men.

I take notes. I'm sitting in the shadows at the back of the shelter, and they've forgotten I'm here. It's a whole new world, a side of some men most women never see.

"And she had these huge gazongas..."

"This little fag, he comes up and goes, 'Ith thith theat taken?' and Jim just up and punches him—"

"So I asked if she was married, and she said no..."

"Sometimes I like a nice quiet drunk, you know, just sitting in front of the TV getting shit-faced..."

"So I, you know, boinked her, and then her husband showed up..."

"And this little butt pirate says..."

"This really hot chick, she was black, and..."

I've heard comments about gay men in shelters before, but it seemed like an isolated outburst. Now it's looking like a trend. I haven't met any men hiking on the Trail who are obviously gay, although if I had to guess, I'd say some of the women I've seen may be. Yet over and over, someone will bring up gay men and then the other guys will all laugh a little too nervously, a little too loudly. I haven't yet heard anyone go on about lesbians, though they seem a more visible target.

I finally figure it out: Here we are, out in the middle of nowhere, packed body to body in a tiny shelter, and apparently they're all horny, or at least want each other to think so. But not for you, man! Not for you! I'm no butt pirate! I want women! Gazongas! Ass! I'm a big man with a big gun!

Steamroller Boy gets up to get a snack and sees me sitting in the shadows. He comes over, sits next to me, and says in a low voice, "You know, a man gets pretty lonely up here. It's hard walking alone. It might be nice to have some company. Don't you think so, Amazin' Grace?"

"I like walking alone," I say. "It's peaceful."

His attention makes me nervous, after all the comments. I think, *Even if I were completely straight and not dealing with the aftermath of a stupid relationship, do you think I'd hike with you after hearing the way you talk about women?* I wonder what would happen if I told him I've been involved with women, that his and the other hikers' comments about gays offend me.

Since I'm a woman hiking alone, I've already forfeited a certain margin of personal safety. Coming out to him would forfeit a lot more. At the least, the gossip would spread up the Trail faster than a wildfire. If you want to keep a secret, don't tell it to a long-distance hiker. Gossip weighs nothing, so it's the easiest thing to carry up the Trail, and it gives everyone hours of entertainment, which is otherwise hard to come by in the wilderness. If I come out to these people, everyone who sets foot on the Trail for the next 2,000 miles will know. Some of them might be psychos who are offended by the news, and they might take it out on me.

Also, I'm too embarrassed by the recent fiasco with Wade. If I tell someone I've been involved with women, what happens when some other hiker gossips and tells about Wade? I haven't told anyone about him yet, but maybe I'll slip. The conflicting stories, like opposing tidal waves, will meet and swamp me in the middle, and curious hikers will pester me to iron out the story. People hate it when you don't fit into their neat categories, and most have no qualms about trying to nail you down. I imagine their inquiry: Well, how could you—? And didn't you know—? And what about the women—? And you really thought—? But what about—?

I don't want these unanswerable questions to follow me up the Trail. I want to have no past, no interesting history. I resolve not to tell anyone anything about my private life until I have it better sorted out. It's isolating not to be able to tell anyone the stories that are weighing me down, but it's better to be isolated than a target.

The woods are full of food. Soon after crossing into North Carolina I find a hillside covered with ramps, which are a kind of wild leek. I've heard of these but have never tasted them, and I gather a handful of the pungent plants to add to my dinner.

I also find peppermint, spearmint, and lemon mint, which, after floating in my water bottle for a few hours, make a refreshing tea. Sassafras roots make a spicy tea; you can chew the leaves too, although they're best for only occasional use—too much may cause cancer. Black birch twigs taste like wintergreen, nettles can be cooked and taste like spinach, only better, and dandelion greens, gathered before the plant flowers, make a great salad. Later in the spring there will be strawberries, raspberries, and cherries.

Finding edible wild plants has been a hobby of mine since I was a child, and on the Trail it's a useful one, though it generally adds only variety and vitamins instead of calories. And I need calories.

For the last couple of nights, I've dreamed repeatedly that I'm driving a car through dark mountains, and the fuel gauge is on empty.

I've always had a fast metabolism. In civilization this is a luxury; on the Trail it's a liability. Even in civilization it can be a drag, since I'm hypoglycemic. When I get hungry, I don't just get tired and cranky, like other people. My heart races, I tremble uncontrollably, and I get dizzy and irrational and forget that I need to eat. If this goes on long enough, I'll pass out. The only treatment is to eat regularly and not get to the point where I'm sick.

On the Trail I'm burning about 6,000 calories a day—the equivalent of running two marathons back to back, every day. It's impossible to carry that much food. My body is undergoing a sort of reverse puberty: My breasts and hips are melting away.

Besides enduring hunger, physical pain, and the steepness of the mountains, I spend a lot of time thinking about Wade. I don't want to, but it's inevitable. You can't go through something like that and *not* think about it. And that's why I'm walking alone, anyway: to give myself time to think and get through this, away from the distraction of other people.

It makes me angry. Here I am, in the most beautiful place in the world, and I have to think about him. In between seeing bear tracks, watching mother grouse protect their babies, and marveling at the stars, I have to watch endless mental replays of the way he squints his eyes when he lies, as if he's looking into a searchlight too bright to bear, or the way he runs water in the bathroom whenever he goes, because he doesn't want anyone else to hear him peeing. I have to reread the letters in his desk or replay every misguided fight we ever had, see every E-mail entry, and watch myself being gullible and believing he's devoted and committed, watch myself spend the money I saved for the Trail to move and be with him. It makes me sweat more than walking up any mountain ever could. I must be using up an extra 1,000 calories a day just from the agitation of this, and although I know it's part of healing, that doesn't help much. I'm as angry at myself as I am at him, maybe more.

I get to the top of a mountain and see a beautiful view, just mountain after mountain rolling away, not a house or a road (or a candy bar) in sight, nothing but dense forest and a far-off river. It's incredible, but instead of being able to enjoy it, I see a replay of the night I left Wade: me pressing his shoulders down onto the bed, leaning into him with a weight of hatred. Now the weight's on me. It's as if he's riding in my pack and I can't get rid of him. It's a far heavier burden than any amount of gear, made heavier by the fact that I can't tell anyone what I'm going through.

I close my eyes and imagine him standing on the mountaintop with me. It's a ludicrous thought because he would never walk up any mountain, even without a pack. (That should have let me know, long before anything happened between us, that he was wrong for me.) Nevertheless, I imagine he's here, ruining my view.

"GET OFF MY MOUNTAIN!" I yell, as loud as I can. My voice echoes down the valleys, bouncing off cliffs far below. A raven, passing overhead, falters a little, startled by the noise, then sails on.

"GET OFF MY MOUNTAIN!" I yell again. It's so satisfying to just let loose; you can never do this in civilization. "YOU DIDN'T HIKE UP HERE, YOU DON'T DESERVE TO BE HERE, THIS IS MY HIKE AND MY MOUNTAIN, SO JUST GET OFF MY MOUNTAIN, RIGHT NOW!!!"

I open my eyes. He's gone. My pack feels about 10,000 pounds lighter. Maybe I'll do this every day. Or every hour. Who cares if anyone hears me? There's no one around, anyway.

Far away, the raven croaks, and others answer. Eventually maybe I'll hike with someone else: not a romance, just a friend. I'll know when it's time to tell my story, when I can trust again, and let go.

April 18
Carter Gap Shelter, N.C.

CHAPTER THREE

"No rain, no pain, no Maine," hikers say, meaning that if you can't put up with the first two, you'll never see the third. It's true, and we all know it, but we hate rain. Cold, wet, adding weight to everything it touches, it's our enemy, and I spend a long day in Carter Gap Shelter with a bunch of other hikers, hoping the rain will stop.

This shelter, like most, is filled with graffiti, written with charcoal taken from the fire pit. Mouse, who's written or carved his name on just about every structure, post, or surface on the Trail so far, has signed in with his knife on the ceiling: MOUSE, the S jagged like a lightning bolt. And MOUSE LOVES WILDFLOWER. Other hikers have since altered it: MOUSE LUBES WEEDPLOWER.

Below this, someone else has written:

MOUSE: I'M LOOKING FOR YOU.
SIGNED, CAT

The shelter is tiny, with a low ceiling, and very cold. I hang my tarp over the shelter opening, and it warms up, though now it's dark inside. With our candle lanterns hanging from the ceiling, and our damp smells and grimy bodies and gear crowded into the narrow wooden space, it feels like we're all shipmates on a long voyage, very far from anywhere. When we move, we limp slowly, painfully. Everything hurts.

"It smells like wet dog in here," someone says.

"That's us," someone else says.

Outside, in the rain, a grouse drums repeatedly, a strange sound, a slow heartbeat speeding up, a flutter you feel in your bones. It's a male, looking for company, persistent and sad.

Ronsonol Man is asleep; Mosquito is lying on his back, his eyes roving over the graffiti on the ceiling, slowly eating one dried apricot after another. "I hate that Mouse bastard," he says, and wearily closes his eyes.

"You know what I heard about that guy?" Steamroller Boy says.

"No, what?"

"He hiked last year and carved his name on everything all the way up the Trail. Every fuckin' bridge, shelter, and signpost. All the other hikers were furious, just like everyone still is when they see all this shit he carved last year. Then he was stupid enough to walk into Trail headquarters at Harpers Ferry and go, 'Hi, I'm Mouse! I'm thruhiking!' And they said, 'That's right, buddy, you *are* through hiking!' and arrested him on the spot for all the graffiti. What a fuckin' idiot!"

Mosquito makes a victory fist, then goes to sleep.

Bearbait, Homer, and Steamroller Boy tell stories about their time in the military. They're the same stories I've heard before. Heavy machinery, women, gays—and a new one: the size of some people's private parts.

I roll my eyes. Bridget, whom I've run into off and on since Georgia, rolls hers. Her friend Terry is sleeping through the rainy afternoon, but Bridget and I have too much energy to sleep. Not enough to hike in the rain, but too much to sleep.

"Wanna play cards?"

"Sure."

We play and play while the rain roars on the roof. The fog is so dense we can't see the Trail, though every now and then a sudden wind blows the clouds the other way and dark branches of trees appear with startling clarity. A large animal crashes around over on the Trail, snapping branches underfoot, but we can't see it. We're playing War, which I haven't played since I was a kid on family road trips: My brother and I played for hours, days, and thousands of miles of American highways, slapping down cards on the backseat, on a picnic table, or on the wet floor of our tent. War is well named: It's stupid, no one ever wins, and it never ends unless the players decide to call it quits.

"Bear?" Bridget lays down an ace of diamonds and takes my queen of spades.

I listen. "Either that or a boar." I lean out and look for our food bags, which we've hung up in trees to keep them away from bears. Bridget's is so weighed down by water that it's pulled the branch it's hanging from almost to the ground. Mine is still high up, the bright red nylon barely visible through the mist. Behind us the men are slowly escalating their military stories, trying to top each other. No one is flexing muscles yet, but you can almost smell the testosterone, like ozone in the air near a lightning strike.

"...and the sergeant said no."

"...I may be horny, but I'm no butt pirate."

"...shit on a shingle."

"...she was marrying someone else."

"...because I was stinking drunk."

All of the stories end at once, and the men sit staring morosely at the rain. I put down a 10 of spades and take Bridget's four of hearts. Bridget takes a bite of her Snickers. I look away. I've eaten all of my good snacks and don't want to look at her candy bar the way a dog looks at your food when you're eating something it wants. The rain is slacking off, just a little; I can see, barely, one white blaze of the Trail, and a stream of running water instead of the footpath.

Bearbait stands up. "Well, I think I'll get going!" The other men swivel their heads and look at him, shocked. He grabs his pack and starts shoving gear into it. "Looks like great weather for a nice 20 miles!"

I lean over and look at Bridget's watch. It's 2:30 in the afternoon. If he's going to do 20 miles, in this weather and terrain, he'll be walking at least until midnight. I'm willing to bet that although the rain has slacked off, that's temporary, and it will pour the rest of the day, all night, and into the next day. It will be dark by, oh, 6 or so. We've wasted a day hiding from the rain, but it's too late to redeem it now.

"Yeah, nice day for a hike!" Suddenly all the men want to be the first to leave the shelter. Bearbait bounds gleefully off the platform and into the mud. "See you in 20 miles!"

The shelter is empty in minutes, everyone but Ronsonol Man—who's still sleeping—packing angrily and stomping off into the rain.

"Sure you don't want to play cards?" Bridget asks Mosquito, the last to leave.

"Shit. I hate rain." He wipes a hand over his stubbly face, pushing water out of his eyes. "What the hell do I care what they think? I'll never see them again anyway. Assholes. Fucking Army jarheads." He throws his pack back down, takes out his food bag and hangs it on a rafter nail, and unrolls his sleeping mat. "I'm in here for the duration. Can you play War three ways? Deal me in."

"Today is another yesterday," Ronsonol Man says the next morning when we all wake up, and he's right. The main difference is that now we've learned our lesson about shelter-bound boredom, and we all pack up eagerly and hit the Trail despite the deep fog and heavy rain.

In the afternoon a fierce storm catches me, Bridget, Terry, and Ronsonol Man as we're climbing down Albert Mountain, a steep and rocky descent. We immediately move as fast as we can: All we want is to get down, away from the lightning.

As we hurtle down the mountain, lightning whips out of the clouds and slashes the treetops. The air smells electric, a combination of ozone and the sharp tang of our sweat. The clouds boil. They're a sickly gray-green, a familiar and terrifying color to anyone raised in the Midwest.

"There's a tornado near here!" I yell as we run.

"What?" They're behind me and can't hear me; my pack blocks my words.

"Tornado!"

"Shit!"

We run faster, sliding and barely recovering our balance on the sharp switchbacks, rocking crazily on slick stones as we cross sudden streams. Huge trees sway as if they'll bend in half. Branches fall, bouncing off other branches lower down. The air is filled with green leaves torn loose. Lightning and thunder hit at the same time, close by, and I wonder if this is how I'll die, struck by lightning on a North Carolina mountain.

There are worse ways to go. The adrenaline rush is exhilarating. Why are terrifying events so much fun? Long after the parasailing incident with my dad, I once jumped out of a plane, and the world had never seemed so beautiful as it did in free fall.

We're in free fall now, racing down the mountain, rain like a wall, cold on our faces. The clouds boil.

"Yeeeeehaw!"

We skid and slip on the packed red clay of the footpath, racing the storm, heading down.

We're in a valley now, protected by mountain walls. Far overhead, the wind tears at the treetops. Thunder rolls, but it has passed us now. The worst of the storm is gone. The rain pours down, *sssssssshhhhhh*, steady as a waterfall. Ronsonol Man checks his watch. We've come three miles in 50 minutes, which must be a hiking record.

The adrenaline rush wears off, and I'm cold. I'm soaking wet. It's still windy, and the wind sucks the heat right out of me. I shiver, and unfold my wet map to see where we are. I need to resupply; I don't have enough food to make it to Franklin, the next big town. I'll have to get off the Trail at the next road and hitch to a campground that also has a hiker bunkhouse and a small store where I can stay the night and resupply.

When we reach the road, Bridget and Terry say that since the storm has passed, they'll go ahead, several miles farther to a road where they can hitch 15 miles to Franklin. They ask again if I want to go with them. Town would be fun; we could eat hot greasy food, and we could split a motel, take showers, and do laundry. But I say no. I don't even have enough food to hike the rest of the day. Ronsonol Man says he'll come with me to the bunkhouse at the campground: A warm, indoor place to sleep, a shower, and food will be welcome. Other hikers have told us there's pizza at the campground—and the best cinnamon buns in the world.

Ronsonol Man and I turn off on the road, waving goodbye to Bridget and Terry, who disappear into the woods on the other side. I hope we'll meet again, but on the Trail you never know.

Still giddy from the storm, we walk down the road, kicking up big sheets of water. It's still pouring, and without the screen of trees over us, there's nothing to shield us from the storm's force. The raindrops are huge, one degree away from freezing, and sting almost as much as hail. With each step, water sloshes out of our boots and onto the road, which is several inches deep in water. I'm shivering uncontrollably but can't stop laughing. We laugh like drunks, turning our faces up to the rain. If only our friends could see us now, they'd know how crazy we are.

A few cars go by. We stick out our thumbs, but the drivers shake their heads, unwilling to have our soaked and muddy bodies and gear in their clean, dry cars. We laugh at the closed looks on their faces.

We walk for a little more than a mile. The road is deserted: no houses, no sign of life. There's also no sign of the campground, which is supposed to be a mile from the Trail crossing.

We check the map again. Sure enough, we've read it wrong,

and the road we want is a half-mile farther down the Trail. Now we have to backtrack a mile on this road, go a half-mile more on the Trail, then hike a mile on the correct road to get to the campground.

A huge wave of giddiness seizes me. We turn around and make up elaborate stories about a scolding schoolteacher. "You should have read your map!" we yell, shrieking with laughter. "You should have read your *map*!"

My hands don't work anymore. My feet seem stupid too, walking in the middle of the road, wandering over to the other side where I don't want to go. It feels like being drunk, only even more stupid and slow. I giggle and watch myself walk, as if I'm a stranger to myself. It occurs to me, the thought squeezing into consciousness from very far away, that I have hypothermia and won't last long in this state. How funny.

Food and shelter, a little voice whispers between the giggles. *Drink hot sugary beverages.*

I have nothing hot, but do I have a Nalgene bottle full of sugary Gatorade.

"Have to drink," I say, slurring the words through numb lips. The rain cover on my pack makes it impossible for me to reach the bottle. I turn so Ronsonol Man can get it for me.

"Can't you wait until we get there?"

"No. Now. Hypothermia. Gonna die."

He gets it out for me. I drink the whole bottle, then take off my pack, set it down in the river that was the road, and fumble out a bag of granola. My fingers can't make the fine motions necessary to open the zip-lock bag, so I bite it open and eat all the granola.

"Feeling better?"

"Good enough."

We hike on, back to the Trail, and reenter the woods. When we reach the other road, we resume our slosh, slosh, giggle, trudge. The granola and Gatorade have revived me for a while, but now I'm losing it again.

Ronsonol Man sings "Singin' in the Rain," more cars pass, and we pray for someone to stop.

A red pickup passes, but we're too demoralized to stick out our thumbs. The taillights flare red, and the truck backs up. A man, his wife, and their two kids are packed into the warm, dry cab.

"Y'all heading for the campground?"

"Yeah!"

"Well, don't stand around in the rain. Get on in back, and we'll take you right there."

The wind chill in the back of the truck must be 60 below. We kneel down as the heavy rain slashes at our faces and the cold water in the pickup bed soaks our butts and knees. My hands are white as bone; I concentrate on them, gripping the side of the truck as we careen down the twisting road. I'm shivering so hard that my whole body is in spasms. *Only a few more minutes. Hang on. You can make it.* The driver is in a hurry to get us to shelter. *Thank God,* is all I can think. *Only a few more minutes and we'll be someplace warm.*

The Trail angel family drops us off, waves, and disappears up the road.

We stagger into the office/store, where a bearded man with a red bandanna tied around his head raises a cup of hot chocolate in salute. He's seated next to a wood stove. Behind the counter, a woman with a no-nonsense face smiles and says hello. She has a two-pack-a-day voice and the manner of one of those people who either love you or hate you: no middle ground. Hanging on the wall behind her are shirts for sale; in huge block letters they say PLEASE FEED THE HUNGRY HIKER.

Ronsonol Man nudges me. "You ought to get one of those."

"Sign in and make yourselves comfortable," the woman says. "We've painted blazes so you'll feel right at home. Follow them down to the bunkhouse. You'll pass the shower house on the way. There's a wood stove down in the bunkhouse. Buccaneer here has already made a fire."

Good, I think, *she likes us*. I take a pen in my fist and scrawl my initials in her register.

Buccaneer raises his hot chocolate again and nods.

I buy a 16-ounce Styrofoam cup of hot chili and head straight for the shower. My hands still won't work, so I unzip my pack with my teeth and claw out some dry clothes.

No shower has ever felt so wonderful. I stand under the hot water, still shivering spasmodically, and eat the hot chili, feeling the cold wash away, both inside and out. Gradually the shivering stops, my hands regain feeling, and my teeth stop chattering. Ahhh....

That evening, lying in a warm bunk, eating Oreo after Oreo, following it with a half-gallon of milk, finishing up with some cold pizza, I feel deeply at peace. Ronsonol Man asks Buccaneer about his life.

"I must have hiked this Trail six or seven times," Buccaneer says. He has interesting gear: a big staff he carved with a totemic face and decorated with feathers he found, and a skunk-skin cap he tanned from a roadkill. He's huge, with legs like tree trunks and wide shoulders. With his dark beard, bandanna, and dark eyes, he looks like his name. I have a friend who's a semi-hermit in Montana; Buccaneer's eyes are like his, kind but distant, the eyes of someone who has seen a lot of pain and has retreated from it.

"How could you afford it?" asks Ronsonol Man.

"Oh, I work for the govmint."

"What, like the Forest Service?"

"No, the govmint. The federal govmint. I check things out. I get around."

I get the idea. He's probably a veteran, on disability, and prefers this hobo life to living in the city. I don't blame him. It's a good life, low-cost, low-hassle, and free.

We listen to the radio. There was a tornado near here earlier in the day, the reporter says. Her voice is generic Middle American, not the mountainy drawl everyone else around here has. Why are local radio stations often so bland? It would be a lot more interesting if people kept their regional accents. I wonder what the local people think, hearing this voice that sounds like it's from Indiana.

Buccaneer stretches and changes the station to NPR. *Prairie Home Companion* is on, and Garrison Keillor is telling a joke about snow. That's where I grew up, that's my home culture: the Great Lakes. Back home. But is it really my home now? Like Buccaneer, I've spent an awful lot of time getting around and checking things out.

Unlike other hikers, I don't have any particular place to go back to after the Trail. When people ask "Where are you from?" I'm not sure what to say. Sometimes I say "Right here," meaning the Trail. I hope I'll figure it out on the walk because if I don't, I'm not sure where I'll go.

The fire purrs in the wood stove. I go outside to look at the sky. It's clear, a crescent moon riding low, near Venus. Spring peepers fill the night with bell-like music, and a stream, flooded by the storm, sings over its rocks. The windows of nearby cabins are warm golden squares in the night.

I'll always remember this, I think. *I love this place. I love what I'm doing. It's the right thing.*

Until now I've been hiking with one hiking stick, the bamboo one I found when I was with Wade, and it makes hiking much easier but feels lopsided. If one stick makes my knees and hips feel better, I reason, two will really help. Back at the campground I picked up a good stick, and now it really does help, since my arms can take some of the weight. The new stick isn't perfect, but it will do for now. I'll keep looking for new ones, and eventually I'll find the perfect one: the one that's made for this walk, the one that fits perfectly in my hand.

According to my journal, I've been out here three weeks, but until I check, I don't know what day of the week it is. I don't have a watch. My clock and calendar are the sun and moon. The plants are keeping time, though; the woods are filled with faint beginnings of spring: mayapples like furled umbrellas, motherwort's green leaves poking up through the fallen ones from last year, lots of bloodroot.

No one in the world knows where I am. I'm free.

Ronsonol Man and I hike steeply down, five miles or so, and it's slippery and cliffy in spots. On the mountaintops it's still winter; I've woken to find snow on my sleeping bag twice, and the high woods are brown and gray and black, with only the barest hint of spring. Until now it's almost felt like spring will never come, and on the way down, before I reach the zone of spring, I stop walking and spend 10 minutes staring up at the tips of all the branches nearby, just to be sure there are at least buds on them. There are: The world will go on. And down in the valley there are leaves on the trees, the dogwoods are blooming, and a goldfinch flutters in a flowering apple tree.

We pass a dead copperhead snake, which is curled up like the letter C in a lesson from a morbid child's book: M is for Murder, C is for Copperhead.

We reach the Nantahala River, where there's a kayak/canoe center, a gear store, and restaurants. The river is wild, and kayakers are paddling in it, their big shoulders moving, their bodies encased in slick wetsuits. They ride the rapids like seals or otters, one with their boats. We stand on the bridge watching them, and some other kayakers walk by.

"Thruhikers!" one snorts. "You can always tell by the smell." They're clean, dressed in shorts and shirts fresh from the laundry. On the other side of the river, cars and trucks shine in the sun; they've driven here from somewhere, and they'll be back home, in bed, by nightfall.

At the restaurant, washing my hands in the bathroom, I look at myself in the mirror. It's the first time I've seen my reflection in more than two weeks. I look different: thinner and dirtier and wilder. My eyes gleam, and I have the odd, intense stare you usually see in old photographs of pioneers or Indians or immigrants.

The food is delicious: big steak, rice, carrots and celery, hummus and rolls and butter, and the waiter, who was once a hiker with a "hoods in the woods" group, brings us each a double portion of chocolate upside-down cake for dessert and tells us he misses the Trail life. He says he passed us on the bridge during his break and heard the kayakers' comments. "Don't mind those kayakers making fun of you," he says. "I hear 'em talking when there are no hikers around, and they all wish they were you."

I look up at the mountains we've come down from. Ravens fly over the summits, which are still lit by the setting sun. I'm glad I'm going back up into the woods, back to cold fresh air and firelight, where I can sleep outside and hear the night animals crying. Civilization has showers and food, but freedom is better.

We've left our packs at the door to the restaurant, and as we put them on and prepare to walk back up the mountain to a shelter we passed on the way down to the valley, the other patrons watch. We bow, salute the clean, well-rested people, and leave.

That night it's nice to be home, nice to be back in the woods with a big fire going, coyotes howling somewhere nearby, and the guys who have showed up telling stories about working for a cannery in Alaska. Ronsonol Man feeds the fire, then pulls out a tiny portable radio, puts on earphones, and scrolls up and down the dial, looking for a hockey game.

"I can get it, but it's mixed in with some guy preaching," he says. "It sounds like the players are making slap shots straight to hell, and Jesus is the goalie."

In the past couple of days I've gotten the feeling that he's getting nervous about hiking in sync with me; we keep ending in the same places every night, we have too much fun together, and maybe it's dangerous. I wish I could tell him not to worry, but I can't say anything because nothing has been said: It's all undercurrents and intuition, and talking about it would merely be embarrassing. What would I say? "I think you're worried that I'm interested in you, but I'm not, except as a friend, so relax." There's no polite way to say it, so I don't.

I've been thinking about the whole male-female thing a lot lately, mostly because of his company. There are plenty of good guys out here; he's one. Ronsonol Man is every straight woman's dream: sensitive, funny, outdoorsy, intelligent. He's good looking, and pleasant under pressure. But the more I walk, the farther I go, the more it becomes clear to me: For whatever reason, I could never be happy with a man, no matter how "perfect." And when I was with men in the past it was for all the wrong reasons, mostly because it was the easy way out, the unthinking response to the social pressure to be "normal." Even when I was with them, I fantasized constantly about women. That's hardly the key to a great relationship with a guy.

Well, I think, leaning my blistered and bandaged bare feet on the wall in the firelight, looking at my toenails, which are blackened and eventually going to fall off, I'm definitely not "normal." If someone is well adjusted and happy in their life, they don't have a compulsion to leave everything and walk over mountains for six months. That's it for trying to be normal. It got me nowhere: stupid relationships, stupid jobs. So now I'll follow my heart and follow the blazes. Wherever they lead me, I'll celebrate it and live it as fully as I can.

The next morning a hiker named Lost John catches me as I cross the bridge over the Nantahala River again. "Hey, Amazin' Grace! You want some breakfast?"

"I just ate a big breakfast, but I'll have another one."

We go into the restaurant and eat. He's gentle, modest, and quiet and has been hiking with a bunch of rowdy, competitive people since I last saw him at the Neels Gap hostel in Georgia. One of them, known up and down the Trail for being a bully, took something that Lost John valued, then taunted him about it.

Lost John tells me about this. His stomach is upset, and he thinks he has giardia, an intestinal disease caused by parasites that you can sometimes get by drinking unfiltered water in the backcountry. His problem seems more like soul sickness, loneliness, or fear; he seems like a shy kid telling you he can't go to school because his stomach hurts.

"Don't hike with those people anymore," I say. "They're ruining your experience of the Trail. Forget all that crap about how many miles you have to hike in a day and who hikes the fastest. Just hike your own way and enjoy it."

"I went whitewater rafting and it was great," he says wistfully. "I loved it. I wish I could stay here a few days and do more. But it's really expensive."

I know that if he stays here, he'll never hike on. Hikers will come and go, he won't know anyone, he'll feel left out and lonely, and he'll go home and feel like a failure for leaving. His telling me he wants to leave is like someone telling you he's going to kill himself, a cry for help: "Save me from dropping off the Trail."

"Just keep hiking. It'll get better. You just need to know better people on the Trail. Come with me; there are a bunch of friendly people around, and you'll feel better."

As we begin the long, slow six-mile ascent out of the valley, I hear his trudging footsteps behind me. We don't talk much; he's too sad.

The wind picks up and sings against my pack frame, whining as it pours through the adjustment holes in the metal uprights. The steep views into the valley are incredible. The sun is out, it's warm, and I'm glad Lost John isn't going home yet. I hate to see anyone leave before they've felt what I feel about this trip.

After about four miles I say, "Hey, John, wanna take a break and have a snack?"

He doesn't answer. My pack is so bulky that it often blocks whatever I say to people behind me, so I turn around.

"John?"

He's not there. I walk a few paces back downhill, trying to see if he's coming around a curve in the mountain. The footsteps I heard behind me turn out to be my pack squeaking and the wind rattling the fabric.

I sit on a log and eat gorp and wait half an hour, knowing he's not coming. At some point during our walk he must have drifted behind and then, too sad to speak about it, turned around without a word and gone back to the valley.

I wish he had continued. I'm convinced it was simply bad company that made him quit. I hope he feels at peace with his decision to leave.

At the shelter that night, Ronsonol Man makes a big fire, and we sit around watching it burn. The military guys talk longingly of their favorite drinks: Tanqueray and tonic versus ordinary gin and tonic; different brands of vodka; the merits of whiskey. There aren't many serious drunks on the Trail, probably because liquor is heavy, and, at least in the South, many of the counties the Trail passes through are dry; you can't buy, sell, or drink liquor there.

Steamroller Boy sighs and whacks the fire with a stick. A burst of sparks rolls up into the dark sky.

"This trip was supposed to be a 'sobering experience,'" he says. "I haven't had a drink since I started, and I can't get any in the towns, but I don't know what's going to happen when we get to a town that has a liquor store."

"I'd sure like a beer," says Randall, a hiker who's hooked up with them. He's a big man from North Carolina, and he was also in the Army.

Everyone sits, watching the fire, thinking.

"This is our TV," Ronsonol Man says, looking at the firelight shining on the circle of hypnotized faces.

"Back home they have a 'fire channel' on cable," Steamroller Boy says. "It's a continuous loop of a fireplace. Can you imagine that? You come home, have a few drinks, turn on the fire channel, and get romantic."

"Yeah, I bet it's just a Duraflame too, not even a real log," says Bearbait.

"What was that about 'You come home, get romantic, have a few drinks'?" Homer says. "I thought you said this was supposed to be a sobering experience."

"Yeah," Steamroller Boy says. "Supposed to be. It sure is. Supposed to be."

In one morning I klonk my head on the low ceiling of the shelter three times, trip twice on my way to and from the spring, drop my water bag and have to go get water all over again, and after hiking a few miles, squat to relieve myself on the steep side of Cheoh Bald, fall backward, and sit right in the hole I've dug and just filled. Fortunately the mess is confined to the long tail of my shirt. There's no water on this mountain, so I take out my Swiss Army knife, use the scissors attachment to cut out the offending portion of the shirt, and bury it right there.

Some short-term hikers come by soon after.

"Hey, what happened to your shirt? There's a big piece missing on the back."

"A mouse ate it."

All day I feel in danger of slipping off a cliff, gashing myself on a rock, or twisting an ankle, as if I'm a puppet with tangled strings. I'm in a good mood, though, feeling so remote from my body that I'm only amused by all these accidents, and it's obvious that I'm exhausted or malnourished or both. The stretch between the Nantahala Outdoor Center and Fontana Dam is one of the harshest, steepest sections of the Trail, and we're all doing big miles for this kind of terrain. A particularly nasty, straight-up mountain, not even named on the map, levels everyone, so that by mid afternoon I catch up with all the military guys, who are sweating up the nearly vertical incline.

It feels impossible to take one more step, but I do, one after the other. This is the Wall marathoners talk about, and we've all hit it. I've hiked nine-and-a-half miles today and have five-and-a-half more to go because I'm nearly out of food and have to get to Fontana Dam, a resupply stop, tomorrow. I can't quit now.

We all keep going. No one talks. Sometimes one of us passes another, bent backs and legs laboring, sweat pouring down our arms and legs, lungs bursting. Periodically I trip on roots, rocks, or my own feet, but manage not to fall. My toenails feel like someone is hammering them. Five of them are black and thickened, due to fall off eventually. I'll be glad to see them go, if the pain will go with them. My knees and hips and feet are in agony. People who see you with a huge pack on your back always assume that it must give you a backache, but my back is the one part of my body that never hurts. And my head. Before the hike I had a headache every single day; it was my standard mode of being. During the hike I've never once had a headache or backache, but everything else is in constant pain.

Late in the day I pass through the Wall, and come out on the other side. I can feel the shift, as if I've tapped into a new source of bright, clean-burning, inexhaustible fuel, which I have: My body, all out of carbohydrates, is burning its fat reserves. I can go forever, and I do, hiking the last three miles in an hour, leaving behind all the men, who watch in amazement as I fly up a hill and leave them behind.

So many times on this trip I've walked far beyond my supposed endurance. It's a stretch. And now that I've stretched this far, I'll never have the same limits again. It makes me realize that a lot of limitations are purely mental: You think you can't do something, so you don't. But in reality you can. Just do it. Just keep going. This trek is painful, but in some ways I love the pain, the testing, the endurance, the hardship of this life. It's real, it's grounding, in a way that the easy life of civilization is not.

I reach the shelter long before everyone else and spend a long time at the spring watching salamanders. This shelter, like many others, has salamanders living in the water source. The Appalachians have a huge variety of different species of salamanders, because the populations are separated by the high ridges, and they all evolved slightly differently. They're quiet little things, harmless, interesting. I wish I knew more about them; for all I know, I could be looking at a completely unknown and undiscovered species. I watch them a while, get water, only spill it once, and go back to the shelter. I bonk my head on the rafters and decide enough is enough: It's time to lie still, not move, not touch anything. The last thing I hear is Steamroller Boy, asking sleepily, "Hey, Grace, what did you say happened to your shirt?"

It's raining, ponging down on the metal roof of the shelter like slow Chinese chimes. Wood thrushes, the most beautiful singers in North America, sing their questioning, flutelike phrases, then pause, like someone tossing a pebble into a pond then waiting for the ripples to spread out before tossing another. I lie in my sleeping bag, in an ecstasy of music. Thrushes always seem to sing more in quiet rain, as if they know it makes them sound even more beautiful. Someday I'd like to lie on cool moss in the green gloom of dense woods and just listen to them all day. No hiking, just bird music.

Last night I dreamed of flying, a release from my body. My hands are so swollen that I can't bend my fingers. Sausage hands. Two of my blackened toenails have come off, with others on the way. Last night I didn't sleep much. My feet and legs were too painful and kept me awake much of the night, in between dreams.

I also dreamed of my grandmother, who has been dead for years, who appeared and said she's concerned about my welfare out here in the mountains. I wake feeling as if she's watching over me, this woman who grew up on a farm and used to ride a horse to school, who never got past the sixth grade because she had to help her parents with the farmwork. She wouldn't understand my desire to be out here, on purpose, when I could be in civilization. Her ideal life, which she never got, was to be a secretary: sitting in a clean, quiet office, in a clean pink sweater, writing neatly on a clean white pad, taking dictation, instead of mucking around in a field, digging up potatoes. In some ways, though, I'm like her. She always knew which phase the moon was in, knew all the species of birds by their songs, knew all the wildflowers in the valley where she lived.

I feel watched over by a lot of departed people on this trip: my father, my grandmother, others I sense walking near me but can't name. This trip does feel like a pilgrimage, one so necessary that even angels are on my side, helping me through. I sense convergences, arrivals, meetings, forces coming together, the slow current of happy fate. Grace, like my name; spiritual gifts. Good things are coming. I can feel them.

I lie in my bag, on my back, holding my hands toward the ceiling to let the swelling drain out of them. I bend my fingers, flex my aching knees, arch my back.

Only six miles to go today, to Fontana Dam. Walking in rain, with bird music, with ghosts.

Fontana Dam is a tiny resort at the edge of a lake created when the Tennessee Valley Authority built a big dam on the Little Tennessee River. It's a beautiful setting, with the lake, and the Smoky Mountains beyond it. There's not much here, other than a post office, a general store, and a cafeteria for tourists, but it's enough.

I get mail in Fontana Dam, for the first time on the trip. My friends all have my projected schedule, and they send me mail care of General Delivery, at whatever town they expect me to be in. The system works, even though I'm behind my schedule by about 10 days: I get a lot of letters and so many boxes of cookies that I can give many of them away. It feels good to have this contact with home, to hear about people living settled lives. It's strange: They're moving in a slower universe. I'm walking and changing so fast, while they're mostly staying the same or changing at a much slower rate.

I look out across the sunset lake, at the cloud-wreathed high places of the Great Smokies, where I'll walk from one lofty summit to the next. The air smells clean—a cool, damp breath of wet stone and fresh flowers. It's getting dark, and the last of the tourists are gone. My gear is packed, and I'm ready to head across the dam and into the Smokies in the morning. I feel blessed to be here, so connected to that deep sweet energy, so blessed to be moving along.

April 27
Fontana Dam, N.C.

Chapter Four

As we enter the Smokies, Ronsonol Man decides he wants to catch up with a group of guys who are walking ahead of us and takes off on a stretch of big-mile days. I keep to my own pace, walking steadily, not too many or too few miles in a day. It's been fun running into Ronsonol Man at the shelters every night, but I don't want anyone, including either of us, to assume we're hiking partners. He feels the same way.

My attitude toward this is paradoxical. I like his company but don't want the baggage that goes with it. I don't want others to assume we're a couple; I don't want to have to hike at someone else's pace; I don't want to get used to hiking with anyone. And I don't want anyone to get used to hiking with me, even if it only means we hike alone but keep ending up at the same place each night.

Still, sometimes I get lonely. Often I get to a shelter and there are two or three or six hikers there, all traveling together, all with that tight bond you can only get through shared ordeals. Invariably they've been traveling together since the beginning of the Trail. They reminisce about Springer Mountain and every mile since then.

As far as I know, the people I met at the beginning of the Trail have all given up and gone home. I didn't have a chance to bond with any of them because we all walked at such different speeds and the dropout rate was so high. Now all the social groups are set up, the cliques are formed, and it's too late to join. I feel like a kid who's moved to a new town and a new high school in the second semester of senior year: Forget it. You're gonna walk alone.

I want to have friends on the Trail. I want to feel like someone cares, like someone would notice and come looking if I fell off a cliff. I want buddies, friends on the trip. But as I walk and think about it, I know the time isn't right.

I'm burdened by all my secrets, by my not being ready to tell anyone why I'm really out here. Maybe people sense this reserve. They feel the barrier, the lack of trust. To make friends I'll have to trust people, but I can't trust people until I've walked through some old pain, and I have to be alone to come to terms with whatever it is that has made me so discontented in civilization. I need time to think about why I had to make this journey.

I'm on a pilgrimage to find out why I'm on a pilgrimage.

One thing I miss, though, is the safety of walking with others. I'm not worried about people attacking me; the terrain is too tough and remote. If you wanted to mug or rape someone, would you bother walking many miles, uphill, in mud and rain, in bear country, to find a target? No, you'd crouch behind a line of parked cars on a Washington, D.C., street, where it's easier to find victims and you can quickly get away and go home to a hot shower and a hot meal after a hard day of crime.

I'm more worried about falling down and spraining or breaking something, or getting hypothermia again. Statistically, I'm more likely to be hit by lightning out here than I am to be attacked.

I fall down more frequently than you'd think. Maybe once a week, maybe more, depending on the weather. Rainy days are the worst, especially on rocks, which are slick, or over fallen leaves, which are even slicker. The cartoonists who draw people skidding on banana peels have never hiked in the rain on fallen leaves. When I fall it's always dramatic, feet flying up, pack hitting the rocks with a decisive *whump!* Like a turtle, I have trouble flipping back over and often have to take off my pack before I can get up. Sometimes I hurt myself: twist an ankle, bruise an elbow, gash a leg. There's nothing else to do but get up and hike on. Alone.

I spend long, quiet days on the Trail, 10 hours of hiking, moving silently except for my breath, the saddlelike squeak of the pack, and the slight scuff of boots on rocks and the well-trod footpath. Sometimes I see the tracks and hiking-stick marks of people who are a few hours or a day ahead, and when I cross streams and see the wet footprints still drying on the rocks, I know the other hiker isn't far ahead. Sometimes I speed up, just out of curiosity to see who it is, but more often I walk at the same pace, following the tracks all day, feeling as if I'm in on a secret.

And at times I feel like I'm flying over the mountains, rocks and roots and birds around me, the rain cold on my skin, wet and itchy, and under my clothes there's deep-down dirt and sweat, as if I'm a part of the mountain and eroding along with it, as if I'm the stream I have to ford, as if I'm the crow calling from the top of the tree or the wet logs I stop to rest on. As if I'm just another animal, an animal moving quietly through the wilderness.

I talk to myself. I talk to the trees, to the sky, to birds, to the animals, especially the ones who are in on the conspiracy to steal my food. There's no one around to hear, most of the time, except the animals themselves.

I've come to love hiking late in the day. I hold my hand up at arm's length, fingers parallel with the horizon, to see how much more daylight is left. Each finger's width above the horizon equals 15 minutes of sunlight. And night comes quickly in the mountains, where the peaks cut the light in half as soon as the sun drops behind them.

Hiking at dusk gives you a feeling of urgency, of secrecy, as if you're witnessing a ritual that the woods reveal to few: the evening ritual of falling sun, of night animals coming out to make their rounds. The sunlight slants low through the trees, lighting patches, as if this branch is special, as if this leaf is meant for your attention. Most people leave the woods at night; few see this special time night after night, few have the dark woods for a bedroom, the stars for their night ceiling. As the trip goes on and I walk farther, I lose my wariness of sitting alone in the woods at night. After all, this is my home.

The Trail in the Smokies follows the chilly ridgeline, so most of the hike is through the piney Canadian summit forest that teems with northern animals: black-capped chickadees, red squirrels, ravens, juncos, and black-and-white warblers. I love the deep-green, leafy, moist environment of the Appalachian cove forest in the bottomlands, and walking along the ridge, where it's still winter, I look longingly, far down into the valleys, where the almost supernaturally green flush of spring creeps up the watercourses. I won't get to walk there, at least not in the Smokies: I'm stuck with winter, up on the cold and lofty summits.

As I walk through the evergreens I sing a lamentful old Appalachian song:

In the pines, in the pines
Where the sun never shines,
And we shiver, when the cold winds blow.

It sounds best when two people sing it together, each harmonizing with the other in a mournful key to imitate the wind. I sing each part alternately at the top of my lungs, hoping that if any bears hear me, they'll run away. There are many bears in the Smokies, and they're so aggressive that the shelters here are fenced in to keep the hikers safe. In between shelters, you're on your own.

At Derrick Knob Shelter, late on a stormy night, I go outside to pee and feel exhilarated, standing on the roaring mountaintop. I put a hand on the outside wall of the stone hut for balance, looking at bright Venus and the partial moon, all the trees bending and swaying in the fierce wind; loving the simplicity and elemental energy of this night, the wild vast view into North Carolina, the lights of tiny hamlets far below, the smell of coming rain. I've walked almost 200 miles to get here.

Inside the shelter, smoke comes down the chimney and twists out into the room like a ghost. The room smells of stone and rain, of hikers' sweat and wet boots, of macaroni and cheese and a fine dust of hot-chocolate powder, blown out of someone's mug by a gust of wind—and ashes, whirling out of the fireplace and settling on us like snow.

"What's the terrain tomorrow?" a short-timer from Cleveland asks his brother.

His brother flicks on his flashlight and looks at the map. "Let's see…up and down, up and down, up and down. Followed by down and up."

Bridget sticks her head up to the upper sleeping shelf, where I'm resting. "You want to go to Gatlinburg with me and Terry in a few days?"

I'm reluctant to go to town, since it's a waste of money, and I prefer the peace and beauty of the woods. But as usual I'm running out of food, and at night I can't sleep because I'm so hungry. I crave fat—anything fried and served in a basket with french fries is all right by me. I check my food bag, which is ominously light, and decide to go.

It pours all night—fierce rain and 50-mile-an-hour winds. The rain, driven by the wind, sprays through the cracks in the stone shelter wall in a fine mist and sounds like stones falling on the corrugated metal roof two feet over my head. In the early morning, before the sun comes up, a muffled *boom!* shakes the entire shelter. An old tree has fallen somewhere nearby.

It's cold and still raining. The shelter is full, and some people have pitched a tent about six feet away, but the wind, rain, and fog are so thick that I can't even see it. They must be miserable in there; it's amazing that the wind hasn't blown their tent away.

Today I'm hiking over Clingman's Dome, the highest point on the entire Trail and a cold mountain even in summertime. The rain will slow the travel, make it arduous and slippery, and if I get hypothermia, there's no convenient town or campground where I could recover. I eat a stick of pepperoni, consider my options, and decide to hike.

By lunchtime the sky has cleared, and I've walked seven of the 13 miles I want to walk today. I'm sitting in another shelter eating lunch inside the safety of the shelter's bear fence when some retired German dayhikers appear. They step tentatively into the shelter and look around with mingled curiosity and dismay.

"Ach! So primitif!" the woman says. They discuss it in German: Do hikers really stay here? But there is only a dirt floor! And what are those curious contraptions hanging from the ceiling?

"Those are against the mice," I say. In a mixture of my high-school German and English, we converse. Where do the hikers sleep? On those wooden platforms. Where do they go to the bathroom? In the forest. Where do they get their water? From streams. Do they ever take a shower? No. Are there that many mice in the shelters? Ach, yes indeed. What is the chain-link fence for?

"Bears."

"Bears!" They're shocked. There are really bears here? Oh, yes, in fact I know people who've been chased by them. I point to the notice on the shelter wall, warning hikers to keep the gate closed; in the past, hikers have returned from a trip to the spring and found a bear in the shelter, eating all their food.

We talk about how big America is—a topic Europeans

always love—and what I'm doing walking 2,000 miles. "Americans are lazy," they say. It's another topic Europeans love. "They never walk. They want to ride in cars, forever, to their shopping malls, and then sit and watch TV all night."

I have to admit they have us pegged. I've always been a walker. Ever since I was little, I would take off and walk all day just for the enjoyment of it, and I often walked back and forth every day to jobs that were five or six miles from where I lived. But I've seldom met other Americans who will even walk across a parking lot if they can avoid it. Think of the people you see shuttling back and forth along the rows in parking lots, crawling up and down so they can get a spot that's 10 feet closer to the store, or who park illegally in the fire lane so they can go inside and buy a diet book and a gallon of fat-free ice cream.

We shake our heads and *tsk-tsk* at the laziness of Americans, as I lift my 50-pound pack and set out for six more miles over Clingman's Dome. As I pass them the woman lifts her hand tentatively, as if she wants to ask just one more question: "Excuse me—but what haf you done to your shirt?"

On Clingman's Dome, said to have one of the best views on the Trail, I go up in the observation tower and observe fog and ice. I knew there would be no view, but I went up anyway, a sort of joke: looking at a blank white screen. I take a picture, but of course it won't turn out. It's just white. All around me, Fraser fir trees jingle as the wind plays the icicles on them like chimes.

That night at Mount Collins Shelter, it's so cold that it keeps everyone awake. We build a fire in the shelter fireplace, but most of the warmth goes up the chimney. Some weekenders, who have a lot of extra food they want to get rid of, amuse themselves by feeding me, Bridget, and Terry. We lie on the upper sleeping shelf, opening our mouths like baby birds, and they pop in Oreos, dried kiwis and strawberries, bite-size candy bars, venison jerky. They're amazed at our unending hunger and our garbage-disposal capacity to eat anything and everything, and they empty out their food bags, trying to find a limit to our appetites. They never do, and finally they wise up and save a few crumbs for themselves.

I lie in my bag, wearing mittens and a scarf and everything else I own. I have one of those little heat packs: Tear the wrapper off, shake it, and it produces heat for the next 24 hours. I put it over my heart and hold it there. It radiates warmth like a little animal. I stop shivering, but just after I fall asleep, something jumps onto my feet. I kick it off, but it comes back. It's fairly heavy: raccoon, skunk, something like that. When I move my feet it goes over onto Bridget, then I hear her sleeping bag swish and it's back on my feet. This goes on for a while. Tension mounts in me: What is it?

"Aaaaaagggghh! Get off me!" I sit up, snap on my light, and am face to face with Bridget, who sits up and switches on her light at the exact same moment. We stare at each other, wide-eyed, then sweep the beams of our flashlights toward our toes.

There's nothing there. Crammed together in the crowded shelter, we've been kicking each other, each of us thinking the other's feet were an animal. We laugh, give each other a few more light kicks just to get it out of our systems, and lie back down.

I think of food: butter, bacon, french fries, ice cream. My body is almost humming; I feel it using itself up, metabolism on high rev. I feel bones I never knew I had. Outside, the wind moves through the cold forest, freezing our footprints on the muddy Trail.

At Newfound Gap I come out of the woods and onto a road. Cars roar past. On the other side of the road is a parking lot packed with buses, trucks, cars, and vans, all filled with people in shorts and loose shirts, all armed with video cameras. When they see me emerge from the woods, they swerve over toward me, almost running, until I'm the center of a circle of lenses, cameras, and gaping children. Terry and Bridget aren't far behind, and when they come out of the woods they're enveloped too. It's the only place in the Smokies where the Trail crosses a road.

"Are you one of those hiker people that walks all the way to Maine?"

"Where'd you come from?"

"How heavy is that pack?"

"What're you carrying in there?"

"Are you walking all alone?"

"Seen any bears?"

"Seen any snakes?"

Behind the crowd, on a rock wall, is a big display about the Trail and the "intrepid souls" who set out to hike the whole way. They've all read it and are thrilled to see us.

Some thruhikers get tired of all the questions, acting as if the people are ignorant or tiresome because they always ask the same things. I love telling people about the Trail, getting them interested, and encouraging them, especially children and women, to walk all or part of it someday. Even if someone only walks the Trail for a mile or a day or an hour, they can be part of something wonderful, can feel that deep sense of adventure and possibility.

The tourists take videos and photos and insist on giving us candy. "How do you get your food?" they ask.

"We have to go into towns to resupply," I say. "In fact, that's why we're at this road right now, because we're all out of food and have to go down to Gatlinburg to stock up for the next week."

Just like that, we have rides to town. Mine is with a silver-haired couple from Tennessee who are just out for the ride and the views. As we drive down the twisty road, they feed me cheese balls and raisins. My hands are scarred from cooking over fire, blackened and rough, and I feel embarrassed to be reaching into their clean bag of cheese balls. They notice and say, "Don't pay that no never mind. We're old campers and hikers, and we've been just as bad off before." True Southerners, they know how to put a guest at home, even if the guest is only briefly visiting their car. They've helped hikers before, and will again.

Gatlinburg is one big touristy strip mall, with Muzak versions of bluegrass piped through speakers on the street, and storefront businesses with pink signs saying:

BASIC SIMPLE WEDDINGS
NO APPOINTMENT NECESSARY
WALK-INS WELCOME

As I stand on the street corner waiting for Terry and Bridget, folks walk by and stare at me and my pack. "I've never seen anyone with one of them things on, except on TV," a man says. "How far do you go with that thing on?"

"I've walked 200 miles to get here."

"No! You're telling me a story."

"It's true." I point at my dirty, muscular legs, which look like a marathoner's. "Do you think my legs would look like that if I hadn't walked that far?"

"Well, that's true. I guess I do believe you!"

He walks away. I stand on the corner, listening to the inauthentic bluegrass, watching people. Everyone in Gatlinburg is very white, very slow, and very heavy. Tourists drift dully up and down the street and in and out of stores, looking dazed and blunted, like fish in a tank without enough oxygen. They seem drugged by the speakers blasting sugary music, by the vast sensory overload of thousands of bright colors all jammed into this one street. They all smell like cigarettes, gasoline, and soap.

We don't have time to resupply, do town chores, and get back up to the mountains before dark, so the three of us get a motel room and suddenly realize that we can't bear being enclosed within four walls. After eating, showering, doing laundry, and resupplying, we sit outside the room, eating ice cream, until it's absolutely time to go to sleep. Even then, with both windows open and a breeze coming in, the room feels suffocating.

I sleep on the bed and wake up in the night from a dream of falling. I put both hands out to feel the ground beneath me, looking for reassurance. Unlike the hard earth or shelter sleeping platform that makes you painfully aware that gravity has a hold on you, the bed is so soft that I can't even feel it; I feel like I'm floating. Every time I relax I have the same feeling of nothing underneath me, of falling. I get up, lie on the hard floor, and instantly fall asleep.

At Cosby Knob Shelter about 15 thruhikers have bunched up. I've never seen so many thruhikers in one place before; some I know, some I don't, some I've been following for the past month, reading their entries in the shelter logs, and some have been following me and reading my entries. It's weird to meet someone who knows all about you through your writing, when you don't know anything about them but their name. Sometimes people "know" things about you that turn out to be wrong: A hiker tells me that the word behind me on the Trail is that I'm an ordained minister. He laughs when I tell him I don't even go to church.

All of us know everyone who's hiking within 100 miles of us—even if we've never met—either through reading their entries in the shelter logs or from gossip passed on by word of mouth from others who have seen or heard of them. We have a community, a culture, and a fellowship that grows stronger as we all walk farther and endure more. It's a long, thin community, spread out over 2,000 miles, but like Gypsies, we keep track of our tribe. "Who did you see today?" hikers always ask when they meet, in the same breath that they ask how far the water sources or shelters are, and we stand on the Trail talking, trading news about who we've seen, and eating snacks, before moving on.

There's a southbounder here, Cloudwalker, who's walked

all the way from Maine and has just 200 more miles to go. We tell him about the mountains he has yet to see, congratulate him, and look at him in awe: Next to him, our 200 miles is nothing. He's friendly but somehow subtly different from us. He's seen all the mountains that we only hope we keep walking long enough to see. He's a different person, someone who's done it.

We won't all be able to feel how Cloudwalker feels, and we know it. It's like one of those statistics about cancer: One in three people will get it. Look around. Will it be the person on your left, the person on your right, or you? On the Trail the odds are even worse: Nine out of 10 drop out. I don't want to be one of them. More than anything, I want to keep walking, all the way to the end.

At this shelter there's a woman who has the same little wood-burning stove I have, and another hiker teases her about how much smoke it puts out. Hers does put out a lot of smoke, because she's burning leaves and green sticks in it. The other hiker, Big Josh, is an acerbic New Jerseyite who reminds me of Rodney Dangerfield, but she clearly doesn't think he's amusing.

I sit next to her and fire up my own stove. "People love to hassle you if you have this stove," I say. "It's so low-tech that it makes the gearheads nervous. It's like a stove Fred Flintstone would go camping with."

"Uh-huh."

She shoves some more leaves into her stove. A wall of smoke eddies out and makes everyone cough. She moves with the rapid, jerky motions of someone who is deeply angry.

"So what made you decide to do the AT?" I ask.

"I lost my job."

"Do you like the Trail?"

"No."

"What keeps you hiking, then?"

"Nothing."

That day, she disappears. Later I hear she hiked back to the road at Newfound Gap and left the Trail for good.

At the end of the Smokies I take a side trip to the Mount Cammerer fire tower, a half-mile off the Trail. I spend a long time sitting on the mountaintop looking into the valleys, where spring slowly moves up the slopes, and looking far off at the mountains I'll cross in the coming days and weeks. A deer appears, walking delicately, like a shy girl in high heels, and stands nearby eating leaves off a bush.

I've been walking for nearly a month. I've never felt so peaceful and right about anything I've done.

How can I keep this peace and trust after returning to civilization? How can I make a living but not have a job that makes me feel as if I'm in prison? How can I keep this simple life, where it's so obvious what's important and what's not?

What's important: a warm fire, clean water, shelter from the rain, food, and the company of others. And the walk. The continuing pilgrimage. I have no thoughts about leaving. The world outside the Trail is like the land beyond a cliff: nothing there, nothing you'd want to leap into anyway.

"You're the kind of person who talks to anyone and is at home with everyone," Bridget told me a couple of days ago. I was shocked. When I was a kid I was like that, then lost it in the years between then and now, when I was living a life that was false in so many ways. Now I feel like I'm coming home to myself, here in this beautiful forest.

I trust that the Trail itself will lead me where I need to go, if I give my heart to it completely. By the time I'm done, I'll know what to do next.

I bow to the deer, who tosses her head at me, then put on my pack and walk. For the first time in the Smokies, the Trail leaves the ridgeline and descends many miles into my dream-forest, that ethereally green, flower-filled, watery cove I've seen from such a great distance while walking along the lofty, wintry summits above. Down here it's deep into spring, the mountainsides covered with dwarf iris, fire pink, ladyslippers, bloodroot, flowering dogwoods, shadbush, golden ragwort, violets, several kinds of trilliums, flame azaleas, Dutchman's breeches, mayapples, buttercup, trout lilies, squawroot, violets, tulip trees, and striped maples. There are so many flowers it looks like the woods are going to a wedding. The path is strewn with tiny, delicate blossoms, petals, leaves, buds, green tips, and tender twigs. This generosity of the forest, its casual strewing of beauty, always touches me, as if someone has done this on purpose simply because it's so lovely and tender.

"Thank you," I say to everything: the mossy, velvet-green stump with a tiny acorn resting on it like a jeweler's display; the magnolia petals, creamy vanilla-lemon scented scoops that look like (but are not) edible spoons; the exquisitely formed maple leaves that are still as small as a fingernail. For the first time on the trip I hear the song of a veery, that elusive bird of damp, rich forests. Its song, a complex, ethereal, down-spiraling whistle, sounds like music from another world, where spirits live.

The shelter in Davenport Gap is full of people, a mix of thruhikers, a group who hiked most of the Trail so far but then hitchhiked up from Fontana Dam, and some weekenders. The hitchhikers, who have a dog with them, couldn't hike through the Smokies since dogs aren't allowed there. So instead of having the dog shuttled around the Park and then kenneled while they hiked through, they simply skipped the Smokies entirely, hitchhiking around the mountains instead of walking through them.

"We're just a bunch of damn yellow-blazers," says one. He's lying in a hammock strung between the rafters, smoking a joint. His buddies laugh.

"No, man, *rainbow*-blazers is what we are. *Rainbow.*"

Two thousand miles is a long walk, and exactly what constitutes a thruhike is debated among hikers as intricately and hotly as the tenets of a fundamentalist religion. There's often more than one way to get between any two points on the Trail. Other trails, usually marked with blue blazes, intersect the white-blazed AT and often reconnect to it five, 10, or 20 miles away.

Some of these "blue-blazes" cut off miles of Trail, thus shortening the walk. Others may be more scenic. Sometimes they intersect with roads, where hungry hikers can find food.

Some people are "purists," hiking the AT and only the AT, passing every white blaze. If a shelter is reached by a blue-blazed loop trail, hard-line purists will backtrack to cover the tiny piece of the AT that's cut off by the loop. Others believe it's OK to take shelter trails, but not to travel on any other blue-blazed trail. And yellow-blazing is out of the question unless you're leaving the Trail entirely and going into town to resupply.

Yellow-blazing is hitchhiking. Instead of following the AT, which is marked by white blazes, you're flying along at 55 miles an hour on the road, which of course is marked by a yellow line. If you hike on that road instead of getting a ride, you're blue-blazing, the equivalent of using a side trail, somewhat less damning than traveling in the back of someone's pickup truck. Bushwhacking, traveling through the woods and not following a trail at all, is green-blazing, and following a trail that used to be the AT, but where the old white blazes have been painted out, is ghost-blazing. Hikers who use a mixture of the AT, blue-blazed side trails, and hitchhiking to travel up the Trail are rainbow-blazers, and some purists look down on them, as if their pilgrimages are less valid.

I'm not concerned about who got here which way. Hikers have another saying, "Hike your own hike," which means mind your own business, do what you're here to do, and don't judge others. I don't think there's any objective way to judge whether someone else's hike is valid; all you can do is make sure yours is valid for you.

The rainbow-blazers pass their joint back and forth, the dog yawns and puts his head on his paws, and the weekenders hand out marshmallows for everyone to toast on the fire. Outside the shelter it's raining flowers, creamy cup-shaped blossoms of five joined petals showering down from the canopy of trees. Limey, a

British hiker, reads us a poem by Rumi, a Sufi mystic, from a book he carries in his pack. The poem talks about the simple life, about living with the moon and planets over your head, about living in a shelter so basic that you could knock it down with one kick.

We all smile at the rightness of it. It's not just a poem, some ideal of simplicity, some metaphor to longingly sigh over. It's a vivid description of our daily life. The only shelter I have, besides the official Trail ones, is a tarp, which weighs one-and-a-half pounds and can be taken down and packed in less than a minute. Others have tents, similarly light and easy. Most of the time our ceiling is the sky. We are never truly indoors, enclosed.

I think of my life before the Trail: enclosed, boring jobs, bad relationships. Like a house of cards on a flimsy table, it was built on the wrong foundation. Behave yourself. Find a man. Get a real job. Be normal.

Go ahead, I think. *Go ahead and knock it down.*

Davenport Gap is a watery, stream-filled, green-lit place, a wonderland of flowers. Showy orchis, dwarf iris, fire pink, golden ragwort, trilliums by the millions, flame azalea, Dutchman's breeches, mayapples, trout lilies, squawroot, violets. I feel my soul widen just from looking at them. I want to draw them all, just as I want to draw or paint the tender leaves and perfect buds scattered on the path. I haven't drawn since I was a child, but this reawakens the urge for art.

Big Josh, the same feisty Yankee who teased the ex-hiker about her stove, is hiking behind me. He talks as we hike, a running self-deprecating monologue: "I don't know what I was thinking wearing these long pants. Jesus, I'm as hot as hell. Would you look at that flower! What is that? It's gorgeous! You'd think a man my age would know enough to wear shorts. What a dummy. Can you believe it? What's *that* flower called? What am I doing hiking this crazy thing? I'm an idiot. Look at that bird. I hope I can make it."

He's enthusiastic, and what might seem like complaining or whining from another person is, coming from him, hilarious. Maybe it's the New Jersey accent. Maybe it's that you know he doesn't mean a word of it and loves it out here.

He finally steps into the underbrush and changes into shorts. We come out onto a road and cross under Highway 40. It's strange to see a white blaze on the upright of the Highway 40 sign and on the underpinnings of the concrete overpass. Overhead, cars drone; in one hour they'll travel as far as we'll walk in five days.

Sweat pours off me as we climb up a seemingly endless hill. Eventually I'm hiking alone, sweating past a strange white humming structure on top of Snowbird Mountain, like a UFO come to rest. Signs warn not to get too close: It's some kind of navigational beacon for airplanes.

I hike on, feeling stranger and stranger, and suddenly I'm lying face down on the Trail, eating dirt. I groan and roll over, and the world spins. I grope around for my water bottle, drink some, lying down, and stay there for a while, sprawled out on the Trail. After a while I get up and hike on, more slowly. The shelter isn't far from here, maybe a couple of miles, mostly downhill.

Groundhog Creek Shelter is on a small stream, and Bridget is already there. We stand in the water and pour potfuls of icy water over our heads and down our backs, right over our clothes. It feels wonderful.

"Where's Terry?" I ask.

"She went off somewhere. She wanted to be alone. I'm worried about her."

"What's wrong?"

"She's been acting weird lately. I'm sure you've noticed."

I nod, thinking of her bizarre entries in the registers. Recently she saw a hiker she didn't even know sleeping at the side of the Trail and wrote to him in the next shelter register: "Are you my Master? My Braveheart? For years I've been seeking my Teacher, and when I saw you sleeping in the greenwood, I thought you might be The One."

"She's just not the Terry I knew, the best friend I grew up with. I don't know what to do. I'm worried about her, but she won't talk to me. She's gonna leave the Trail, so I'll have to hike alone, and I don't want to."

We pour more water. Ahhhh. Another hiker appears, a white-haired man named Fullabeans, and sets up a tent in the bushes. He watches us wash but keeps his distance.

"I don't want to leave," Bridget goes on. "I always start stuff and never finish. I have to finish this, I have to prove to myself that I have it in me. But you know, I keep missing my boyfriend Bo, and without Terry to hike with, I'm afraid I'll get too lonely and leave."

"You can do it," I say. "There are other people out here. I'll watch out for you, and if you want to go to the same shelters at night, we can keep track of each other's safety. I walk alone, and it's really peaceful most of the time."

"I don't know. I guess I'll do it...because I have to."

Other hikers show up: Blister and Red Hot. Blister is a beautiful but tough-looking woman who never smiles; she usually seems angry, and I'm wary of her. Red Hot is a sociable, voluptuous woman who's thinking of leaving the Trail; she only came on the trip because Blister wanted to do it and didn't want to do it alone. It's hard to find friends who need the same pilgrimage you do, and at the same time.

Dances With Mice, a mild-mannered guy who seems to do whatever Blister and Red Hot ask, is with them. There's also a retired section hiker named Cletus, and a retired couple named Yertle and Turtle. And Big Josh, who delivers his Rodney Dangerfield monologue as he approaches through the brush.

The shelter is crowded, but I sleep deeply. Heat exhaustion really wears you out. I have a strange dream of being enveloped, crowded, with blankets twisted over me. I wake up, and the dream continues. Someone is lying with their arms around me.

I lie there, half-asleep, confused. When we went to sleep, Blister was lying on that side of me. Surely this isn't her. It doesn't feel like a woman, anyway.

I jump out of the shelter and go around back. It's pouring rain, and I have to pee. When I'm done I stand there, letting the rain clear my head, and consider my options. It's pitch black, as the woods always are when there's no moon and you're miles from the nearest artificial light. I don't know where my flashlight is. I feel my way back to the shelter and stand in front of it counting heads, moving down the row and tapping each one, since I can't see them: one, two, three, four, five...*six*.

When we went to sleep there were five people in the shelter, besides me. Someone new has snuck in during the night, and his head is on the fleece I've wadded up for a pillow. I feel like I'm in "Goldilocks and the Three Bears": *Someone is sleeping in my bed.*

I smack the thick hair. "Hey, who are you? You're on my pillow. You're on my sleeping mat. You're halfway in my sleeping bag. What the hell are you doing?"

The other hikers, who are already half awake from my tapping head-count, burst out laughing and snap on their lights. Fullabeans freezes in the crossfire of their beams, caught in the act: He is, indeed, on my mat, his head on my pillow, his body halfway on top of my sleeping bag.

"Way to go, Grace," someone says. "You tell him."

"It started raining," he says weakly. "My tent leaked like hell, so I just came in here."

"Oh, right," I say. "Well, just get the hell away from me."

He rolls away, but then Blister, who's on the other side of him, gets territorial. She doesn't want him all over her either. He lies tensely between us, trying not to occupy any more space than necessary. As I go back to sleep, I hear the other hikers laughing.

We wake to storms and rain and wood thrushes singing their

counterpoint to the dense green-sounding *sssssshhhhh* of falling water. Yet another hiker has crept in during the night, chased in by rain, but he's lying at our feet. We all huddle there, crowded and damp, and cook our breakfasts, hoping it'll stop before we begin hiking, but it doesn't, so eventually we all straggle onward.

The Trail is a tunnel of rhododendron jungles, flower-scented wet woods and cedary-mossy-scented hollows, where I use rolled-up rhododendron leaves as funnels to divert water from springs into my bottle. I meet a troop of Girl Scouts in brightly colored rain gear; I hear them long before I see them, shrieking and laughing like distant jungle birds. They're thrilled to see a lone woman thruhiker, and ask about my gear, the walk, whether I ever get tired or scared. "I didn't know a woman could do this," several of them say. "I'm gonna be just like you and hike the whole Trail someday!"

I think of my dad, who encouraged me to do things like this. I'm passing on his legacy of adventure, risk, and connection with nature. *Way to go, Dad,* I think. He would be proud.

I get to Roaring Fork Shelter just as a storm rolls in. Bridget, Blister, Red Hot, Dances With Mice, Fullabeans, Big Josh, and Yertle and Turtle are there, along with Cletus and two other hikers named Mr. Fixit and Pancake. Twelve of us are packed into an 8-by-12-foot space. The ceiling is so low that when we lie down our food bags hang inches from our faces: an ominous, crowded feeling of some terribly heavy object suspended over you, ready to fall and crush your skull.

We hang our wet gear outside, where it will get even wetter, and cook our suppers, elbow to elbow, wet shoulder to wet shoulder. All the women are on one side of the shelter, the men on the other. Fullabeans is the cause of this; everyone's wary of him now, but we're not holding a serious grudge. The hiker community is on to him. He won't bother any of us again.

Packed in as we are, there's no privacy, but we're used to it and don't care. We sample food from each other's suppers and butt into each other's conversations, as if we're some kind of collective life-form. Big Josh makes noodles, the last supper in his food bag, and then when they're almost done, he knocks the pot onto the dirt floor. Noodles splay all over his boots.

"Oh, Jesus," he says. "Would you look at that? What kind of stupid thing is that? I can't believe it. What the hell am I doing? Look at that mess. What an idiot."

Desperately he rakes the noodles up with his hands and tosses them out into the rain like confetti. For some reason this strikes the rest of us as funny, and we laugh uncontrollably as we help him fling the muddy noodles outside.

"Here, Noodle Boot, eat some of my supper," I say. "I have macaroni and stuffing left over."

"Noodle Boot!" Everyone bursts out laughing. "That's your Trail name, man! Noodle Boot!"

"Oh, Jesus," Big Josh says weakly. Other hikers are already passing him food.

"Noodle Boot, Noodle Boot." The sleeping platform quivers; we're all ready to pee our pants at this. The name fits him: his self-deprecating humor, his air of confusion and disarray, his secret sensitivity. We all think he's the funniest man on the Trail, but he would never believe it. He thinks he's a terrible hiker, a know-nothing, a boring middle-aged guy who's an idiot to even think he can make it out here. Somehow that endears him to all of us. Noodle Boot. He's our mascot—if he only knew it.

He's hiking, I find out, in the aftermath of an unpleasant divorce. And he's also dealing with grief over the loss of his son, who died in an auto accident. The Trail name he's been telling everyone to use for him, Josh, is actually his son's name, as if he's living the life his son could not, as if he's taking on his son's identity for the duration of the Trail. For some reason no one ever uses it, as if they sense it's not really his name, that the task behind it—living the life his son could not—is impossible and perhaps even unhealthy. Trail names are like that; people only use them if they fit.

"Was your son a hiker?" I ask.

"No." He looks away. "If he hadn't been so interested in women and alcohol, maybe..."

I wonder if the accident was alcohol-related, and if it was his son's fault, but don't ask. What a tragic waste to endure, to see your son die before he's had a chance to get himself together. A lot of kids go through that sex-drugs-and-rock-n-roll phase, but most of them live long enough that it's just a phase. I think he's hiking now because he wishes his son could have been like this: outdoorsy, healthy, motivated toward a goal. Strong. And if he makes the hike in his son's name, maybe it will help him get through the pain.

He eats the food we've given him and apologizes for the noodle residue on the dirt floor of the shelter. We all tell him it doesn't matter.

Rain pours through a leak in the ceiling. Mr. Fixit puts on his headlamp and reads a tattered copy of *Travels With Charley.* Blister and Red Hot whisper together; others sleep.

I go outside to get water. The world is beautiful in the rain. I stand in the downpour and savor it. For most of this trip I've been unable to think and walk at the same time. It sounds ridiculous, but I've spent most of the time just trying to breathe, just concentrating on getting up the mountains and down again, consumed by various pains. I still have the pains, but I'm used to them now, finally in Trail shape, and today and in the past few days I've been able to walk and meditate at the same time, just take in the woods and the mountains, not fight them. My pack is so much a part of my body that without it it's hard to balance. Even in the dark I know every pocket in it, like my tongue knows my teeth. And I know these wet woods, and all their secret places, in the same way. I've been walking almost a month and have come 255 miles.

At the stream, leaves cascade over a lip of smooth rock. I throw in my filter intake hose and start pumping, watching the stream, the leaves, the rain joining the stream, everything in motion, everything flowing. I watch the water so long that when I look up, everything still seems to be moving.

Everything: the trees, the rocks, the green and mossy banks. The sky. And me.

Chased by thunderstorms, wet red poncho slapping at my legs, I cruise 11 miles, mostly downhill. The woods are filled with the sound of running water and the valleys are full of clouds. Thunderstorms come in waves, one after the other, and I race to get down a mountain, or stop halfway up, until the lightning passes.

It's weird to be out here in the storms, alone. Sometimes there's nowhere to hide, and I crouch right there on the red clay of the Trail, arms wrapped around my knees, head down, as lightning bolts chase one another across the sky and the trees sway and groan overhead. If the storm is really bad, I take off my metal-framed pack, get away from it, and crouch on my rubber sleeping mat, hoping it'll ground me.

Other times I find shelter under the tipped-up lean-tos formed by the upended root masses of giant fallen trees. I crouch in these caves, looking at the tangled weave of heavy roots, counting the stones clenched in their fists, timing the lightning, flinching when it's nearby. I feel a strange kind of peace, hiding like this: I'm involved, I'm part of the forest. I don't know anyone else who's been out in storms like this, alone, in the middle of nowhere. I've always wondered what wild animals do in storms; now I know. Hunker down and wait.

I get to Deer Park Mountain Shelter around noon, in record time. No one's there. It's only three-and-a-half miles to the town of Hot Springs, but I'll stay at the shelter tonight and head into town early tomorrow. Someone has left half a copy of a Kurt Vonnegut book in the shelter, and I spread out my sleeping bag, lie on it, and read. A rare luxury. The book ends in the middle, and the second half is nowhere to be seen, but it doesn't really matter; Vonnegut isn't big on plot. Hikers do this a lot: read half of a book, tear off the part they've finished and leave it behind for other hikers in order to save weight in their own packs, then walk on with the second half. When they finish that, they leave it behind too. I've seen several half-books during the trip, but never matching ones.

A wet, muddy beagle limps out of the woods, jumps onto my sleeping bag, and curls up, right at home. When I cook some lunch he hops up, limping in an exaggerated, theatrical manner, and begs. I give him a serving of mac and cheese, and miraculously he stops limping.

"You big phony," I say. "Where did you come from?"

Fullabeans shows up, looks at my spot, sees the expression on my face, and sets up his sleeping bag on the other side of the shelter, as far away from mine as possible. The dog limps over to him, gets a handout, and is miraculously healed again.

Cletus, the section hiker, comes in and tosses down his pack. "I hate this damn Trail," he says. "I'm awful sick. I'm gonna quit this damn thing."

He looks at me. "How long did it take you to hike here?"

"I don't know. I got here around noon, but I don't know what time it was when I left."

He sets up his bag next to Fullabeans and coughs all over Fullabeans's lunch. Fullabeans flinches.

I shut them out and read. Through the screen of Vonnegut's prose comes a steady stream of their complaints, both of them bitching and moaning about jobs they once had, bosses they had, how various companies dicked them over, and what a pain in the ass the Trail is. Too much dirt, too much rain, too many ups and downs, all these damn mountains we have to walk over. I roll my eyes and wish that either I, or they, were elsewhere. If it weren't still pouring, I'd go sit in the woods.

Finally, Blister, Red Hot, and Dances With Mice appear, and eventually Yertle and Turtle show up too. I'm overjoyed to see them all. They're optimistic and alive.

"Hey, we're glad to see you," Red Hot says. "We thought you'd speed ahead to Hot Springs and not even stop here."

"I'm just as glad to see you. I need some fun."

Blister, Red Hot, and I go into the woods and wash our hair: girl bonding.

"So you've spent the whole day with Fullabeans?" Blister asks as she scrubs her head.

"Yeah, he didn't say anything. He's not gonna bother anyone."

"He'd better not, or I'll kick his ass," Blister says. "I love what you said the other night: 'Your head is on my pillow. Your butt is on my mat. What the hell are you doing?' Way to go."

We go back to the shelter. It's small, and although Yertle and Turtle are tenting out back, it's crowded with six people: me, Blister, Red Hot, Dances With Mice, Cletus, and Fullabeans.

"None of us are sleeping next to *him*," Blister says, jerking her head at Fullabeans. "Cletus, shove over."

Cletus shoves over until he's jammed up against Fullabeans. He really is sick. He coughs uncontrollably, right in Fullabeans's face. Fullabeans is clearly unhappy with this, but there's nothing he can do; he's outnumbered. He's broken the hiker community's shelter rules: There may be no physical privacy, but you keep your hands and eyes to yourself.

Big Josh, alias Noodle Boot, shows up a while later, and we have a cheery campsite. The rain stops, Blister makes a big fire, and we sit around it eating and talking. The beagle reappears.

"What's wrong with this dog?" Red Hot asks. "Poor thing, he's limping. Whose is he?"

We look at his collar and find the name and address of a man in Hot Springs. Red Hot ties up the dog, saying that the next day she'll lead him into town and return him to his owner. He curls up at the foot of the shelter, right at home.

It's getting dark now, and all around the shelter, foxfire glows. It's a fungus, glow-in-the-dark green that fills the night with a million little shining eyes. Even though I know what it is, it's still eerie. Entire logs glow like ghosts. A whippoorwill calls, obsessive and sad, then makes an odd boinging noise, like a broken cuckoo clock winding down, making us all laugh.

The dog tries to come up on my bag, but he's muddy and wet,

and I push him away. He wanders over and tracks mud all over Fullabeans's clothes. Blister grins, her teeth flashing in the fading light, and gives me a thumbs-up.

Out back, Noodle Boot wrestles with his tent, and his voice drifts through the shelter wall: "...an idiot. What was I thinking? I ought to know better than to walk this crazy thing. Would you believe it?"

May 9
Hot Springs, N.C.

Chapter Five

After a day and a half in Hot Springs, Dances With Mice, Blister, Red Hot, and I leave town, straggle across the bridge over the French Broad River, and haul ourselves weakly up the cliffs on the other side. It's so humid it feels like I'm trying to breathe through a plastic bag. I don't think I've ever hiked this slowly, not even at the beginning of the Trail.

It takes all afternoon to drag ourselves five miles to a campsite at the edge of a pond. We'd planned to go farther, but this is it for now. All the way here I've fantasized about swimming in the pond, which is a cool blue circle on the map, but in real life it's thick as soup, green with algae. The drinking water source is the scummy spring that feeds the pond. No swimming there either.

I lay out my sleeping bag on the soft needles under a grove of pine trees. The others set up their tents, and when Blister is done she points up the hill. "What is that thing?"

There's something white up over the rise, very close to us. Wearily we slog up the hill to investigate. It turns out to be the roof of a camper, which is parked in a little clearing at the end of a red dirt road. Raft guides from the French Broad River have the afternoon off and are setting up for a party. They look a lot like hikers: lean young men in tattered clothes, with wide-awake outdoor faces, except they're a lot cleaner than we are since they've been in the water all day. Reggae music, alternating with bluegrass, pulses out of their tape player.

"Hey, hiker dudes! Want a beer?"

They turn on the radio, open coolers, and toss beers to all of us. We stand there dumbly with the beers in our hands, looking at the vehicle and the road, slowly realizing we've walked all afternoon, thinking we were in relative wilderness, to reach a place that's 10 minutes away from Hot Springs by this dirt road. I feel like I'm in a beer commercial, stumbling out of the woods into a sudden party.

We go back to our camp, bring our food up to the party, and eat supper. We tell them hiking stories about bears, lightning storms, and long mileages. They tell us river stories about close escapes from rapids, capsizes, and people who almost drowned. After a while I'm happy to just sit watching the dark come down, listening to the slow talk and the music. Some hikers carry portable radios, but I don't. Music is a rare treat, almost overwhelming. I close my eyes and savor it.

When it's almost completely dark, someone lights a Coleman lantern. It startles me, this sudden portable sun. I had assumed that since it was dark, we'd just sit in the dark talking, the way hikers do, and then go to sleep. I'd forgotten about artificial light.

The next day, after a six-mile hike that feels like 12, we find that Cletus, who swore he would get off the Trail at Hot Springs, is still hiking. It's been hot, humid, and threatening rain all day, and shortly after he arrives at Spring Mountain Shelter, a few spats of rain come down. We all go outside to move the wet clothes we've hung out on trees to dry and to cover the rest of our gear. First Cletus complains because it's threatened to rain all day, then he complains because it's raining, and when the rain stops he says, "It'd just figure, after we move all this stuff, that it stops raining."

Red Hot rolls her eyes. Blister makes a fist, like she wishes she could punch him, this man who finds a way to complain even when he gets his wish. He has a cracked, cawing voice like a mule's. Worse, he's a shelter hog, spreading out his gear until he's taken far more than his share of space. Clouds of tiny, biting flies swirl into the shelter. Cletus slaps and mutters, rumbling under his breath like the constant distant thunder.

Boxcar Willie shows up. He's a courtly man with a neatly trimmed white beard and an interesting story: He was a train engineer until one day he hit some guy who was parked on the track in a pickup truck. Most people don't realize that it takes a train a long distance to stop; it has a lot of momentum. Boxcar Willie says he slammed on the brakes as soon as he saw the guy, but there was no way he could stop in time. The man in the truck either couldn't or wouldn't move. Boxcar Willie got a good, close-up look at his face at the moment of impact, the moment the man died.

His supervisors told him it happened to everyone, sooner or later. But he couldn't let it go. He took early retirement, and that's why he's out here walking, trying to make sense of such a senseless thing. Unlike Cletus, he's hopeful and positive; every hiker who's met him likes him.

Cletus keeps complaining. Finally, Red Hot, Blister, Dances With Mice, and I leave the shelter and camp on a rise nearby.

"I'd rather be rained on than listen to that all night," Blister says.

I set up my hammock between two trees and rest, after putting on extra clothes to keep the no-see-ums from biting. Slowly the sky clears. Down at the shelter, Cletus keeps on cawing.

I go back to the shelter and get the logbook. Noodle Boot has signed in; he left Hot Springs ahead of us and is still a day ahead. His entry says he's definitely going to leave at Erwin, Tennessee, the next town.

"Let's catch up to him and get him to stay on the Trail," Red Hot says. "I love that guy."

"Me too," I say. "What is it about him? He complains all the time, but somehow it's funny, and you know he doesn't really mean it."

"He's a million miles away from Cletus," Blister says. "Now, there's someone you could do without."

I swing in the hammock, writing in the logbook. Blister looks out at the trees. "You know," she says, "this is gonna sound weird, but I don't feel like we're in the woods anymore."

I know exactly what she means. It's not that we don't feel like we're in the woods, but the woods have become so familiar, so *home*, that we don't feel we're somewhere strange or special anymore. We're just home, where we belong. Like sitting in your bedroom back in civilization—you never think, *I'm in my house*. You're just *there*. Here, the woods are a given like that, the ground of our daily life. We don't even notice that we're camping; we're just living, and it feels like we've always lived this way.

It's clear when we wake the next day, with a front rolling in from the west.

"Grace, what's the weather gonna be?" Red Hot asks.

"Clear, then cloudy, then the clouds will go away without any rain, but in the late afternoon another front will come with thunderstorms, and it'll rain like hell all afternoon and night."

"How do you know?"

"I'm not sure. But I've watched clouds since I was little. I just know."

I hike alone all morning, but later Blister, Red Hot, and Dances With Mice catch up to me, and we all bunch up at a little gas station at a road crossing, right on the border between North Carolina and Tennessee. Inside, there's a wood stove, a couple of beat-up couches, and a pleasant elderly woman, with a soft mountain accent, in charge. We buy snacks, then go outside and sit at the edge of the gravel parking lot, eating as we watch the approaching afternoon storm.

A hiker named English Pete passes by. "Have you seen Vampire?" he asks. "She was supposed to be heading this way."

None of us know her, and none of us have seen anyone else that day.

"Well, I'll go south for a while and see if I can find her. I'm rather worried about her."

It turns out that he has a crush on her and gave her a gift, a necklace he always wore, at the last town. She was supposed to catch up with him but never did, so now he's backtracking, 20 miles out of his way, to look for her.

"She said she was going to buy me a gift up ahead in Erwin. I'm really worried," he says, then heads into the woods.

"True love," Blister comments.

"Yeah," says Red Hot, "but somehow I have the vibe he's a nice guy, too nice, and is about to get burned."

As soon as we get halfway up the first mountain, the storm slams down, throwing lightning bolts all around us. The forest is very dark, down here under the trees.

"Should we run back to the store?" Red Hot asks. Her face is white in a sudden strobe-flash of lightning.

"Nah. The lightning'd get us crossing the road. We're safer among the trees."

We take off our packs and get away from them, and spread out, so that if one of us gets hit by lightning it won't travel through all of us.

I lay out my rubber sleeping mat and crouch on it, face buried in my knees. It's the first time I've been with other people in a storm. It's kind of a relief, not bad at all.

The lightning passes, though it keeps raining. The woods are always beautiful in the rain. All the colors are bright and deep, saturated. I love seeing all the creatures who live here: red-and-black-striped millipedes, caterpillars, slugs, little orange efts, all the flowers. Yesterday I spotted a mutant trillium, with four petals instead of three. I love the sound of water moving under rocks, over moss, and the clarity the rain gives to the air.

Blister, Red Hot, Dances With Mice, and I all end up camping in the same place, near a shelter but not in it, since it's full. I string up my tarp to make a roof to keep the rain off, and we build a fire to dry our clothes and warm ourselves up; I cook on it too. It's cozy under this little pavilion, as the rain comes down in sheets all around us, in the dark. I hold out my rain-drenched fleece to the flames, and gradually it dries.

A woman comes out of the dark. "Hi, I'm Vampire," she says. The rain has plastered her hair to her face, and she's wearing a big, soaking-wet pack and improbable clothes: hiking boots and a very short dress that shows off her deep cleavage. "Can I share your fire?"

"Sure."

We make room for her, and she huddles in with us. "I have cancer!" she says brightly, scanning our faces to see how we're taking this news.

"What?" Blister says.

"And this morning I almost died. We were naked"—she giggles—"and we were standing on the train trestle over the river back at Hot Springs, and when a train came we jumped into the river, just before the train hit us. Only, I almost didn't jump in time. I almost got hit."

None of us say anything. She adds, "And then this guy and I, this 17-year-old, we rented this boat, and went out on the river? And I'd never been in a boat before? And we, like, capsized, and I got stuck with my leg caught under a log underwater, and if he hadn't dove in and saved me, I would have drowned. Really!"

I look around: Are there any trees about to fall? This woman seems like a disaster magnet. That is, if what she's saying is true.

"What kind of cancer did you say you have?" I ask.

"Oh, it's in my, you know, womanly parts. I haven't had a period since I was 16."

Dances With Mice turns bright red and looks wildly around for an avenue of escape, but outside our little tarp-shelter it's still pouring.

"—and I went to this doctor, and he said my cells were funny. So I have cancer!"

She leans over, exposing her generous cleavage, gives a little wiggle, and looks up at us from under her lashes.

"So anyway, I had this accident in the boat this morning, and then I, like, couldn't even walk!"

We're several miles up in the mountains, so this is obviously untrue. If anything, she can walk better than any of us, since it took us three days to get here, not one.

"And the thing with the train—that was scary!"

"That was *stupid*..." Blister says, "*if* it ever happened."

"Better not tell Boxcar Willie," I say. "He's at the shelter over there, and he's out here because some idiot was on the tracks and didn't move out of the way in time, and Boxcar Willie hit him. He saw the guy's face, right at the instant he died."

Vampire's eyes widen. "Oh!" she says.

"Listen," I tell her, "my dad died of cancer, and if you really do have it, you ought to get off the Trail at the next town and go to a doctor. If you have cancer and aren't being treated for it, you're stupid to be out here. You'll die, and it won't be very funny."

Vampire looks away and flaps her wet rain jacket over the fire to dry it.

"Did you see English Pete?" Red Hot asks. "He was looking for you."

"Oh, was he?"

She seems subdued. She doesn't say much after that. Eventually she gets completely dry and heads over to the shelter to sleep.

"What's up with her?" Blister says. "Is she a pathological liar or what?"

"Maybe just pathological," Red Hot says. "Do you think she really has cancer?"

"Who knows."

We hear voices coming from the shelter. "What do you suppose she's telling them?" Red Hot asks. "Do you think she'd be stupid enough to tell Boxcar Willie she was playing on the tracks?"

"No," Dances With Mice says. He flaps his rain jacket up and down over the fire. "She's probably telling Cletus that she never has a period. Man, I'd love to see *his* face."

It rains constantly for the next three days. My food bag is getting very light, and I begin rationing: counting out my snacks, eating smaller and smaller meals. I wasted time at the beginning of this stretch, on the slow days out of Hot Springs. Now I'm paying. Erwin, Tennessee, looks like a promised land. I think about all the food there: ice cream, french fries, fresh fruit, milk.

The three others have begun bickering among themselves. One morning I pass Blister and Red Hot, who are standing on a mountainside screaming at each other; the fight is so intense that they have no breath left to walk. It's either fight or hike, but not both. In camp near Low Gap, they don't speak unless they have to. Dances With Mice sits to one side; both women ignore him completely, and they also ignore me.

"Pass the salt," Blister says. It's three feet away from her, closer to her than to Red Hot, who's on the other side of the fire.

"It's right next to you," Red Hot says. "Right there."

"I can't reach it."

With elaborate courtesy, Red Hot gets up, walks all the way around the fire, picks it up, hands it to her, bows, then walks back around the fire and sits down. Dances With Mice ducks his head and looks away as if to minimize his chances of being in the line of fire. I eat my small supper and try not to look at their food.

The rain pours down. I hold my fleece over the fire to dry it, watching steam come off it, shivering. We're camped in a natural bowl near a stream, which is steadily rising. I hope we don't get flooded during the night.

When it's almost dark, English Pete shows up.

"Did you ever find Vampire?" I ask.

"No. Well, actually, I did, but she wanted to stay back at the river. She's met someone there, some raft fellow."

His arrival cheers everyone up. He's a neutral party, a new face. Blister and Red Hot thaw and begin telling stories, mostly about Cletus.

"I saw that chap a few times," Pete says. "He always asked me how long it took me to walk from here to there, then he told me he had done it in less time."

"All lies," Blister says.

"Well, of course I knew that," Pete says, "but I never told him so."

The next day it's still pouring. The silence-alternating-with-bickering between Blister and Red Hot continues. Dances With Mice is morose. No one says a word to me, and I have the impression they're all heartily sick of me, or offended because I walk alone, as if they think I think I'm too good for them. I eat a candy bar, the only breakfast I have left, and leave.

I don't stop all day. I don't have any snacks to eat anyway so there's no point in taking breaks, and if I stop I'll just get wetter and colder. The only thing that's keeping me warm at this point is constant motion. Paranoia is creeping up on me. Everyone hates me. Nobody loves me. Something is wrong.

The woods are dark and gloomy, the rain like a big heavy hand on top of my head. The day is a big blank because I'm so distracted; it's like my short-term memory is gone. Every place looks like every other place, as if I'm walking in circles. My socks are soaking wet, and I'm beginning to get serious blisters from their constant rubbing.

Fourteen miles later I reach No Business Knob Shelter and eat my last remaining food, one packet of Cream of Wheat. Other hikers show up, including Steamroller Boy and Homer, whom I haven't seen in a while.

Blister, Red Hot, and Dances With Mice arrive a little later. They seem to have reached a truce and cook an elaborate meal together, although they're still ignoring me. I look the other way as they pass food around and compare tastes. My stomach cringes. I feel lost and alone, as if they're doing this on purpose to torment me and it's too late to appeal the decision.

Outside, somewhere in the woods, there's a high-pitched, endless drone. I sit listening to the rain and the underlying whine. It sounds like someone mowing a lawn, but there are no lawns up here, and even if there were, no one would be mowing at dusk on a long, rainy day. The sound seems to swirl around me, cutting me off from everyone. I feel like I'm in a bad horror movie, like I should clutch my ears and fall to the ground, writhing, from this sound that is driving me mad, which no one else seems to hear.

Perhaps I'm hallucinating. If I ignore the sound, maybe it'll go away.

That night I'm too hungry to sleep. Dances With Mice snores, full of mashed potatoes, stuffing, and instant gravy. Far away the ominous humming drones.

Someone's walking outside the shelter, stepping softly, rustling. Definitely a person. I hear the footfalls and the breathing. Who would walk around in the woods on a starless night without a flashlight? It's a good way to get your eye poked out.

"Hey, you out there!" Steamroller Boy yells. "What's up?"

No answer.

The rain has stopped, and other hikers are camped nearby, with a dog. The stealthy footsteps sneak off in that direction, the dog barks, and flashlight beams cut the night. I go outside, get my pack, and bring it into the shelter. If someone wants to steal packs, they'll take the ones outside, not bother to come in and step over sleeping hikers.

The snoring is a torment; people mocking your insomnia, keeping you awake by sleeping. The night walker, whoever he is, is gone.

I grab my bag and the fleece I'm using for a pillow, and go down the Trail, then lie down near the other hikers' camp. The dog goes into a fresh seizure of barking, the people lean out and spotlight me, decide I'm harmless, and go back into their tent.

I lie there, eyes wide. I'm so hungry I can't think straight. The distant humming makes me twitch. It's very dark: all clouds, no moon.

Just as I doze off, it starts pouring. I drag my bag back to the shelter and lie awake all night. My hands are shaking, I can't keep a thought in my head for more than a few seconds, my mind races. On some level I know this is because I'm hungry, but that thought keeps slipping my mind. Over and over I think about how much the other three hate me, how they ate all that food in front of me, how they're doing it just to get me. I know this is irrational but keep forgetting.

As soon as it gets light I pack up and leave. The others, just awake, are startled to see me put on my pack, say goodbye, and take off.

It's six-and-a-half miles to the Nolichucky River and a road, then four more miles on the road to Erwin. I hope I can hitch once I get to the road. If I don't get food soon, I'll pass out.

It's still pouring. The Trail is slick and muddy, and my blisters feel like someone is sticking knives into my feet. On the steep descent to the river I fall repeatedly, over and over, skidding into the mountain laurel, crashing into just opened white azaleas.

Finally, I stand up and scream, as loud as I can: "I just want to get down this goddamn mountain!"

It echoes down the mountain, bouncing off the river. I hike around a steep switchback. A local man is standing frozen in the Trail, eyes wide with fear: The crazy woman of the woods is on the loose.

"Howdy," I say, and rush past him.

By the time I get to the road I'm talking to myself. The

humming is real, it turns out. There's some kind of industry on the river, and the sound is coming from there. At least I wasn't hallucinating, though I don't know how I heard it from six-and-a-half miles away.

It's still pouring rain, and no one stops to give me a ride to town. I walk along the edge of the road. Wild strawberries are growing in the ditch; only two are ripe. They're the size of my little fingernail. I eat them; it's like trying to fill up a swimming pool with an eyedropper.

Ahead of me, two big black dogs race back and forth across the road, heads low, bodies tensed, wheeling and eyeing me, unable to contain their tension as I slowly advance, muttering to myself. When I get closer they charge, leaping at me.

I swing at them with both my hiking sticks, baseball-bat style, and yell, "GET THE HELL AWAY FROM ME, YOU BASTARD DOGS! I'LL KILL YOU! GO HOME! GO HOME! BAD DOGS!"

The dogs back up: Here's a real psycho. I bark and howl like a wolf, swing my sticks, and chase them back to their yard.

Shaking, I totter away, on the lookout for more. This part of town is strung-out, flat, and has an unloved, "No one's going anywhere" feeling; from the corner of my eye I catch a flicker of curtains as people peer out at me, then close the drapes again. Finally, I get to the motel I've heard other hikers talking about and check in.

Noodle Boot has been here; he checked out this morning. "Going home," the proprietor tells me. "Said he'd had enough."

"Is there any food around here?"

"There's a grocery store down the road. You can see it from the parking lot."

I don't have any cash, just a credit card and an ATM card. The store is filled with the smells of fruit and bread, fresh fried chicken and chocolate.

"Do you take credit cards?" I ask the clerk.

"No, ma'am. I'm sorry."

"Can you tell me where the nearest ATM is?"

"Oh, you just get on the interstate and go to the next exit. It's right there."

"I don't have a car. Is there one I could walk to?"

"Where'd you come from today?"

"The Erwin Motel."

"You don't have a car back at the motel you could use?"

"No, I walked there. I walked here all the way from Georgia, and I don't have a car."

"From *Georgia*!"

"Maybe I could walk to the one you told me about. But isn't it illegal to walk on the interstate?"

"Not here! Shoot, they'll just think you're fishing off the bridge. They don't care. Did you really walk here from Georgia?"

I limp back to the motel in tears. The owner says there are ATMs, food stores, and restaurants on the other side of town, but that's four-and-a-half miles away. One of his employees sometimes shuttles hikers over there, but he's not here now. He should be here any minute.

I go to my room. The ceiling spins, and my hands are shaking so badly that when I try to get a glass of water, I drop the glass. I talk myself through it and drink water from my cupped hands.

The shuttle guy doesn't show. I'll have to walk. I don't think I can make it, but there's no other choice.

Out in the parking lot, the world looks slanted. I stand there, watching the asphalt sway, feeling my feet bleeding into my socks. I'm shaking uncontrollably, crying. At least it's stopped raining.

"Hey, Grace!"

It's Bridget.

"Grace! What's wrong?"

"I—I'm hungry—no food—or something—I don't know—"

She takes her pack off, dumps her food bag on the ground, and starts handing me candy bars. "You're sick, aren't you? That hypo-whatever thing you told me about? Eat these."

My hands are trembling so much that I can't unwrap the

bars. She tears them open and hands them to me one by one, as I sit down on the wet asphalt and eat them almost whole.

"What happened?"

I sit and breathe, eyes closed, feeling the sugar take effect. "I ran out of food on that last stretch. I haven't eaten much for the past two days, and I got really sick."

"Weren't there any other hikers around you could get food from?"

"Yeah, but it was weird. Everyone's been in some kind of mood. I've been irrational because of the hunger thing, and I don't know what's really been going on. It's been a hard week."

"That's for sure! This rain is getting to me!"

"Are you staying here?"

"Yeah."

"Where's Terry?"

"She left the Trail. She's going to go find herself somewhere else—some commune where they do yoga. But I'm going to keep walking. Wanna split a room?"

Blister, Red Hot, and Dances With Mice show up, and we sort things out. It turns out they were just so sunk in their own misery that they had no idea about the hell I was in, and they didn't notice that I wasn't eating or that I was sick. It's been a bad stretch for everyone, with the rain, the tough terrain, the isolation. We're all friends again. Just the same, I'd better go back to hiking alone, if hiking with people is going to make me this paranoid. And this hunger sickness thing, if I don't get it under control, is really going to make me crazy.

We get a ride to town from a kind local woman, a Trail angel who drives around looking for hikers and offering them rides. It's amazing how many people like this there are, scattered up and down the Trail. I vow that in the future I'll help out strangers whenever I can.

I eat two bean burritos, a foot-long sub, a bag of chips, some Oreos, a milkshake, and a 32-ounce cola before I even begin to feel normal. Then I get a 12-piece bucket of fried chicken and fixings and head back to the motel.

It's a relief not to be in the rain, a relief to have food and be clean and be isolated from the elements.

Bridget and I lie on the beds and eat greasy chicken while we watch cable TV. My sleeping bag is mummy-shaped, so on the Trail I have to sleep neatly and can never really relax. Now it's an unbelievable luxury to lie in the shape of an X, with my arms and legs sprawled out. Bridget does the same on her bed, and we eat and watch talk show after talk show.

The commercials alone are sensory overload. We feel vaguely guilty doing this. After all, we're supposed to be having this purifying wilderness experience, and here we are watching *Jerry Springer.* It's something most travel writers never talk about. You read about someone going trekking in Nepal, or to Tibet to meditate, and she neglects to mention the time she called home just to see how the Packers were doing, or how she spent four days and nights in a hotel in Singapore on the way there, downing tropical drinks and swimming in the pool. Or you read about someone who built his own cabin in Alaska, but he leaves out the two weeks when he visited his family in Indiana for Christmas or the time he spent on the Internet checking his stocks.

We stay in Erwin two days, eating nonstop, walking back and forth to town. It's typical of the Trail that even while we're "resting" in town, we still walk 10 miles a day—but with no pack it's easy. My blisters heal. I buy a lot of food, and while we watch a talk show host interview people who are extremely overweight, I add up all the calories in my resupply then divide by five, the number of days the food is supposed to last. I've gotten the most fatty, calorie-laden foods I can find, but it only works out to about 3,800 calories a day, a 2,200-calorie deficit from the 6,000 a day I need. Slow starvation is inevitable, but this at least will hold it off a little longer.

We see on the news that a murderer has escaped from the nearby Tennessee state prison and is believed to be hiding out in the mountains, either near the Trail or on it. I think about the stealthy footsteps near the shelter the other night and hope my mother isn't watching the news. I call home. She chats blithely;

she hasn't heard. In case she does hear about it, I tell her I'm hiking with a big group of burly men, and that we all look out for each other, no one's ever alone, and it's so much fun.

I get off the phone, and Bridget raises her eyebrows. "I don't see any big group of happy guys here."

"Worry insurance," I say. "You ought to try it—your mother will love it."

Outside Erwin, up on Beauty Spot, a mountain that's aptly named, I sit with other hikers and applaud the show: a thunderstorm over the next mountain. Lightning slashes the treetops, clouds boil, rain comes down in a slanting wall. It's like a cartoon; the storm is so concentrated it looks portable. Over us the sky is clear blue. We congratulate each other on picking this spot to camp, instead of the unfortunate mountain a few miles away.

We've built a fire, and a runner dressed in shorts and a tank top comes trotting by on the Trail, dropping beads of sweat on us as he passes.

"Mighty hot for a fire," he says as he passes.

"Mighty hot to be running," a hiker named Sun Ra says. The runner laughs and runs on, turning his head to watch the distant storm.

Sun Ra rolls a cigarette and lights it. "Some guy was giving me a hard time the other day because when I finish a cigarette I peel open the butt and drop the tobacco in the woods. I don't drop the paper, but this guy was hassling me because he said tobacco isn't a native plant, and I shouldn't be littering it around."

"What did you say?" a hiker named N'Yawk asks in a deep Brooklyn accent.

"I said, 'Tobacco isn't a native plant? Hey, in case you haven't noticed, we're in North Carolina!'" He laughs. "Besides, the Native Americans still sprinkle tobacco on the ground. It's a sign of respect for the Earth."

Beauty Spot is worthy of respect. It's a bald, a mountain covered with grass and flowers. No trees grow on balds, for reasons still mysterious to science, and they're all beautiful, high-sky meadows. The water source here is a dark and swampy spring down the hillside; we all go in a group and take turns waiting for the slow, dark brown flow to fill up our water bags so we can filter out of them, and despite the water's inkiness, we're grateful for it. It's a social event; I haven't camped with this many people in a long time.

We go back up to the spacious hilltop, cook, and chat. Blister and Red Hot sit by the fire and talk about Vampire. "We were in a public bathroom in town the other day, and Red Hot and I were talking about her," Blister says. "I said, 'That girl must be crazy or on drugs, to act like she does,' and she heard me and figured I was talking about her, and started screaming at me. I was like, 'If you're not crazy or on drugs, why would you assume I'm talking about you? If the shoe fits, wear it, and don't get in my face about people talking about you. Just quit doing stupid shit that makes them talk, is all I have to say.'"

"There were these two girls on the Trail before who were bi," N'Yawk says. "They were very out about it. Anyway, Vampire heard that, and she was flirting with them and flashing her cleavage and shit like that, and they got fed up. So one morning they get up and they're having breakfast, and she walks up, and they sort of *stare* at her chest, you know, and say, 'Well, how about it? Wanna get in our tent?' like they're calling her bluff, and all of a sudden she's like, 'Oh, *no*, I was just *kidding* last night, ha ha ha, just a *joke*,' and she was out of there. It was fuckin' hilarious."

"Did you know her family is really rich?" he goes on. "She had to get off the Trail at one point—I think it was her birthday or something—and we all get to this gap and there's a limo parked on the dirt road and it's her family's *driver*, come to take her home for the weekend. I heard she just decided she wanted to do the Trail, spent like 4,000 bucks on gear in two days, and then came and started. It was just a total whim."

Just then Vampire shows up, walking over the hill. She's hiking in a minidress with a cleavage so deep it makes the mountains look flat, and a male hiker is following her, hypnotized. She cocks her head. "Hi, guys," she says in a little-girl voice.

People mumble hello, then ignore her. It seems everyone has heard her near-death stories or been the target of her flirting, and they've grown tired and jaded.

She stands at the edge of the campsite, hands on hips, watching everyone, then she and the guy disappear down the hill. A short time later they come back, and they've switched clothes: He's wearing her dress; she's wearing his shorts and shirt.

"Anything for attention," Sun Ra sighs.

She sits at the edge of the campsite with the guy who came with her, and that's that. She seems disappointed. I wonder again why she's out here and how much truth there is in the stories people tell about her. And how much truth there is in the stories she tells about herself. She reminds me of a roommate I once had during a summer at college, a Southern girl from a very wealthy family, a girl who had two lives: one as a beautiful, graceful debutante who volunteered at the local art museum and hobnobbed with art collectors and artists, another as an angry, confused young woman who, banished to her room by her father, took out all the bulbs in the lamps in her room, smashed them against the wall, then slit her wrists with the shards of glass. Two days later she was back at another ball, wearing an off-the-shoulder gown with elbow-length white gloves to hide the wounds, smiling, dancing.

I make a rough, floorless A-frame tent with my tarp, using my hiking sticks for supports, tying it down against the wind in case the rain comes over here. But I lie with my head outside so I can watch the stars. I always plan to watch the stars but never do. I can't stay awake long enough to do much more than trace the outline of the Big Dipper.

I think again about my summer roommate. The bathroom in that apartment had two sinks, so we could both get ready in the morning at the same time. She took hours sculpting her face and hair, examining her body and clothes, critiquing all her nonexistent flaws. I would take a shower, put on jeans and a T-shirt, comb my hair, brush my teeth, and figure that was enough.

"How did you escape?" she once asked me, leaning over the sink and touching up her eyebrows. "Do you think I like doing all this? It's a prison I can't get out of. What people think. What *guys* think. Why should I care what they think? Do they obsess like this? No. Do you? No. You're like a guy. You don't obsess about how you look. You're just yourself. You look fine the way you are, and I know I would too, but I can't seem to believe that enough to live it. How did you escape?"

At the time I didn't know. I was just grateful that I *had* escaped. But really, I think now, lying on my back looking at the bright span of stars, in other ways I haven't. I'm still under society's thumb, or only a recent escapee, still ignorant of what I want and need in life. I might not wear makeup, I might not care about diets or fashion, but I've spent more than enough time in relationships with men, because that was the socially easy thing to do, even though I've known for a long time that it's not what's going to make me happy.

I envy the two bi girls N'Yawk was talking about; I envy their openness. I feel a huge respect for them, whoever they are. I wish I could just say, "Yeah, I'm like that too" or "Yeah, I've been with men and women, but you know, the more I think about it, the more I think I need to be with a woman to be truly happy." But I don't say it. The story is too tangled to explain, too painful and confusing.

There's another thing about secrets that no one talks about: how when you keep a secret, the weight of your *not* telling grows. I've been walking for so long and have said nothing about this topic, so everyone assumes I'm straight. If I told people now that I'm gay, it would be a big deal. *Guess what Grace told us!* Whereas if I'd had the sense to be open from the beginning, no one would care. *Oh, yeah, Grace. She's gay. So what?*

Secrets carry power, but too often if you keep a big part of your life a secret, it gives people power over you. The power of fear, the fear that they'll take your secret away and expose you. It's better to expose yourself, and do it early on.

Roan Mountain is a steep climb. Getting there from the shelter I've slept in, and climbing its craggy south slope, takes most of a day. As I get higher the woods turn to balsam fir, and the air is filled with the northwoods aroma of their resinous needles. I stop, pick up a fallen bough, and fill my pocket with the needles to make a sachet.

This mountain is famous for its hillsides covered with wild azalea and rhododendron, but they're not in bloom yet, so the tourist parking lot on top is empty. At lunchtime I join a hiker named Thoreau and a group of pleasant hikers called the Fun Guys, who've caught up with me.

Going down the other side I lose track of everyone and hike alone, peaceful and content, taking deep breaths of the scented air. Down in the valley, at the bottom of the north side of Roan, the woods end.

When I reach this gap I cross a road. There's a sign nearby that marks the border between North Carolina and Tennessee, and three rustic-looking men are leaning on it. The mountain on the other side of the valley is a bald and it's beautiful, a vast rounded sweep of tall grass and low shrubs.

I hurry down the slope, cross the road, and start up the bald mountain. The three men, who until now have shown no interest in going up any mountain, start after me. Their sudden eagerness to hike is unsettling.

I hike faster. They hike faster. They're in their 20s, 10 years younger than I am, and have no packs. Between breaths they discuss the possibility of catching me: It will be easy.

"She's a little bitty thing, and look at that big pack she's toting. We can catch her."

At least they don't know I've already hiked seven miles

today, most of it straight up and over Roan Mountain.

They're about 20 paces behind me. I hike faster and mentally inventory my potential weapons. I have pepper spray, a Swiss Army knife, and two heavy hiking sticks. There are three of them and one of me. If they catch me I'll fight for my life. Even if they eventually win—and they probably will since there are three of them—they'll have scars.

But first they have to catch me. Steadily, using my panic as fuel, stabbing my hiking sticks into the ground and pushing my weight upward, I run up the mountain. Are there trees on the other side? Maybe I can get over the summit before they do, run off the Trail, and hide.

My breath burns in my throat. My heart is hammering so hard it's dizzying.

They pant behind me, laboring up the mountain. The distance between us is widening.

"Shit," one says. "She's fast."

"We can catch her."

Fury and fear war in me. Fight or flight. I haven't hiked all this way just to be raped or killed by a bunch of rednecks. Concentration. Use the adrenaline. Stay in the rhythm. Don't slow down. Keep. Going. Up.

"I—can't—walk—no more," one of them gasps.

Good, I think.

"Come on—it's just—a little—way," says another.

Keep. Going. Up. Please, God, don't let them get me—

One drops out. The other two keep coming, though they're farther behind now; I can't hear their heavy breathing.

Crows fly up from the other side of the summit, calling, and sweep away.

Keep. Going. Up. Almost there. On the other side you can hide in the trees.

I reach the summit. All the way down the other side, as far as I can see, up the next mountain and the one beyond that, there are no trees. There are scattered rocks, but the men will see me heading for them. No place to hide. I can also see there are no other hikers for miles; I'm completely alone.

I run down the mountain, not looking back. The terrain, covered with long flowing grass, seems to glow. I'm in a bowl between the mountains now; they haven't yet reached the summit behind me, and there's no way to tell whether they're still coming. If they catch up, I'll tell them there's a bunch of people hiking behind me, that if they make any trouble for me, they won't know when those hikers will catch up, come over the mountain, and find them and me in the bowl.

Up the next mountain. Any other time it would be beautiful. Now I curse the lack of trees.

At the summit of the second mountain, I look back. Only one pursuer is left. He has just reached the summit of the first mountain. He turns, looks over at me on the next mountain, and his whole body sags with disbelief as he sees the great distance between us. He's not coming any farther.

I tighten my pack straps, tighten my waist strap, say a quick prayer of thanks, and keep on going.

The South is famed for its hospitality, and rightly so. Hikers walking into town get rides without even putting out a thumb; old men in pickups pull up alongside as you trudge down the road to town, and ask if you need anything; people lie in wait on abandoned dirt roads just to give you a cold soda and a candy bar. In towns, people are pleasant, warm, helpful, and easy to talk to.

The section between Elk Park, North Carolina, and Hampton, Tennessee, is different.

There are stories about this section, and warnings posted in the shelters. A shelter in this area was burned down and never replaced because it was clear that the local people didn't want it there and would continue to burn down any replacements. In the late 1980s someone strung fishhooks across the Trail at eye level on near-invisible fishing line. Women have been raped. Walk through quickly—that's the word on the Trail. Don't stop, don't camp, don't leave the Trail, don't build fires. Go through in groups and get the hell out.

On one mountain the Trail zigzags tightly down between fences marking the boundaries of private land. At the edge of this land, facing the Trail, hand-painted signs warn:

BEWARE OF SHOTGUN
THIS MEANS YOU

Other hikers tell me they told some locals who had driven a four-wheel-drive up to the Trail that vehicles aren't allowed on the footpath. The locals said "Is that so?" and fired their guns into the air. The hikers, rules forgotten, hastily retreated.

Just after crossing the road that leads to Elk Park, I run into a woman named Inchworm and hike with her for a while. She tells me Bridget has left the Trail; she hated hiking alone and missed her boyfriend too much to continue.

We come out of the woods onto a narrow road. Someone has slapped the word TRIAL and an arrow pointing to the left on the road with blobby strokes of white paint. On the map the Trail goes right.

"Trial, eh?" Inchworm says. "Look at that."

We stop and consult the guidebook. Sure enough, the Trail goes right, not left, on this road for half a mile. We look for blazes and see none, but a fence along the road is missing posts at regular intervals. On one, only half-destroyed, we can see a few flecks of old white paint, remnants of a blaze. Someone is trying to get us lost. I wonder what's at the end of the "Trial" and am glad we won't find out.

Uncertain, we turn right and follow the missing blazes. The road is lined with rundown houses with cars in the yards. Chickens roost in the sprung seats, and in the yards, dogs bark and run to the full length of their chains, slavering and choking in their eagerness to bite into a meaty haunch of hiker. Remembering the dogs that attacked me in Erwin, I get out my pepper spray, and we advance cautiously.

People stare as we pass. When we wave they don't move—they just watch, as if they don't trust us out of their sight for a second. When we finally turn off into the woods, it's a relief to get away from their eyes.

The map for this section makes it look like the day's 14-mile hike is nearly level, but the Trail climbs and falls all day through a series of hills and gaps. It's difficult to follow the map and figure out where we are.

"This mapmaker is gonna go to mapmaker hell," I say.

"What's that like?"

"He has to walk 100 miles a day, in 100-degree heat and 100% humidity, with 100 pounds on his back, using only his own map as a guide."

Obviously he's never walked through here. Secretly I don't blame him.

We stop at a brook to eat, and Inchworm decides to stay there and rest a while. I walk on.

Many of the counties in this part of the country are dry, and moonshine is still a thriving enterprise. The official guidebook for this section, which is a written description of the Trail sometimes giving landmarks down to the tenth of a mile, includes directions such as "At stream to left of former moonshine still, turn hard right, and continue straight down hollow" and "Cross boggy branch. About 30 feet to left are remnants of old moonshine still. Soon, descend through white pines."

The stills mentioned in the guidebook are there, obviously defunct, but three times that day, passing through hollows near brooks, I smell sour mash cooking.

I don't see anything, I don't smell anything, I know nothing, I'm out of here.

The day is humid, hot, and long. The endless ups and downs are getting on my nerves, and paranoia is making me jump every time a bird flies over or a squirrel runs up a tree. I'm afraid the moonshiners will see me near their stills and take it the wrong way. *Dead women tell no tales...*

Several times I think I'm almost there, only to go downhill

again, then up, in the sweltering heat. I pass a hiker named Sailor Dan, who's sitting on a log wiping his face with a bandanna.

"I'm camping right here," he says. "I don't care if we're not supposed to. I can't take another up and down. Say hello to the Old Man of the Mountain if you see him, and tell him I'll see him at Laurel Fork Gorge tomorrow."

Finally, just when I'm about to give up and camp right on the Trail, I reach the shelter. It's full, except for one space next to the Old Man of the Mountain, who refuses to believe that Sailor Dan isn't coming.

"I'm saving this spot," he says petulantly. He pats it like a third grader saving a seat for a friend.

"You can't save spots in shelters," I say. "Besides, I told you he's not coming. He's camped three miles back."

"I'm saving it for him!"

"You can't save spots! First come, first serve!"

The other hikers, wiped out by the day, lie in their bags, watching this spectacle. "She's right, man," someone murmurs.

"I don't care," he says. "If Sailor Dan comes, he'll want this space."

"He's not coming, you crazy old man!"

The Old Man of the Mountain puts his pack over the spot. In a rage, I leave and string my hammock between two trees. It's going to pour tonight, and I really want to be in the shelter, instead of soaking wet out here. I know my rage is inordinate and ridiculous, but can't stop myself from acting like a fool. PMS. Low blood sugar. The hazards of the Trail. I need to eat.

After eating, I've cooled down, but the Old Man still refuses to budge. I string my tarp over the hammock to make a roof, then get in. It's actually very cozy: enclosed, safe, floating, like the best fort you could ever have made as a child.

Lightning flashes, too far away for thunder; then slowly the thunder rolls in. The trees sway and the hammock rocks. I look out and see the moon, still owner of half the sky, but now the wall of clouds is advancing, erasing stars one by one, reaching for the moon.

The clouds come over, and rain pours down on the tarp like insistent beating hands. Some water starts flowing down the support ropes and along the hammock, wetting my back. I pick up my Teva sandals and hang them from the support ropes to guide the rain off the hammock and down to the ground. It works.

In the shelter the Old Man snores. Someone shushes him. I turn on my side, rocked gently by the storm, and sleep.

The next morning I hike through the rain to Laurel Fork Gorge, where a waterfall cascades into a river in a deep gorge. The shelter up on the cliff above the gorge is deserted at first, but eventually Thoreau shows up, and we both decide to go down to the river to swim and wash our filthy clothes.

I love swimming in rivers, love the way the water touches you all over, like a lover; love the way a river demands you to push back. I sit on the bottom with just my head out of the cold water and feel the water pressing at my back, my arms, pushing me inch by inch downstream. I put my head underwater and hear the cold clink of pebbles on the bottom. Ahhh. I tense my feet and dig them into the bottom so I won't be swept away.

"Do you mind if I take my clothes off?" Thoreau asks.

"Nah, I don't care."

He strips and splashes in the water. I keep my clothes on, letting the river wash them while it washes me.

Thoreau decides to move his gear out of the shelter and camp down by the river. I go back to the shelter—still no one there. Shelters have only one thing in common with hotels: Someone always leaves a Bible in them. I pick up the Bible, open it at random, and read, "If someone forces you to walk a mile, go two." A nice verse for hikers. I look for more verses on walking but can't find any, and put the book down. This shelter has other reading material: improbable excerpts from very old issues of *Harper's*. I change into my dry clothes, hang out the wet ones, put up my hammock, and read "The Little Laborers of New

York City," by Charles Loring Brace (written in 1873) and "Lord Macauley on American Institutions" (1877). This selection turns out to be not as odd as it seems. People in civilization read about the wilderness, but when you've been in the woods for a long time, there's nothing as escapist and relaxing as reading about the Victorians.

A storm arrives and so do other hikers, chased by rain. One is a woman called Nomad who's traveling with a man, Dough Boy. The Fun Guys show up, but later all of them but a hiker named Paul leave, heading out into the storm. A man who's running the entire Trail, not hiking it, shows up, and so do some weekenders.

We string ropes from the shelter rafters for our wet clothes, and huddle in the spaces between the laundry, talking, shivering, looking out at the storm.

The runner has a fanny pack with a very light and compact down sleeping bag, and for food he has only a can of sardines and some saltine crackers. He also has a tiny cell phone and offers to let us call home in exchange for some of our food. We give him food, but no one uses the phone.

He tells us he has a support crew who meets him at road crossings with a van that has a bed in it, fresh clothes, and food, but some days, like this one, he doesn't reach the road and has to camp. He's amazed by our camping skills and ease in the woods.

"I learn from you guys every day," he says. "I could never do what you do. I sleep in a normal bed almost every night. It spooks me to be out here at night, and I don't know how you carry all that stuff. But I do wish I had more food, like you have."

I don't envy him. He's moving so quickly he can never be part of the Trail community, since each hiker sees him only once, then he's gone. He's moving too quickly to really see anything: no sitting to look at views, no swimming in the river—not enough time. He's in a specialized world, even more specialized than the hiker community, and more lonely.

Other people have run the whole Trail; he's heard about them. He's not trying for the record, which is 52 days, set by

David Horton in 1991, just trying to do the entire Trail in under 70 days.

"When did you start?" Paul asks.

"Two weeks ago."

Most of us have been on the Trail between one and two months; I've been walking for six weeks.

If I ever had to set a Trail record, I'd want the prize for walking it in the slowest time. I'd hike two miles a day and look at every flower, every stone, every view and every footprint, and I'd spend every afternoon watching clouds, talking to birds, and chatting with other hikers. Of course, on a thruhike, you have to move more quickly than that if you're going to get to Maine before it snows, but I can dream.

In the morning I wake early to the sound of thunder. The runner is already gone, and I wonder how he's doing; he said last night that the one thing he hates worse than anything else on the Trail is rain.

I get up, startling a mouse back into its hole in the wall, and pull my clothes off the line we've strung up in the shelter. They're still soaking wet and cold. This is one of the unpleasant aspects of the Trail that I never get used to; even when it's not raining, I sweat enough to keep my clothes constantly wet. Every morning I put on clothes that are wet and crusted with salt and dirt, like soaked sandpaper against my skin. And last night I dreamed over and over that I needed to take ibuprofen. Now I finally do, but it doesn't help much. Everything hurts.

Thunder! The woods are filled with the sweet, rushing sound and smell of rain. It's a nice change from the reek in the shelter. We're all beginning to smell like ammonia; our clothes have been soaked with sweat and rain for so long that the sweat is breaking down. The bath in the river yesterday, instead of helping, only sped this process along. Except for our wide-awake faces, we look, and smell, like zombies, dressed in tattered, rotting clothes.

In the logbook, southbound hikers have written about a Chinese restaurant in Hampton, Tennessee, the next town. "Cheap, plentiful, and good" is the consensus.

As soon as I see the word *wonton* in the logbook, I know where I'm going. Paul decides to go too, and catch up with the Fun Guys later.

Before hitting the Trail we hike down the steep cliffs to see Laurel Falls, a dramatic waterfall. The official AT actually passes through this gorge; I took the blue-blazed side trail to the shelter yesterday and missed it. And it's a good thing: The river is so swollen with rain that the Trail is underwater. Out in the river, a white blaze on a rock in the middle of the stream marks the submerged and dangerous AT.

I look back in the direction we've come from. A double white blaze on a tree marks a turn in the Trail; beyond that, the way is veiled by mist. Double blaze. A turn in the path, a bend in the Trail. A change in direction. It means more to me than just a direction for hiking, as if it's a symbol for my life. *You're changing. Pay attention: The way turns here.*

Hampton is a nowhere town of speeding cars, barking dogs, and suspicious glances, but the Chinese food lives up to its reputation. Two other hikers are here, middle-aged women named Angie and Moira. We all sit together and go back for plate after plate of food.

The owners tell us they only opened two weeks ago, and almost all of their customers have been hikers, who stagger down from the mountains and eat so much it threatens to drive their all-you-can-eat buffet out of business. They had never heard of the Trail before they opened, and they're mystified by this parade of filthy pilgrims.

We try to explain the shelter logbooks, the word-of-mouth hiker information network, but they don't quite understand. "You mean you all walk together?"

"No, we're all separate, but the word gets around." I think about the hoboes who crisscrossed the country during the Depression, making chalk marks on fences and doors to mark houses where someone was a soft touch. The restaurant owners don't know it, but they've been marked.

Hampton has a hiker hostel, and I decide to stay there to get a break from the rain and take a bath. The only catch is, it costs $10, I don't have the cash, it's Saturday, there's no ATM nearby, and the bank isn't open until Monday. I sit on the hostel steps talking with Angie and Moira, trying to decide what to do. I cross my legs, resting my booted foot on the opposite knee, and pick idly at the mud stuck in the cleats while we talk.

Something's stuck in the mud in my boots, something brown and folded, like a leaf or a moth's wing. I pick it off and unfold it. It's a $10 bill. I can stay.

Things like this happen often on the Trail, so often that hikers have a name for it: Trail magic. Happy coincidences, mysterious gifts, kindnesses or breaks that seem to come from nowhere. I wonder how long the money has been stuck to my boot and where it came from, and know I'll never find out. It's enough just to accept it and be here, in a warm, dry place.

The hostel has a small library of books, mostly religious. One is an inspirational book by an American soldier who was a prisoner of war in Vietnam. I open it at random and read: "I was in an enemy prison camp in the middle of the enemy's country. I remembered from the long trek up here that it would be a hike of several hundred miles in any direction before I could expect to reach friendly hands."

By now I've walked 400 miles, not in enemy territory—at least not until the last few days—but I have no doubt he can do it. I settle down happily with the book.

"You know that convict who was running around in the woods?" Angie says. "The murderer?"

"Yeah, what about him?"

"Well, I heard yesterday that they caught him. Apparently he was hiding up in the mountains, just like they thought, near the Trail, but he avoided the Trail and hikers because he figured if any of us saw him we'd turn him in. The guy was born and raised in the mountains around here but didn't know how to survive in them. So the other day these state troopers were driving along the road, and this guy was just walking along the side, and they stopped and were like, 'Aren't you that guy?' And he didn't even resist or run, just turned himself in. He said he hadn't eaten for a week and it was raining and cold all the time, and he figured it would be better to go back to prison where he could have a bed and be warm and dry and get three square meals a day."

"Ha," I say. "That just shows you we're all tougher than convicts." I wonder what I'd do in his situation—probably sneak up to shelters at night and steal food bags and gear. But then, I already know how to survive in the woods and use the gear once I have it, and he didn't.

I lie in the bathtub and read. The book is good, but disappointing from the point of view of hiking stories—every time the soldier escapes, he gets captured right away. Eventually he's freed and gets to go home, without ever having to walk all that way, in rain and heat, through hundreds of miles of strange country. I almost feel sorry for him.

Conditions the next day are a simulated Vietnam, without the war: very hot, very humid, and rainy. I pass two old men fishing at the edge of Wautauga Lake.

"How's the hike?" they ask, tipping their caps.

"Great. How's the fishing?"

"Turrible. Ain't caught nothin' but turtles."

I hike through the rolling terrain and spend a lot of time crouching on the Trail as lightning comes and goes, as waves of storms cross the mountains. Even the wind is hot, a big sweaty hand pushing at the trees, and the rain is warm, like a shower in civilization. My skin is cool and clammy, on the edge of heat exhaustion, even when it's raining. I ride this edge all day, trying to drink enough water and not hike too fast.

As you walk alone all day, your mind can play tricks on you. More than once before now, walking along, I've had incidents where I look up and see—briefly—someone standing on the Trail ahead of me. Just waiting. Just looking. Or I see someone sitting on a big rock, watching my approach. I look away, usually down, to make sure there are no stones or roots in the path. And when I look up, the person is gone. Whether it's an effect of exhaustion, a trick of tired eyes, a lone hiker's wish for company, or maybe something more, I don't know. But some shelters, like Vandeventer, have real ghost stories attached to them.

The story is that a woman hiker was attacked and killed in the shelter by a man with an ax. He was obsessed with her pack and wanted it for himself. After he killed her he took it, put it on, and hiked down the Trail, happy to have it at last. He was caught, and died in prison 20 years later, but the hiker's ghost is said to return to the shelter at 5:30 each morning, in the shape of a whippoorwill that lands in the center of the fire circle and sings.

Whippoorwills are strange birds. They sing only at night. Their eyes shine blood-red when you catch them in the beam of a flashlight. They're low, compact, and oddly shaped, with big heads and gaping mouths. Their song—a loud, quavering *WHIP! poor-will!* repeated over and over, sometimes thousands of times in a row—is haunting, obsessive, and extremely loud; if you brought one back to civilization it would make a dandy car alarm. In Appalachian folklore, they're associated with hauntings and ghosts.

The shelter is full, with only one spot left. Besides me, there's Nomad, Dough Boy, Sun Ra, and a section hiker named Ron. The rain pours down, and no one wants to hike a mile round-trip in it to get water, so we filter the runoff from the roof to get drinking water.

Sun Ra tells us he's going to leave the Trail. "I'm totally bored with it," he says. "I'm bored with rain, bored with mac and cheese, just totally bored with hiking and being out here. This life, it's not any fun anymore."

"Maybe it's just because it's been raining so much lately," Nomad says. "It's getting on everyone's nerves."

"No, I'm just bored. I'm gonna find a road tomorrow, hitchhike to Damascus, hang out a few days, and then bail."

I'll be sorry to see him go; he has a good sense of humor and a kind of solidity and groundedness—despite the rootlessness he shares with all of us—that's unusual on the Trail.

"What are you gonna do when you get back to civilization?" Nomad asks.

"I don't know. Any suggestions?"

"You could work for Habitat for Humanity, building houses. I did that for a while. It's a blast. They give you room and board, you learn all this stuff about building, and the people are great. And it's a good cause."

"I'll think about it."

Nomad and Dough Boy, who have the best food I've seen yet on the Trail, make popcorn and pass it around. We savor it, watching the storm outside as if it's a movie, and since it's so dark, go to bed early.

We sleep peacefully while it rains. Near morning, the rain stops. Someone is screaming—no, crying—no, screaming.

We all sit up. What is it?

WHIP! poor-will! It's loud, as if it's right in the shelter with us.

Disoriented, we squirm upright in our bags. It's close to morning but still not light enough to really see. Someone grabs a flashlight and flings a bar of light out into the dark.

In the center of the fire pit, in the middle of the circle of stones, the whippoorwill is singing. Its red eyes shine.

"What time is it?" Sun Ra asks.

Nomad checks her watch. It's exactly 5:30 A.M.

Since Nomad and Dough Boy are hiking together, cooking together, and sharing gear, I assume they're a couple, but if they are, something's wrong. Nomad is a striking woman, six feet tall, strong, and blond, like a Nordic goddess, whereas Dough Boy looks like his name, with tiny dark eyes in a pale face, like raisins sunk in a bun. They cook together like they've been doing it all their lives, but there's no happy chemistry between them; it seems like an old, stale marriage. He's young but acts like one of those disappointed, and disappointing, old men who spend their lives hiding behind the newspaper and grunting.

"Great hike today, huh?" Nomad says.

"Mmmff."

"Isn't this curry fabulous?"

"Mmmff."

I can't figure out how they've achieved such monumental staleness at such a young age. I don't have to wonder long, though, because when we're getting water at the spring, Nomad explains.

"He's my cousin. Our families thought it would be safer if we hiked together. And God, is he getting on my nerves! What a downer!"

For her sake, I'm relieved she's not involved with him. Lately I've felt lonely at times, but seeing them, I realize there are definite pluses to hiking alone.

I reach Damascus, Virginia, after a 20-mile day, just before Quincey's pizzeria closes. The Old Man of the Mountain is there, along with several other hikers; he and I apologize to each other for our run-in back in North Carolina, eat huge pizzas, and buy each other a beer.

I've walked 450 miles to get here, and I'm very tired, emotionally as well as physically. "Head is more important than heel," said Grandma Gatewood, the first woman thruhiker. She was 68 when she hiked the entire Trail in 1955, and she knew what she was talking about; she hiked the entire Trail twice more before she was 77, and hiked many other trails, including the 2,000-mile Oregon Trail, in her 70s. It would seem that in order to walk more than 2,000 miles, you'd have to be physically tough, some kind of superathlete. But what you really need, even more than physical stamina, is emotional and mental stamina.

Lately it seems like all I do is get up, eat oatmeal, walk, eat some more, walk some more, get to a shelter, get water, filter water, gather twigs, make a fire in my stove, cook supper, eat it, wash my cooking pot, brush my teeth, and go to sleep. Then the next day I get up, put on the same clothes, which get dirtier and more painfully crusted with salt as each day passes, and do it again. It's like a job, or school, except that my duties aren't very well defined, and no one is making me do it. The daily chores, both of walking and of surviving, take so much of my time and energy that I have very little left to think about the transformation I'm supposed to be going through. I feel like *something* is changing in me, or in my attitude toward the Trail or life in general, but I can't say what it is. It's like water deep underground: It's there, a source of life and renewal, but I can't reach it yet, even though I'm terribly thirsty.

"Have you ever thought of quitting?" Thoreau asks me as we rest in our bunks at The Place, a hostel run by the Methodist church. Outside on the hostel lawn, new arrivals who don't feel like staying inside are setting up their tents. A dog barks, and tent poles click as a hiker dumps them out of a stuffsack and connects them one by one. Down the street, someone is mowing the lawn, and the sweet green smell drifts through the window. This is a spacious old house, with plenty of bunk-bed-filled rooms and high ceilings that make you feel like you've gone back in time to a gentler place. Inside the house, I hear the shower running nonstop as people wash off a week's worth of grime, and other voices of hikers in the common room downstairs running through the recognition ritual:

"When did you start?"

"April 8th. How 'bout you?"

"March 25th. I got slowed down back in Tennessee. I sprained my ankle and had to get off for a week."

"Where'd you go?"

"That hostel in Hampton."

"The one like a castle? Near the Chinese food?"

"That's the place. Hey, do you know Starbuck? He got ahead of me then, and I've been chasing him, 'cause I owe him 10 bucks. He never writes in the logbooks, so he's hard to find."

"You'll never catch him, man. He's like a week ahead. The dude is in a hurry. I heard he got some job offer or something, so he has to be done by September."

Thoreau has been lying on his back staring at the ceiling, but when he asks me about quitting he rolls onto his side and looks at me intently. He's not wearing a shirt, and his chest looks thin and vulnerable, like a boy's.

"I can't quit," I say. "I'm doing this trip for a reason, and if I quit, I'll never get where I want to go. I'll just have to come back and do it again, so I might as well do it now or I'll be stuck until I do. So I never even think of quitting, because I can't."

"What do you mean?"

I explain about the place I need to get to and the trip being a pilgrimage to it. Secretly I believe something dire will happen to me if I quit—not necessarily anything dangerous or evil, just stagnation and general unhappiness in life. I don't know where I'd go or what I'd do if I quit now, but I know for a fact that I'd be miserable, whereas if I just keep going, I'll find happiness. I know this sounds absurd and escapist, but I feel in my bones that it's Truth.

"Have you thought of quitting?" I ask him. I've seen him a few times before but have never really talked with him. He's in his early 20s but seems younger. His eyes are wide and filled with daydreams, and I'd make a bet that in civilization he reads science fiction and is a member of one of those groups that dress up and reenact medieval times. I have friends do this, so I know the signs.

"I think about it," he says. "But I don't have anything else going for me. I've messed up my life. If I have to leave, I'll kill myself, because I have nothing else to do."

"What've you done to mess up your life?"

"Oh, you know, the usual. Drugs and drinking. Have you gone to college?"

"Yes."

"Well, I haven't, and it bothers me. I'm trying to educate myself by a program of reading out here. That's why I call myself Thoreau. I have *The Education of Henry Adams* and a book by Jung in my pack. Do you understand his theory of the collective unconscious?"

"I've read some of his books," I say. I can't imagine bringing any of these books on the Trail; they're too heavy, in more ways than just physically.

"Listen, there are a lot of ways to get educated besides being in school," I say. "Like right now, being on the Trail. This is an education that you could never get in a book. You're learning about the woods, you're learning endurance, you're learning about people and yourself. Besides, some of the people I know who've had the most schooling are also some of the stupidest people on earth. They have no common sense and no real skills except reading and talking about the things they've read. They don't have sense enough to fix something that's broken or cook a meal. Are you still doing drugs and drinking?"

"Just pot. And I drink when I can get it. I have some good bud in my pack if you want to share. I carved my own pipe—it's cool, you ought to see it. I call it my medicine pipe. I'm part Indian, you know. Cherokee. My grandmother was a Cherokee princess."

"Maybe that's why you're depressed. Not your grandmother, I mean, but the pot and alcohol. Maybe you came out here to really listen to yourself, but you can't hear it. You know how it is when you're high: You think you're having all these profound thoughts, and you even write them down, but the next day you look at the piece of paper and it says, 'My feet hurt.'"

"How'd you know?"

"What else would a hiker think about? The only alternative would be, 'I have the munchies.'"

"Maybe we're just born to suffer," he says. "It's part of our animal nature. We're all just animals." He throws back his head and strikes a pose. "How many years was I beast before I was man?" He likes the sound of this, so he repeats it.

Downstairs, a woman is yelling. The words "Hell!" and "Sinners!" and "Abomination!" come punching up through the wooden floor like sharp nails. "Jesus Christ!" she yells.

Boots clomp on the floor, hikers laugh, and the woman starts singing "Amazing Grace."

"Hey, it's your song," Thoreau says. We go and stand on the stairway, looking over the heads of the crowd. The woman is standing on a low table, ranting and rolling her eyes. She's not a hiker. She looks like a hippie, with long flowing hair and a flowered skirt and tight shirt. The way she looks doesn't match the way she talks. She looks like she should be saying, "Groovy, man. Pass me that joint." From the way she talks, you'd expect her to be dressed in a plain black skirt, heavy black shoes, and white blouse, with her hair in a bun.

Through the window I see a van outside, painted with psychedelic swirls and flowers and bell-bottomed letters that say:

GOD SQUAD

THERE IS ONLY ONE WAY TO TRUTH.

Some hikers are laughing; others are heckling her; and some just watch. The general gist of the sermon is that because we're wanderers in the wilderness, we're godless and need to be saved. This seems to be a common assumption about hikers: There are Bibles and tracts in almost all of the shelters, as if we're in special need of spiritual help. It's gypsies versus townies; wanderers are heathens.

The hostel caretaker comes in and tries to get her to leave. She refuses. She's not connected to the church that runs the hostel. She may be motorized, but she's just a wanderer like the rest of us and has showed up out of the blue not knowing where she'll go next. She's not a townie, she's a gypsy like us, and she hates herself for it.

When the hikers find out she's one of the transients she's denouncing, they drift away, make meals, gather laundry, and disappear for pizza. One stays, talking earnestly with her. He calls himself Saul. "The Lord directed me to walk this Trail," he says. He adds that eventually he'll build a church, when the Lord tells him to. He looks and talks just like Sylvester Stallone—an unlikely missionary.

The woman wrinkles her brow and stares at him, puzzled. Neatly, swiftly, he has done some kind of spiritual martial art on her, and she's gone from being the preacher, in charge of the crowd, to the woeful penitent.

I go back upstairs. Thoreau is lying on his bunk, his unlit pipe resting on his chest. I wonder if he'll really kill himself if he has to quit. I don't think so, but you never know. I wonder what secrets he's carrying around. I realize that I don't know his real name and perhaps never will.

A hiker named Lioness is on the phone in the common room of the hostel. Her voice is thin and whiny:

"Sick, sick, sick. That's all I hear, how sick you are. You never ask how I am. I'm tired of hearing it. I'm out here suffering, and all I hear is how sick you are."

She's an improbable hiker. Extremely overweight, with big blond curls, she has the air of a victim: Use me. Most hikers seem relatively tough and self-sufficient, especially those who have survived until now. Her name seems almost like a joke, the most unlikely handle she could have.

She slams down the phone, pooches out her lips, and exhales a gust of breath. "What should I do?" she asks.

"About what?"

"My father is in intensive care back in Montana, and I'm fed up with it. He's just doing this to get me to come home. He just wants me to feel sorry for him. He's faking it. He always does."

"But if he's in intensive care, there probably is something wrong with him."

I think about my dad in intensive care for the two-and-a-half weeks before he died. His breathing had failed, so he was on one of those machines that breathe for you. *Whoosh,* the pump in the machine came down, and his chest went up as his lungs filled. *Whaash,* the pump went up, and his chest went down. It was frightening and nauseating, watching the machine breathe him, seeing the tubes and wires keep him alive, the dark screen with the tenuous green trail of his heartbeat. The tube for the breathing machine prevented him from speaking, so he never did get to say goodbye.

I can't imagine not wanting to see him, or speaking to him the way she talks to her dad. I ask her what she does back in civilization. She says she works at a nursing home, which doesn't answer any of my questions; it just adds to them.

She decides not to go home. "What are your plans?" she asks.

"I'm taking tomorrow off," I say. "A rest day. Then I'll head out the next day."

"Oh, good," she says. "That's what I'm doing. What time do you want to leave?"

Just like that, she's suddenly declared herself my traveling partner. It takes me by surprise. No way do I want to walk with her; she's unpredictable, to say the least, and her neediness is frightening.

"Uh," I say, "we'll see."

A butterfly lands on my hand as I sit with my feet in a creek, eating gorp and writing in my journal. I'm being bad. I'm not on the AT at all. I'm on the Creeper Trail, a rails-to-trails path that leads out of Damascus and eventually reconnects to the AT. I'm a big bad blue-blazer, and it has the same wicked thrill as skipping school or calling in sick to work when you're well. Suddenly hiking is fun again. Lioness left the hostel before I did, so I'm off the hook.

The butterfly is black and gold, a great spangled fritillary. It looks like concentrated sunlight and night. Looking at it is almost painful, as if the sight of something so beautiful so close makes your soul expand too quickly and you get the spiritual equivalent of the bends.

It jumps from my hand to the page, unrolls its proboscis, and checks my words to see if they're tasty. Clouds of other butterflies, tiger swallowtails and more fritillaries, orbit my head and shoulders and settle on my pack and my arms. It's not magic, it's dirt and salt that attract them, but the bicyclists rolling past on the Trail don't know that. They stop and point and stare. I wave, and the butterflies swirl up, then resettle, drinking my sweat.

Last night I dreamed of Wade and woke up angry and annoyed that even in sleep I have to waste time thinking about how stupid I was to spend any time with him. Back in Damascus someone had a car identical to his, and it was such a small town that any time I went anywhere I had to see it, parked on the street across from Quincey's, a little reminder of an evil time. Now it's following me in my dreams. I know that to get through this, I have to think about what happened with him, and while I'm walking out here it's as good a time as any, but I'd rather think about the butterflies.

I sing as I walk, old hippie songs from the '60s, and incidents from my childhood float past: Big Wheels bikes, banana seats, how all the kids would stick baseball cards and colored straws in the spokes of their bikes. Christmas. We used to go skiing in Colorado every year, and on Christmas Eve the ski patrol would ski down the mountain in a long chain, each person holding torches in both hands, a river of red fire flowing down the dark mountain, and my dad and I would stand under the stars, watching until the lights went out.

Coming around the side of Mount Rogers, I slip off the edge of a rock and twist my ankle so badly that I fall down, the weight of my pack crashing on the stony trail. I lie there, resting on the reassuring bulk of my pack, trying not to think about the injury. If I fall, I reason, it must be because I'm tired. I wasn't paying attention. I'll just rest here a while, since I'm already down. My pack is so heavy and my body so slight that when I fall I always land on my pack, which cushions me. How convenient.

Birds fly over. The trees bend back and forth in the wind. My ankle screams. I wonder if this is the Big One, an injury that would force me off the Trail. I can't leave now. I don't want to leave.

When I was about 10, my family went camping on the shore of Lake Superior. That night a huge storm swept in, creating waves the size of houses. We crouched over our portable radio listening to the weather: There were five tornadoes in a circle around our location. In the morning the road to the campground was washed out, so we were trapped until trucks could get through to fill it in.

My mother went walking along a 30-foot cliff, but she didn't realize the earth had been loosened by the storm. It gave way, and she fell off the edge and sprained her ankle. My father wrapped it, and my brother and I went into the woods and found a forked branch that we padded with an old sweatshirt and made into a crutch for her. She's my role model for dealing with this occasion: the woman who broke her leg skiing on her honeymoon and sprained her ankle on a camping trip, and went back for more.

I wonder if anyone is coming along behind me. If not and if I can't get up, I'll have to crawl around, set things up, and camp right here. I don't have much water, which could be a problem. I do have two heavy hiking sticks, almost as good as crutches.

I send little feelers of thought down toward the injury. Is it broken? Can I move it? I can, so it's probably not broken. I lie here for about a half hour, then get up and limp on, leaning heavily on my hiking sticks, toward the nearest shelter. I'll rest there tonight and hope it's better in the morning.

Thomas Knob Shelter has a request posted on the wall: Don't make fires here, because it's a fragile habitat and rare wild salamanders need the dead wood to survive. Since my stove uses wood, I can't cook, so I eat cold snacks and borrow hot water from other hikers who have fuel-burning stoves. The shelter is busy: me, Thoreau, a young woman named Little Star traveling with an old man named Pappy, a hiker called Popsicle, and another named Maine Event.

Wild ponies live here. At dusk they come up to the edge of the shelter, snorting warm breath, their hooves clicking on the stony ground, and lick the salt off our arms and legs. There are seven of them, including a shy, dark brown colt. We wish we could pet him, but his mother would kick the daylight out of us, so we keep our distance. It's intimate, this being kissed by horses, and makes us giggle.

In the back corner of the shelter is a white bone sculpture, the pelvis of a horse that some hiker must have found and left here. Thoreau puts it on his head, where it makes a frightening mask. His eyes gleam out through the symmetrical openings, and one piece comes down over his nose like the face-protector on a Viking helmet. "How long was I beast before I was man?" he roars. He beats his chest and looks around at us as if we are his subjects.

It's cold up here, a northern, glacial, unforgiving, and beautiful place, the soil thin and rocky. It smells like balsam fir. I sit on the stone step in front of the shelter, take off my boot, and look at my ankle. It's black-and-blue and swollen. It's painful, but by now I'm so used to various kinds of pain that it hardly seems to matter. I can bend it, it will get better, and I can keep on walking.

In the morning my stomach screams for food. The cold, hard floor has spread an ache up through my bones; I've lost so much weight that all my bones grind into the floor, right through my thin sleeping mat. I'm in the loft of the shelter, and it's cold up here. The wind, which has been roaring all night, is flapping my tarp, which I've tied over a hole in the wall to keep out some of the cold. Near my hand is a pile of chewed string a mouse has left, and a coverless romance book set in Ireland. I pick it up and read: "Oh, Deirdre, but don't you see,

Colin is gone! I've looked all over the estate—I asked the gamekeeper..." and toss it into the corner. The mice can use the paper for a nest.

I shiver in my bag, thinking of food, wondering what to eat for breakfast, since I can't use my stove. Nutty Bars, instant lemonade, and Chex Mix are the only alternatives. I crave bacon; if I had a stick of butter, I'd eat it whole. I now know why Arctic explorers and Inuit tribes ate whale blubber.

Suddenly a man says, "I have some summer sausage and cheese, and also some bagels and muffins."

I hop down the ladder one-footed, wincing with pain. But what a great breakfast: blueberry bagels, jalapeño jack cheese, summer sausage, all in one big sandwich. It's the best thing I've ever eaten.

The Trail angels are two elderly men. They're just out for the weekend and are heading home today. They're modest and low-key, but we pump them for information anyway, and from their conversation I gather that one of them is a wealthy gentleman who lives on an estate somewhere nearby, and the other is his valet. They often go camping, hiking, and hunting together.

Oh, Deirdre. You never know what, or who, you'll meet on the Trail.

I wrap my ankle in an elastic bandage and hike with Pappy and Little Star through the beauty of Grayson Highlands State Park, which looks more like Montana than Virginia. Odd rock formations and buttes jut out of the ground, and wild horses chase one another over the wide grassy swells and come delicately to us for handouts. Little Star loves animals; she's like a little girl, trying to get close to the foals, petting the aged mares. We stand still while the horses wash us with their tongues.

We walk past a strangely familiar place. I've been here before, with Wade. It was the only time I went camping with him other than the time in the Shenandoahs, and one morning I left him in camp and went hiking by myself.

It was August, and the wild blueberries were ripe...

I decide to go blueberry picking by myself. I bring a big metal bowl, and set out to fill it.

I pick for a while, moving steadily farther and farther up the mountain. I know the Trail is somewhere nearby, and want to see it. I want to feel it, to be on it, feel the electric immensity of standing on a path that could lead me over the mountains either to Georgia or to Maine. I have a feeling it's up on top of this ridge. I hike up the steep incline, careful not to spill the berries, and sure enough, there it is. I stand on the footpath and look at the white blaze on a hawthorn tree. It's a symbol of something huge, like those dreams where you discover a new door in your house that leads to a whole wing of rooms you never knew existed.

A man is walking toward me on the Trail with something in his hands. Something big and dark and alive. The thing lifts a wing. It's a hawk, and the man is holding it with one hand over its eyes and the other in a sure grip on its feet. I've never been so close to a hawk, and feel awe at its strong claws and patterned feathers. It radiates intensity, even with its eyes covered.

The man is a rehabilitator of injured animals and birds. This hawk has broken a wing, but now it's healed and ready to fly again. He's going to let it go. He invites me to come and see, and tells me he's also up here to scatter the ashes of a young friend who died in a car crash. The dead friend loved birds, hawks most of all. The bird's release will be a part of the funeral, a sign of the soul flying free.

More people come straggling along, breathing hard as they come up over the brow of the hill. I'm glad I have the berries; it seems rude to attend a funeral and not bring any food. They greet me cordially, as if they were expecting me, and take handfuls of the berries to eat.

The hawk release is first: The rehabilitator doesn't want the bird to wait any longer. We all stand in a loose half-circle. Two people say short prayers, one Christian, one pagan. The man lifts his hand off the bird's head and lets it look around. It stares at each of us intently, as if memorizing our faces, then lifts its wings and lofts away, gathering speed.

I feel something in me tear loose. "Take me with you!" I want to call. The bird circles, then comes down in the dense top of a pine, as if it needs time to look around from a safe place and decide what to do next.

I know how it feels.

The funeral guests set off for the scattering of the ashes, and I go the other way. It's too intimate for me to see. I want to stay up here forever, just keep walking, north or south, it doesn't matter, just so I don't have to go back to the campground where Wade is.

I touch the white blaze before going back down toward the campground.

"I'll be back," I say.

As I go back down the hill, the hawk flies over my head, and I hear its distant scream. It's an omen, I know: If I come to the Trail, I'll also have another chance at life. Like the hawk, I can fly free, and find my home.

Now we pass that exact spot. It's a strange kind of déjà vu, as if it were just a week ago, yet also millennia ago. I feel I could just walk down the hill and Wade would still be sitting there in a folding chair, bored out of his mind by the woods. He'd be the same, but now I'm changed. I've been walking slowly, but damn, I've walked far since then. There are a lot of miles between that life and this one. Thank God. Now I speed up and leave the place behind. The miles go by faster in such beautiful terrain.

Old Orchard Shelter sits at the edge of a big meadow, and I get there early. Popsicle, Pappy, Maine Event, and Little Star show up too. Popsicle has a stash of half-smoked cigarette butts he picked up back at a road crossing where someone in a car dumped out their ashtray, and he's in heaven. He peels them open, pours out all the tobacco, and rerolls two new cigarettes, then smokes, exhaling luxuriously.

"You're one tobacco-happy guy," Pappy says. "You've got to be addicted to smoke those road butts."

Popsicle shoots smoke out through his nose and puts water on his stove for coffee. "Hey, man, there's nothing wrong with it. I don't pick up the ones that are all yellow, just the clean white ones. And I reroll them so it's not like I'm touching someone else's germs. Besides, it all gets burned anyway, so it's sterile."

Pappy looks dubious.

"Grace eats old M&Ms she finds on the Trail," Popsicle says.

"Is that so?"

"Yeah," I say. "If they're not all rained on and faded. Never refuse free food. I once found a half-eaten apple that some tourist had left at an overlook and I ate that too."

"Yecch," Little Star says. She's a very feminine woman, recently married. Her husband was delayed by work but will be joining her on the Trail soon. In the meantime, she and Pappy are hiking buddies.

I hang up my hammock and lie in it drinking coffee, reading *The Red Badge of Courage,* courtesy of Thoreau, but am immediately bored and instead just lie there, looking up at the trees. This is what my friends think I do every day: a life of ease and pleasure and painless strolls in the woods. It's impossible to explain the physical harshness of this life to someone who hasn't lived it. It's rare to get into camp in time to relax before the evening round of chores: laying out my sleeping gear, getting water, collecting wood for my stove, cooking and eating supper, doing dishes, washing up, hanging up my sweat-soaked clothes, and writing in my journal.

Late in the afternoon, Lioness shows up. She spreads out her sleeping bag, sits on it, and sorts through her pack.

Out in the meadow, Pappy and I are laying out our sweaty

hiking clothes and socks on bushes, with the irrational hope that they'll dry by morning. Pappy studies Lioness thoughtfully.

"For a big gal, she sure don't sweat that much," he says.

It's true. Her shirt is dry, her pack is still crisp and relatively clean, and she looks fresh.

"How did you get here?" I ask Lioness when we go back to the shelter. I'm curious, because although she disappeared from Damascus before I left, there has been no record of her on the Trail. No journal entries, and no one has mentioned seeing her. And this shelter is relatively close to a road: only one-and-a-half miles away.

She looks up, startled. "I hiked all the way here. What are you insinuating?"

"Nothing. I don't care if you hiked or rode. I was just curious because you look so clean."

"I hiked!"

Behind her, Pappy holds out a thumb and flails his other arm, desperate to flag down an imaginary car. Then he waves his index finger in circles, the "crazy" sign.

"I used to play in a band," Pappy says later, when Lioness is down at the spring. I can picture this: He's lean, with white hair in a crisp ponytail, and even now he would look good onstage. "I played lead guitar and sang. We were pretty good, back in the '60s, and we traveled from town to town for gigs. There were always women. Groupies. They'd follow us. I'd see the same gals in the audience every night for a while, then they'd disappear, and you'd know they were following some other band. They couldn't be in the band, but they wanted a piece of the action."

"They just wanted a piece of your action, Pappy," Popsicle says.

"Well, yeah, some of 'em did. But that's not the point. What I'm saying is, this gal here, what you've got here is a hiker groupie."

It makes sense. I think about Vampire, the "poor little rich girl" I met back in North Carolina. Yeah, she was a groupie too. How odd. I've never thought of hikers as a sexy group.

Lioness comes back, and while we're all making supper she

begins to talk, rambling on until I'm not sure whether she's talking to herself or if we're all supposed to be having a conversation.

"He's younger than me, you know," she says.

"What?" Popsicle says.

"He's younger. A lot younger. I've got a younger man." She giggles and stirs her noodles and sauce.

"Where'd you meet him?" I ask.

"Oh, we've never met. We just talk on the phone. But we're going to get married and have a big wedding."

"You've never seen each other?"

"No, but we know we're in love. Isn't it beautiful?"

"How did you, uh, meet this guy?"

"Well, he hiked last year, and he left a notebook in a shelter with his name and address in it, you know, for a shelter register, and I saw it and wrote him, and he wrote back, and I said I wanted to hike but didn't have anyone to mail my food drops to me, and he said he would do it for me, you know, like passing on the Trail magic. And we wrote back and forth, and called. He's younger, you know."

Behind her, Pappy nods as if to say, *See? I told you so.*

Lioness talks on about her love, on and on. She jumps from topic to topic and sentence to sentence so much that it's hard to follow. She chatters through the evening and on into dark, and doesn't stop until everyone is asleep, or pretending to be. Everyone is too polite to tell her to be quiet, as if we all have some unspoken understanding of her frailty, and the others are so tired they fall asleep anyway. I lie in the dark with my eyes wide open, listening to the steady run of her voice, afraid to roll over because then she'll know I'm awake and talk even longer. Finally, her voice winds down like a worn-out toy.

Even in sleep she's annoying and somehow pathetic. As she breathes out she sighs, a high, sexual-sounding moan, over and over, as if even in sleep she has to prove that someone wants her. I sit up and look at her in the starlight. She seems asleep, but you never know. She could be doing it just to get attention. She doesn't seem to be able to tell, or doesn't care, when no one is listening, so the fact that everyone else is snoring so loudly that the floor is trembling might not matter to her. Between their snores, her moans, and Popsicle's coffee jittering through my veins, it's impossible to sleep.

I get up and walk around. Down at the end of the meadow the embers of Maine Event's fire gleam through the trees. He's smart to camp apart from everyone else.

Stars are scattered across the sky; quick as a minnow, a meteor slides between them and disappears. It's a gift from the cosmos: bright and beautiful, then gone. A compensation for insomnia.

Lioness is still moaning. Her cries carry out across the meadow, getting thinner as they go, rising to heaven. All the men snore on. Point and counterpoint: songs of longing, and sleep.

Perseverance

Do not imagine that the journey is short; and one must have the heart of a lion to follow this unusual road, for it is very long.... One plods along in a state of amazement, sometimes smiling, sometimes weeping.

—Farid ud-Din Attar, *The Conference of the Birds*

June 4
Troutdale, Va.

Chapter Six

Two women have been killed on the Trail.

Popsicle and I stand at the road crossing, gaping at the local who's just told us this news. We've hitchhiked into the tiny hamlet of Troutdale for a quick resupply and big baskets of burgers and fries at the local diner, and the owner is kind enough to offer us a ride back to the Trail. Just before he drops us off, he says, "Y'all be careful out there. I heard two girls got themselves killed up in the Shenandoahs."

"What?"

We've been carefree until now. Oh, sure, there was a murderer loose back in Tennessee, but somehow we never took him seriously. Now we're hiking straight toward the Shenandoahs. It's a little more than 300 miles, or three weeks, away. Not far enough.

"Where in the Shenandoahs?"

He rummages in the front seat of his truck and finds a

muddy newspaper. "Think it's in here...yeah." He folds the paper and hands it over. HIKERS KILLED IN SHENANDOAH NATIONAL PARK, reads the headline. Two women, Julianne Williams, age 24, and Lollie Winans, age 26, have been killed at a remote campsite. They were out for a long weekend, not on the Trail but close to it, on a side trail. They were experienced woodswomen, both teachers at an outdoor school for women. Police became suspicious when their families and friends reported that they had not come home when they were expected. Their dog was found running loose in the woods nearby.

The paper says it's believed that the women were lesbians and that the killing was a hate crime.

Oh, great.

We lift our packs out of the back of the truck, put them on, and thank the man. "Be careful now," he says, and pulls away.

We head into the woods. We don't talk much. I've always loved the Shenandoahs. I went to college in Washington, D.C., lived in D.C. for several years afterward, and went to the park often. When the city got to me I'd get up at 3 in the morning, be deep in the park by sunrise, and spend the entire day exploring or just napping in a secluded spot. I know most of the trails and many of the mountains there. I've always thought of it as a sanctuary of safety and peace.

For Julianne and Lollie it wasn't. This news is saddening and disturbing, and personal. This is the very reason I've walked so far keeping secrets about my personal life.

There's a man out in the woods, and he's waiting to kill you.

Popsicle and I walk fast.

"How far do you think the guy could get in a day?" he asks.

"On foot or in a vehicle?" I ask. "I doubt he's a hiker. They weren't really on the Trail. If he has a car, he can go anywhere."

Even here. We walk faster. Our packs are filled with treats I bought in town to give to other hikers: For once, we're going to be the Trail angels. But that's not the only reason we're in a hurry to be with other people. There's safety in numbers.

The shelter we're headed for is supposed to be two-tenths of a mile off the Trail, but when we get to the blue-blazed trail that leads to it, it seems farther. Happy to be home, Popsicle and I almost run down the blue-blazed side trail, singing the theme from *Rawhide* at the top of our lungs and yipping like cowboys. We finally get to the shelter; it's secluded, almost a secret.

When we get inside, we see a man lying on his back in a sleeping bag with a shirt over his face. He doesn't have a pack, or if he does, it's not in or near the shelter. Popsicle and I figure he's asleep, so we take off our packs and sit on the picnic table outside the shelter, eating gorp and wondering out loud where everyone else is.

"Who's there?" The man in the shelter doesn't sit up or remove the shirt from his face. His voice is muffled, disembodied.

"It's Popsicle. How you doin'?"

"I thought I heard a female voice. Is there a woman there?"

I back off and say nothing, and signal to Popsicle, "Let's go."

Popsicle doesn't see me. "It's Amazin' Grace," he says.

Mentally, I curse him. This guy is spooky. I don't want him knowing anything about me.

"Amazin' Grace," the man says. "There's a love note for you up at the next shelter. Someone's in love with your pretty face. You have friends too, Popsicle. They're heading for that ranger station. Gonna get pizza."

He names several other long-distance hikers. He knows their destinations, their recent petty arguments, their injuries; he knows too much for a stranger.

"I hear you're heading for that ranger station too, tomorrow. You're gonna eat pizza too."

Popsicle and I exchange glances. I try to see the guy's face. The shirt completely covers it except for a piece of salt-and-pepper beard. His left hand is sprawled out on the scuffed wood, like a corpse's. He's wearing a wedding ring.

I pick up the shelter logbook and read the most recent entries. Several hikers have signed in and written not much more than "Moving on." I know why.

"You hikers," the man says in a low voice. "All you ever do is talk about your *gear*, and your *boots*, and your *Trail.* Then more of you show up, and you tell the same stories about your *gear* and your *boots* and your *Trail.* And your *miles*. That's all you ever do. You disgust me."

Popsicle coughs and lights a cigarette, a half-smoked butt he picked up in a parking lot in town. "So what brings you out here, amigo?"

"I've been…fasting. For a week. Looking for…vision. I was up at that other shelter I told you about, but I couldn't take it. All those hikers. It's a nice shelter… You ought to go there. I've been…thinking about some things…I did. My wife and I…had a fight… I have some...regrets."

I'm definitely ready to leave. I don't care if we have to walk four more miles. I would go 20.

"You smokers." He half-sits up but doesn't remove the shirt from his face. "You're doing that on purpose. You're blowing the smoke in here on purpose. That's what smokers do. You want to hurt me? You want to kill me? You smokers want to kill everyone."

"No, man, it's the wind," Popsicle says. "I wouldn't do that. I'm a considerate smoker."

"You lie. You're doing it on purpose. You're blowing that smoke right in here. That's what you people do. You're killers."

I hoist my pack. "Well, it's been a nice break, gotta go, happy trails," I say, and start walking swiftly down the blue-blaze toward the AT. Popsicle is right behind me.

"What a freak!" he says.

"Do you think he'll follow us to the next shelter? It's only four miles."

"He even told us to go there. What if he sneaks back in the middle of the night and kills us? He's fucked up."

"We could get off the Trail somewhere between this shelter and that one and then stealth-camp," I say. "You know, go off the Trail and into the woods where no one can see us. Not make a fire. Eat cold stuff and stay quiet. He'd never find us."

"If there are other hikers at the next shelter, maybe it'll be OK."

"There'll probably be 20," I tell him. "Look at it this way: Anyone who thought they were going to stay here, like us, has moved on. If they stayed at the last shelter, like us, they had to do 14 miles just to get here. The next shelter makes it 18. Most people aren't going to go beyond that because the next shelter after that makes it a 24-mile day. Every hiker on the Trail is probably bunched up four miles from here."

"Good. But if there's any less than eight people there, I vote that we hide."

The terrain is up and down, roller-coaster hills. I'm glad. Even if that guy is a murderous psycho, there's no way he can keep up with us or catch us in this terrain, as long as we keep hiking. I think about the rednecks who chased me back in Tennessee, who thought that a lone woman carrying a big pack would be easy prey. No one can catch a long-distance hiker going uphill.

We're in good shape and flying along, fueled by adrenaline and our recent resupply and pig-out in town. We'll only be in danger if we stop: Then he can catch up with us. In the middle of the night. Stealth-camping sounds like a good idea.

There are 12 people and a dog at the shelter. Eight of them saw "Spooky Joe," as they're now calling him, and decided to move on. Four simply bypassed that shelter altogether.

Popsicle talks about hiking on and hiding, but I decide I'll be safe with so many people—and a dog to warn all of us if anyone approaches. I get out my Swiss Army knife, wrap my fingers around my heavy hiking sticks, and fall into a dreamless sleep.

The Trail passes right by the Mount Rogers ranger station, and we go inside and tell the ranger about Spooky Joe. He's a classic cop: thick, wide-shouldered, all business. He takes detailed notes in a tiny black cop notebook as Pappy, Little Star, Popsicle, and I tell him our story.

"Do you think he's still up there?" the ranger asks.

"We don't know. It was a couple of days ago. He could be gone. Plenty of other hikers saw him, though, and he may have written something in the log."

The ranger slaps his notebook shut, thanks us, then hurries outside, revs his car, and speeds off. We know what he's thinking, the same thing we thought: Maybe this guy is connected to the murder of the two women. We hope the murderer is caught, and soon.

Soon after this, all the rangers go home. They let hikers camp on their back porch, where there's a water spigot, a public phone, and even a roof to sleep under in case of rain. We take turns bathing under the spigot, call home, and drink sodas we bought from the machine inside the ranger station before they closed.

We order pizza on the phone, and Popsicle tells me about his stepfather, whom he detests, and his mother, who apparently has bailed him out of every trouble he's ever gotten into. She's paying the complete cost of his Trail trip—at every town stop he gets a box of food and $20 spending money. The $20 doesn't go far; evidently she suspects, correctly, that he'll spend any money on drugs or drinks, so he has to "borrow" them, or the money to get them, from other hikers.

Today he got a joint from some people at a road crossing. I saw them too; they were camped in a tent and had a big black dog who barked viciously as I passed. Popsicle, unbothered, simply called "Hello?" and within minutes had a joint, free of charge. I can tell the weather and find edible plants, abilities that mystify other hikers, but his drug-detecting ability seems more uncanny to me, and so is his ability to tell when someone is an easy mark. Back at Troutdale he borrowed money from me for the meal, and the pizza is also a loan. He says he'll pay me back at the next town, but I have my doubts.

Pappy tells us stories about his life. He's been a hobo, a Hell's Angel, a Vietnam vet, and now owns a farm back home.

"What did you do in Vietnam?" I ask.

"Mostly flew. I was lucky. I never got down on the ground where it was really bad."

We talk about Trail life, how sometimes it's lonely.

"These guys," he says. "You hear 'em all the time talking about how horny they are. What do they expect? I don't have a problem—I just get to know Rosie Palmer and her five sisters." He holds up his hand and waggles his fingers. "There's more to do than run after women all the time."

Lioness shows up; as usual, she's not nearly dirty enough to have been hiking. She dumps her gear and heads for the phone. She talks animatedly for a while, quickly, too fast for anyone on the other end to say a thing. Pause, as she looks out over the ranger station lawn, listening. Then the wind shifts, and her half of the conversation drifts over to us across the summer evening:

"Well, if you're avoiding me because you're busy, that's one thing, but if you're avoiding me because you're just tired of me, that's another. I don't like that. Are you avoiding me? Why do you have that tone in your voice? I thought you loved me. If you loved me you wouldn't talk to me that way. Well, fine."

She hangs up, crying.

"Uh-oh," Pappy says. "Bad news."

The next day it's 11 miles to Atkins, Virginia, where the Trail crosses Interstate 81. It's an easy, breezy day, and there are so many rhododendron thickets that the Trail becomes a lavender tunnel, made of flowers. A few times I stop for some "flame azalea worship," just sitting and staring at this plant, which is a bush or small tree covered with deep orange flowers. These are some of my favorite wild flowers, deep orange, exotic blossoms, always a surprise in the dark woods. I eat some wild strawberries, and crush some jewelweed stems and apply the juice to my poison ivy. It's almost gone; something in the jewelweed dries up the rash.

There's no hostel in Atkins, but there is a truck stop with a restaurant and motel, and a Dairy Queen. The Dairy Queen is filled with people from the highway, people who've been driving all night, who started their day in Massachusetts or Georgia or Missouri and who have the speeded-up, slightly disoriented air of people who have been moving at 75 miles an hour for too long. I stand in line, dirty, my shirt soaked with sweat, smiling as I look at the fat-filled menu. "That woman looks like a hobo," an old man behind me remarks. "I am," I tell him.

Ten hikers have showed up, including Lioness, and we all chip in on one room at the truck-stop motel. This might seem like a lot of people, but we don't notice; it's still more luxurious and less crowded than sleeping in a shelter. We all take showers, leaving a sludge of mud in the tub, do laundry, bring out our sleeping mats and sit on the walkway outside the room. As usual, no one wants to be inside a building unless they absolutely have to.

A trucker, Raiford, is fascinated with us. He sits at the edge of our circle and asks us about the trip. His job seems filled with freedom, but it isn't, he tells us. There are deadlines, people to report to, routes that must be traveled, regulations. And it's lonely. He has a wife, but she's far away. "And we, you know, we go our own way," he says.

"I like a woman with substance," he goes on. "A woman with meat on her bones." He points at me. "You there, you need to eat more. You ain't nothin' but skin an' bones. It's a damn shame. You got to put some meat on you." He looks back at Lioness. "Now, this gal, she's a *woman*."

Lioness glows and giggles.

Popsicle, who's been to town on an unusually unsuccessful quest for dope, returns and hands me a phone card worth $20, which his mother put in his resupply box. Maine Event takes me aside and whispers, "What did you do? You must be the only hiker he's ever paid back. He still owes me $40 from like two weeks ago."

We all go to the restaurant, and Raiford comes with us. He sits across from me, next to Lioness. It's pretty obvious that he has his hand on her leg. Typical hikers, the rest of us alternate between taking in this juicy gossip-in-action and looking greedily at the other diners' food. The people next to us have huge mountains of mashed potatoes and gravy on their plates, and when they see us looking they protectively slide their plates out of grabbing range. I'm on the verge of asking them, "Are you going to eat that?" when our food shows up.

I eat my dinner as well as the bread the people at the next table leave behind in a basket, and most of Raiford's dinner. He's so excited, he can't even eat. He leans over, whispering things to Lioness that make her giggle and toss her head. His room number is one of them. She's aware that the rest of us are watching, though, and her tension is obvious.

"You always eat like that?" Raiford asks me, momentarily distracted.

"On the Trail, yes."

"And you ain't gained a bit?"

"No, I'm losing."

"A damn shame."

He gets up to pay for his dinner, and then Lioness goes to the cashier. When she comes back, she still has her $20 in her hand. Raiford has paid for her meal.

He saunters back to his room, whistling. Back at our room, we take bets on whether Lioness will sleep in our room or his.

She chooses ours. If we hadn't been here, watching and laughing, what she would have done? It's a lonely world, and for some people, compliments and company are hard to come by.

The next day, feeling greasy and slow from the truck-stop gluttony, I slide out of town. It takes all the energy I can muster to drag myself the 2.8 miles to the first shelter out of town, where I lie down for a rest. Someone has hauled one of those hospital egg-crate mattresses up here, and it's the bed of heaven. Popsicle, who's also dragged himself reluctantly out of town, is right behind me. He sits down and begins telling a long and rambling story about getting arrested for being intoxicated in public, which he says he wasn't, and anyway it wasn't his fault, someone else gave him the booze. Just as his mother is bailing him out of jail, I fall asleep.

Hours later I wake to find visitors: Grateful Dread the rainbow-blazer, his dog, Elvis—who was a stray that Dread found on the Trail—and another hiker named The Alchemist. They've packed in 15 beers and an undetermined amount of pot. While they fire up their pipes and pop open more beers, I lie dazed on the mattress, hungover from too much sleep, or not enough. The sun is low, too low for me to reach the next shelter tonight, and the clouds say it's going to rain, which precludes camping out somewhere in between. I'm deeply disappointed in myself for the small number of miles today, but it's too late to reclaim the day now.

Resupply choices back at the truck stop were limited to things like cookies, Slim Jims, and chips, so supper is not inspiring. I make some instant tabbouleh that another hiker left in the motel laundry room. It's too horrible to eat, so horrible that garbage-disposal Elvis won't even lick it. None of us has any water, and this shelter is one of the few without a water source. The topo map shows water far below the shelter, in a deep ravine. One by one we try getting down there, but none of us make it: too steep, too crowded with thorny underbrush, and too many hidden rocks and deadfalls. The clouds continue to threaten rain, but it's an empty threat. I leave my cooking pot outside, just in case the rain comes to fill it up.

The guys make a fire, and drink and smoke. Their stories ramble further, trailing off, all loose ends. It's only about 6 o'clock, but I can't stay awake. Tomorrow I'll really hike.

The next morning there's a quarter-inch of rain in my pot. I drink it and set off hastily down the Trail in search of more. According to the map, the nearest water is three-and-a-half miles away, in a stream in Crawfish Gap. The three guys are yawning, beginning a "wake and bake" session of pot smoking. I doubt they'll hike today.

I get water and walk up and down, up and down, down and up the mountains. Despite the rain, it's hot and humid, and even when it's not raining I sweat so much that on breaks I can wring a cup of sweat out of my tank top. When it rains, I don't get much wetter than I already am.

As I'm coming down through the woods toward Knot Maul Shelter, I have the feeling that someone I know is there. I'm right: It's Thoreau. We sit and eat lunch together while it pours outside. I've come 11 miles today and am not yet tired. The next shelter is Chestnut Knob, nine more miles, up on top of a high, grassy mountain. I feel like I could walk forever, so I get up and keep going.

Thoreau hikes with me for about four miles. Among the yellow irises bordering the Holston River I find wild spearmint, clean and fresh as chewing gum. We both chew some and put more in our water bottles to make tea.

The woods are full of smaller streams, runoff from the rain. They're thick with red mud, and my water filter clogs and breaks when I get water from one of them. I drink unfiltered water, hoping it won't make me sick, and leave Thoreau, who says he's going to stop and cook supper, then head up the last five-mile uphill to the shelter. In the next town I'll have to call the filter manufacturer and get a replacement sent to me.

The rain tapers to a fine drizzle. I'm in the "stretchable last mile," the section right before a shelter that seems to defy the laws of physics by getting longer and longer as you hike, as if you're walking on a vast rubber band that some giant is stretching out: The longer you walk, the farther you seem to be from your goal.

The shelter I'm headed to, like the last one, has no water source, so I stop at a spring on the way and fill up my bottles. The water is iron-red and rusty tasting, but I can't filter it, so I accept my chances and drink it.

Finally, the shelter looms up through the fog. It's an

enclosed stone building, with actual glass windows, completely sealed in from the rain, a rarity on the Trail. It's tight and cozy, heated by the body warmth of the eight hikers holed up there. Shortly after I arrive, Thoreau shows up, making nine in all. Pappy and Little Star are here, as well as a man named Mousetrap, Maine Event, and three others I haven't met until now: 911, Sacajawea, and Julie the Wimp. I wonder about her name; it's one of those unfortunate Trail names people would be better off without.

The rain comes back, pounding on the roof. I put on my dry set of sleeping clothes, eat some noodles and candy bars, then light my candle lantern and study my map. Bland, a small town that hosts a bluegrass concert every Sunday afternoon in the town diner, is 20 miles away. Tomorrow is Sunday. Could I make it there by 1 tomorrow afternoon? Only if I get up at 3 in the morning—not likely, and especially not likely if it's still pouring. Damn, I've been planning to get there on a Sunday for several hundred miles now. I love bluegrass.

Disappointed, I lie in my sleeping bag. I can feel bones deep in my pelvis, bones in my back. The angles of my face feel sharp, like cliffs. When I lie on my side, my hipbones, elbows, shoulders, and ankles grind painfully into the sleeping platform through my thin mat.

The Wimp is making a set of miniature playing cards, drawing the symbols and numbers on paper folded and torn to size. She picks up a tiny book someone has left in the shelter. "Hey, this Gospel of John is card-sized! Anyone for a game of poker?"

No one takes her up on it. Instead, they discuss their least favorite mountains:

"That mountain has more false summits than a chorus line of female impersonators," Mousetrap says of one summit.

"I hate mountains like that," 911 says. "Remember Kelly Knob back in Georgia? I kept thinking I was almost at the top, and then the Trail would turn and there would be more of it."

"Bly Gap was the worst," his partner Sacajawea says. "That Sharp Top mountain. I hated that."

"What about Roan Mountain? It took me five hours to get up that thing."

Thoreau isn't listening to any of this. As the others talk, he paces and sings, stops to spin the lid of his pot like a top, fidgets with some string, whirls and paces some more, back and forth, in a space the length and width of a coffin, ducking and wheeling like a boxer through the wet clothes hanging from the ceiling. He sings loudly, tunelessly, like someone wearing earphones. The wet clothes swing and bounce, flinging drops of water everywhere. The Wimp looks up from her stack of flimsy cards, 911 stops talking, and we all look at Thoreau.

"Feeling restless?" 911 asks.

"I like to sing," Thoreau says. He grins, enjoying our sudden attention. "It makes me feel good."

Maine Event smiles, stroking his black beard. "I like to fight," he says in a mild voice. His voice is naturally hoarse, like that of a gangster or blues singer.

Silence.

"Uh-huh. It makes me feel real good."

"Who do you like to fight?"

"Singers," Maine Event says. "I kill singers."

He's joking, but the singing stops. We take inventory of our collective water supply: It's low. We all take our cooking pots outside and set them in the rain to fill up.

In the night, I'm woken by a sudden, uncanny silence. The rain has stopped. Quickly I run outside to pee. This may be my only chance. The long, wet grass soaks my legs and feet. The mountaintop is eerily still, wrapped in fog so dense I don't dare go more than a few feet from the shelter for fear of getting lost. Our pots are all full of water, except for the ones the wind has blown over. I set them upright again, go inside, and hook the bungee cord that holds the door shut.

Wham! The rain hits the roof like one of those safes people are always dropping in cartoons.

"How many ibuprofens do you take a day?" 911 murmurs

in his sleep as I pass by on the way to my place on the sleeping platform.

The Wimp mumbles back, "I just mix them in with my gorp, like M&Ms."

This has happened before: hikers conversing across the miles of sleep. I've done it too, waking up to realize I'm having a dream-conversation out loud with someone I hardly know, a hiker I've never met before and may never see again. In civilization we might think we have nothing in common, but out here in the dreamlike woods, we're all on the same road, all pilgrims walking, our shared pains and the mountains we've already been over tying us together on a level deeper than waking, even deeper than sleep.

The next day I hurry down the ridge. The hike is harder than it looks on the map because of the rain, all slippery mudslides and sharp rocks. I'm weak from not eating enough recently, and I'm rationing snacks—always a bad situation.

Rhododendrons arch over the footpath, and their lavender petals are strewn all over the Trail, like some kind of pathway to beauty or love. I sit on a rock and look at this, and wonder where it will take me.

The woods are still; all day I haven't seen any sign of the hikers ahead or those behind me. If they left footsteps, they've all been erased by the continuing rain.

I pass through a deep, dark ravine, where unseen water gurgles under rocks. Spooky. I reach the shelter at dusk. It's empty. The area has an uneasy, neglected feeling, and I feel nervous being there alone.

I get water at a nearby stream, then go into the woods and rinse off, pouring the cold water over my head. I put on dry clothes. I sit in the shelter listening to owls, imagining I hear footsteps in the soft rain. Why am I so paranoid? My thoughts are tangled, confused, running in smaller and smaller circles. I look in my food bag: nothing. Hunger sickness is setting in, and it's making me crazy. I decide to ignore my thoughts and not take them seriously until after I've been to town and eaten.

Lightning comes and goes like some flashlight-wielding voyeur. The shelter has more mice than I've seen—or heard—in a long time. When they start running up over my sleeping bag and onto my face, I get out my unused canister of pepper spray and draw a circle on the wood around my sleeping bag. They won't cross this nasty scent barrier, but they still scrabble and leap across the rafters and fight in the corners. When the rain doesn't sound like a person sneaking up on the shelter, it sounds like a million little animals snapping twigs, scuffling up the leaves.

The people in the Laundromat in Pearisburg are very local, very Southern; they look like a New York movie producer's image of Southern rural people: missing teeth, straggly hair, worn clothes. They're also very kind, asking about the trip, giving us advice. I think about taking their picture as examples of local color, but it seems disrespectful, so I don't.

"Y'all ought to be careful," a man in overalls tells us as he folds his clothes. "There's a lot of rednecks around here. Not meaning any disrespect if any of y'all are rednecks, but you know what I mean. It's a good idea to be careful."

His wife, who's my age but looks like she's had a lifetime of hard work, says, "I've met some of them hikers before. They was nice folks. They took my picture. I didn't know why. How come you think someone'd take my picture?"

"Maybe just a reminder of a nice person they met here," I offer.

"That's nice," she says.

A biker named H2O and I sit in the hard plastic chairs, watching our laundry whirl around. The caretaker of the Laundromat is a shy, shirtless man with a large belly, and now that the other folks have gone it's just us and him. He takes out the garbage, checks the change machine, and sweeps the floor. Popsicle's laundry is there too, whirling around in the machine next to ours; he and another hiker named Chocolate Chip hitchhiked here to catch up with us, and they've gone to a nearby bar with Bigfoot.

H2O and I drink sodas and debate whether, if they don't come back in time, we should take their laundry out of the wash when it's done and put it into the dryer, using our own money. If we don't, and if they don't come back in time, the Laundromat may close before they have a chance to dry their clothes, or even retrieve them.

If it were anyone else, we'd do the laundry for them and not care about the money or the favor; that's the hiker way, because we all help each other. But we've both seen how Popsicle is: He's a user. Maybe it's time for him to be responsible for himself instead of drinking beers someone else has bought and assuming other sober buddies will pick up the laundry. There's a fine line between helping someone out and being taken advantage of, and we decide this situation has crossed it. So we decide to leave Popsicle's laundry where it is. If he doesn't come back in time, so be it.

Finally, just in time, Bigfoot comes and moves his laundry, Popsicle's, and Chocolate Chip's, then goes back to the bar.

Our clothes finish drying, and H2O folds his neatly before placing them in his pack. He has separated colors and whites, something I haven't bothered to do on the hike.

"What did you do before the Trail?" I ask, figuring that whatever it was, it was probably precise.

"I'm a scientist. A chemist. I did research for a big corporation, but I hated it. That corporate atmosphere. I'm supposedly on official leave, so I could go back after the Trail if I wanted to, but I don't think I will."

The other guys return, drunk. Bigfoot is a happy, quiet drunk, but Popsicle and Chocolate Chip are the obnoxious kind. By this time other patrons are in the Laundromat, and they turn and glare at us balefully as Popsicle hauls his laundry out of the dryer and stuffs it into his pack, yelling, "This town's full of rednecks. Did you see that old guy with no teeth?

And the women! Jesus! Tits down to here. There are hillbillies everywhere."

The big-bellied laundry attendant's shoulders grow tense as he sweeps. He's a mild-mannered guy, with the sense not to fight a stupid drunk. If anyone's acting like a redneck, it's Popsicle.

"C'mon, let's go," I say, wishing there were some big old hillbilly boys in the back room who would beat the crap out of him, but unfortunately there aren't.

We go down the street, and Popsicle keeps roaring; every other word is "fuck," and locals cross the street and walk on the other side as we approach.

I walk far behind them, and Chocolate Chip drops back and walks next to me. He leans over and smells my shoulder—fresh laundry—and presses his face into my arm. Then he puts his arm around me and asks, "Will you sleep with me?"

"No."

"Oh..." He takes his arm away. "It gets lonely on the Trail, you know, you kind of want...you know, something, you know, and there are so few women up here, and it's like a need, and, uh..."

I say nothing, just keep walking. I'm starving. I just want to get to Pizza Hut, eat, and get away from all of them.

At Pizza Hut, Chocolate Chip tries to shove the condiment basket, parmesan cheese holder, cutlery, and sugar into his shirt, looking over at me and grinning as if this is a feat. I glare at him and he puts it all down, confused.

"Hey, babe, whatcha doing after work?" Popsicle asks the waitress.

She taps her pen against her pad, says, "I'll just give y'all a few more minutes to look over the menu," and departs.

I sit, elbows on the table, thinking of a thousand places I'd rather be. Like in the woods, hiking and camping by myself.

"Hey, Grace!" Chocolate Chip yells. "C'mon, Grace, smile! Enjoy yourself! C'mon! C'mon! Let's see that smile! I wanna see that smile!"

"Look," I say, "leave me alone. Let me eat my dinner in peace. Don't tell me what kind of look to have on my face, don't tell me what to feel, don't tell me what you want. I don't care what you want. I'm fine. Just leave me alone."

This startles Popsicle awake from a long ramble about how all the gear manufacturers will pay him to walk the Trail again, with their free gear. "What? Huh? Who did what? What's going on, Grace?"

"He's hassling me, and I told him to lay off."

"Hey, man, don't hassle her!" Popsicle says. He shoves Chocolate Chip in the shoulder. "Leave her alone! Don't hassle her, man!"

Everyone argues about what they want on their pizza. I'm getting an individual one, for this very reason, and finally everyone else does the same. Chocolate Chip gets up, head hanging, and shuffles out of the restaurant.

"What? What's up with him? Why'd he leave?" the guys ask.

I eat my salad and marvel at how this kind of thing is lost on men. A table of women would have known he was going to leave before he even thought of doing it, and no one would have wondered why after he was gone.

The waitress reappears, and Popsicle asks, "Hey, what size bra do you wear? It's a joke, baby, just a joke! Can't you take a joke?"

I apologize to her for my obnoxious fellow hikers, especially him.

"Don't apologize for me," he says.

"Someone has to," I say. I decide it's time to hike a day ahead of or behind him and Chocolate Chip, since they're both so annoying and I keep running into them.

On the way back to the hostel, which is run by the Holy Family Catholic Church and has a strict no-alcohol policy, we pass a Texaco station that sells beer. Popsicle veers toward it, feet slowing as he looks in the window and sees the shining cans.

"Hey, H2O, you got any money?"

H2O, honest to the core, says he does.

"How 'bout getting some beer? I'll pay you back at the next town. My mom's sending me 10 bucks."

"No."

"No? C'mon, I'll pay you back."

H2O keeps walking. "The hostel says no drinking on the property. We're guests there, and I'm not drinking on the property."

"We won't be on the property. We'll go off it and drink."

"No, because we'll still be drunk when we go back there, and that's what they mean."

"No, it says 'on the property.' And we won't be on the property. And rules are made to be broken. Are you Catholic?"

"No."

"Then why do you care? It's not your religion—you don't have to follow their rules. You don't even have to drink. Just lend me the money, and I'll take the consequences."

"No. I'm not going to contribute to it."

I admire H2O. He's so dry, so calm, so reasonable that it's impossible for Popsicle to pick a fight with him. If he were to argue back, forget it. But a flat no, said without emotion, is hard to argue with.

As we walk up the hill, Popsicle turns, looking back at the station. "I can pay you right away. I can give you a 12-roll of film. It's not even opened. How about that?"

"No."

"What if I paid you, cash, at the next town? You could go to the post office with me and get the money right away."

"No."

"There's too many damn rules in the world. Don't you want to live a little?'

"No."

"What, are you some kind of anti-alcohol puritan or something?"

"Popsicle, you've seen me drink beer. It's a question of hospitality. We're their guests, and they don't want us to drink, so I'm not going to drink."

"You don't have to! No problem! You know, I really respect you, man. You're a real man. If you could just lend me the money, I'll just get one. I won't even be drunk. Just one."

"No."

The days after Pearisburg are hot and humid, long June days of sweat and dehydration mixed with images of nature: wild strawberries, butterflies, a scarlet tanager in a tree—so red it looks like a mistake—a lot of snakes, and a brightly patterned turtle digging a hole at the edge of the Trail, presumably to lay eggs and make more turtles.

Once again I'm low on food, and suffering from lack of sleep from bugs biting me all night. I feel sluggish, stale, almost but not quite depressed. *Hey*, I say in my mind to whatever synchronistic force it is that seems to oversee the Trail, *I could really use some Trail magic today. Just some encouragement. I'm not picky. Anything. Just something nice to help me get through the day. Please.*

I hike up a steep hill, then along a ridgeline, and H2O and Bigfoot catch up to me. We hike along the ridgeline some more in the sweltering heat, then down to Laurel Fork Shelter, where we stop for lunch. Popsicle and Chocolate Chip are long gone, delayed by a drinking binge back in town; they're somewhere behind us, and we may never see them again.

"I need to go to town," Bigfoot says. "I have to call my brother. He's gonna meet me and hike with me and H2O for a while. I have to tell him where I am."

We've heard there's a store 1.6 miles from the next road crossing. Sounds good to me. He can call, and I can get food.

We hike through fields of black-and-gold butterflies to the road, where a handmade sign says the store is closed. H2O goes ahead on the Trail, and Bigfoot and I stay on the road, hitching, hoping to get a ride to another store.

No cars come, but a storm does. We hunker down, watching the approaching lightning, bending as the wall of rain hits us. After the heat it feels good, although the lightning is scary.

A farmer comes along in a pickup truck. He tells us he had been going to cut hay, but the rain stopped that. His name is Ralph, he lives just over yonder, and if we want to come to his house to get out of the rain, why, he'd be glad to have us.

He gives us dry towels, fried chicken, and Dr. Pepper, and tells us how his family has owned this land for generations, including the land around Laurel Fork Shelter. Then the Trail people came along and the government took the land away to make the Trail. He's mad at the Trail organizers, but remarkably has nothing against the hikers; he helps all the hikers he runs into.

His nephew is visiting for the day, and runs in and out of the house, giving us weather reports: "That storm is broke in two, but it looks like another's coming right behind it!"

The rain finally stops, and Ralph wraps up the rest of the chicken for us. We go back out and stand on the road, which is steaming, and eat the chicken while we wait for a ride.

A student from a nearby technical college picks us up. He drives us to the next town, to the store, then suggests that we all go to an all-you-can-eat restaurant in Blacksburg, where we stuff ourselves. Then he gives us a ride back to the Trail and stands talking with us.

"I want to live a dream," he says. "You guys inspire me. I've been sober for a week, longer than I've ever gone before. I want to make it, I want to be clean. If you guys can keep going, so can I."

We congratulate him and encourage him to keep with it, to get through the tough time; it's worth it. I have friends who used to be alcoholics or drug addicts, and quit. I admire them, because it's not an easy thing to do.

We head into the woods. We're just going a short distance away from the road, then camping. We meet a Trail maintainer, a volunteer who comes up here to cut the brush that threatens to overgrow the Trail.

"There's a lot of poison ivy up there," he warns. "Oh, and by the way, someone left a six-pack of Coke in the creek, and it's all yours."

The grass is wet, so I string up my hammock and tie the tarp over it like a roof, and swing peacefully in the sweet evening air, listening to Sinking Creek. *Thanks,* I say to the Trail. I asked for one little bit of Trail magic and met three kind strangers in one day. On the Trail these things don't seem random; it feels as if there's a larger pattern to the trip, something too big for me to understand, as if I'm walking at the edge of a mystery, part of some large, intricate spiritual ecosystem.

I lie in the hammock and watch fireflies light up the nearby trees. The creek sings. Something is moving me forward, some current; I'm like a stick in the creek, and motion is with me.

I pass a sign tacked to a tree: a WANTED poster offering $25,000 for information leading to the arrest of the murderer who killed Julianne and Lollie in the Shenandoahs. Instead of a picture of the murderer, who is unknown, there are photos of the two women, who look happy together. I know some of what they've been through to find that happiness. I admire them, and grieve for them, because it was so short.

Last night, in the logbook at Niday Shelter, I read a warning about a man who assaulted a woman hiker near McAfee Knob, a mountain I'll hike over soon. The news about the rapist, who travels with a big vicious dog, and the WANTED posters, make my pack seem a lot heavier today.

I'm low on water, and after nine miles of hot, sweaty hiking, when I go down a long descent and end at a river called Trout Creek, I stand there looking at it, debating whether to drink from it. I still don't have a working filter and have been drinking water as it comes, from springs. Rivers are something else; they have a lot more runoff from possibly disgusting sources. But I'm dehydrated and it's hot, and there's really no choice.

As I'm going down the bank, I accidentally drop my water bottle into the river. It bobs away like a toy. *Damn,* I think, *I need that!*

I sprint down the bank, pass the bottle, and plunge into the rapids, grabbing it just before it sweeps past me. Popsicle shows up on the bank. He's caught up with me.

"Whatcha doin'?"

"Rescuing my water bottle."

I climb out of the river. He squats and filters water, lets me use his filter, then scouts along a nearby road for cigarette butts, examining the ground minutely, like Sherlock Holmes scanning for clues. Pickings are slim. "You see these piles of butts all over, where people dump out their ashtrays," he says irritably. "Why the hell couldn't someone dump some here?"

We hike up the next mountain.

Two separate thunderstorms, which I've been watching all morning, converge overhead, and once again the Trail is made up mostly of wet, slanted rocks. If curses were fuel, I'd be a rocket. We hike over a mountain called Dragon's Tooth, the rain stops, and I take a break. A black swallowtail butterfly lands on my hand, and there's a rainbow below me, down in the valley.

The rain returns, and climbing down Dragon's Tooth is difficult; it's more like rock-climbing than hiking. I've had a vision defect since birth that makes rock-climbing very difficult: no depth perception. On the one hand, this is a plus: I can stand on the edge of a cliff, look over, and feel no worry, because it doesn't look like a drop-off to me; on the other hand, it makes climbing down cliffs and rock piles difficult. I can't tell how far away a rock or foothold is from my foot; I have to guess and then jump, and hope the guess was right. I sweat over every footing and lever myself down, trembling, wishing I had a Dr. Pepper and something hot and greasy to eat. My blood sugar is low and getting lower, and I'm feeling shaky and anxious.

Finally, I'm down, and the Trail is more like a trail. I come to an intersection, AT versus blue-blazed trail, and check the map. The AT leads ahead over more steep cliffs; the blue-blaze leads to a parking lot and road, and the road leads to a store, where there's food.

I'm off like a shot, down the blue-blazed trail. Suddenly I have energy. I feel like I'm skipping school, Dr. Pepper and food getting closer and closer with every step.

The Catawba general store and feed shed is a busy place, with two retired men who are hiking a short section, a young hiker named Scooby Doo, and three bicyclists who are doing the Transcontinental Bike Trail.

We all sit in front of the store looking out over the green countryside, eating and watching pickup trucks go by, our wet socks and clothes flapping on the fence. The bike guys tell us they do a maximum of 80 miles a day, but usually do about 60, compared to hikers' 20 and 15. Their trail is 4,000 miles and takes three months, and they don't have to be nearly as self-sufficient or isolated as we are, because they're much more mobile.

It's a pleasure talking to them. They're like colleagues, and even though we're traveling differently we feel a sense of camaraderie as fellow pilgrims.

When the store closes for the night, the owners open the feed shed to us. I set up my sleeping bag and sit on it, peaceful. There's a radio nailed to one of the beams, tuned to a country music station. All around are piled sacks of Reliance 12% Horse Feed, Reliance 10 Horse Feed, Hi-Tech X-L-A, Pullet Start & Grow, Super Lay Crumbles, whole corn, salt blocks, oyster shell, and Safe-Guard cattle dewormer.

Lately I've had the most fun when I've been doing things that are "against the rules"—blue-blazing, hitchhiking to all-you-can-eat restaurants, skipping off the Trail to this store and feed shed. All my life I've hated pointless rules and fences and boxes, and I've made the Trail into one, trying to be a purist, trying to stay on the white-blazes, worrying when I don't.

I'm still walking from Georgia to Maine along the Trail, but the Trail to me is now a corridor, not just the footpath in sight of the white blazes. The Trail is also the land and trails around it, the towns, the people, the local drivers and farmers and storekeepers; it's everyone you meet, especially those who help you along. It's an experience, a state of mind more than a single white-blazed line.

John Denver comes on the radio, singing, "Hey, it's good to be back home again," and I couldn't agree more. Right now my home is this shed, and I'm at peace. I love the way I've learned to be so happy with so little. I don't know anyone else who's had the privilege of sleeping in a feed shed in a tiny Virginia town.

Scooby Doo and I talk about the murders and agree to hike together tomorrow; he's as nervous as I am.

"Also," he says, "did you hear about that scary dude who's wanted for sexual assault near McAfee Knob? It freaks me out. That and those two girls getting killed. Even though I'm a guy, I'd rather not walk alone."

Scooby Doo is a born-again Christian, and as we walk the next day we talk about religion. As we trudge uphill, clouds gather around the mountain. This doesn't seem like a coincidence; storms seldom hit while you're safe in a valley. Like cats, they wait patiently until you're at the top of a mountain and then attack.

Somewhere along the Trail, Scooby Doo has met a beautiful girl and her family, who are also Christian. He's fallen in love with her, she has fallen in love with him, her family loves him, and he's going to stay with them when he finishes the Trail. He wants to marry the girl. He's so in love with her that I wonder if he'll be able to finish his hike. He shows me pictures of her: blond, sweet, her family smiling benevolently over her.

We talk about his religion. He became a Christian in high school, and it changed his life. He's happy now. He's found a community and a sense of spiritual wholeness.

"I have no fear of death," he says as we ease out onto a long cliff. It's only a few feet wide. On one side is the top of the mountain; on the other, a huge drop-off into a beautiful valley. (If we fall, at least we'll be treated to some gorgeous views along the way.) We'll have to walk along this precarious edge for a half-mile before the Trail descends on the other side of the mountain.

"If I die today, I know I'll go home to heaven, and I'm right with God," Scooby Doo says.

Slam! Lightning whips out of the clouds and strikes the mountaintop. Scooby Doo turns, gives me a quick panicked look, and starts running. I'm right on his heels. So much for being at peace with death. Who needs death? Being alive is a lot more fun, and besides, I'm comfortable that way. Evidently Scooby Doo is too.

We run hunched over, like commandos evading enemy fire, while lightning rages around us. *Kaboom!* We can smell the electricity in the air. The advancing line of clouds is a solid black wall, swirling with voltage. Some nerdy little inner voice reminds me that lightning bolts are 54,000 degrees, six times hotter than the surface of the sun.

Rain pours down, soaking us instantly. The cliff is only a few feet wide, not exactly the kind of place where you'd want to run, in the rain, in a lightning storm, with a big pack on your back. Visions of all the ways we could slip and fall off the mountain play out in my mind: We could fall upside down, sideways, or backward. Backward is the most likely; I would land on my pack, a few hundred feet down.

The hairs on my arms stand up, charged with electricity. We keep running. The lightning blows the top off a tree a hundred feet behind us. The shock wave of the thunder vibrates in my chest.

We reach the end of the cliff, crash through the bushes, and run desperately down the switchbacks. The rain floods down, streaming over rocks, over logs, across the Trail.

I race around a turn. In the middle of the Trail is a bobcat, hunched up tight, as frightened by the storm as we are. In the storm, it must not have heard or smelled us coming. It turns its head and sees us, and I get a good view of its beautiful spotted fur as it leaps gracefully up the mountain and disappears.

"Yeeeeeeeehaw!" I scream, dancing in the mud. "We saw a bobcat! There are people who spend their whole life being rangers or whatever and never see one! What a gift! Yahoooooooo!"

I wake up in the middle of the night, disoriented. Where am I?

On Springer Mountain, Georgia, the southern terminus of the Trail

first water I drank on the Trail came from this waterfall on Long Creek in Georgia.

Hikers treat blisters and cook supper at Low Gap shelter in Georgia.

Filtering water and soaking sore feet in a North Carolina creek

A rare afternoon break in Virginia

Mail call in Hot Springs, North Carolina

Eating a snack on McAfee knob in Virginia

When it was clear, I occasionally slept out in the open.

rossing the Potomac at the 1,000-mile mark, between West Virginia and Maryland

t Pine Grove Furnace State Park in Pennsylvania. The wooden spoon says "Member f Half-Gallon Club." I've just eaten a half-gallon of ice cream, and I'm still hungry.

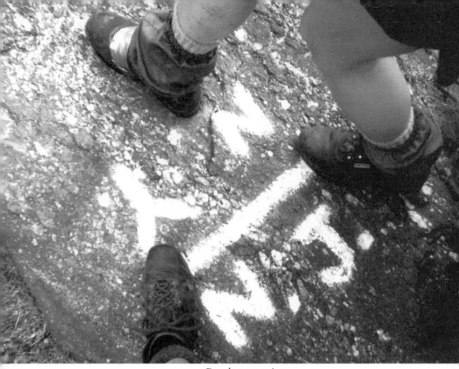

Border crossing

Getting ready for a night's sleep on the tables in a greenhouse in Great Barrington, Massachusetts

Nomad gets ready to carry a cheesecake (perched on top of her backpack!) up the mountain in New Hampshire.

The Trail in Maine goes where it looks like it goes—right over the edge.

In Maine. The sign says it all.

What's that light overhead? A star? A firefly? Which shelter am I in? I don't remember walking here, don't remember getting water or setting up my sleeping bag, don't remember making a fire or cooking. And I feel strangely levitated, as if I'm floating.

Overhead, little green lights glow, near the shadows of wooden beams. What are those lights? Foxfire? I pat the ground around me; it's so soft it's frightening.

Slowly I realize: I'm in a building. In a motel. The lights up above are the smoke detector and the glow-in-the-dark light switch, and the ground is soft because it's a bed. I did walk here, but since I didn't end the day by fetching water and making a fire, this place feels unconnected, like a dream.

I go back to sleep, but a short time later a noise wakes me. A scrabbling, a thumping. Some animal is in my food! I feel around for my flashlight and finally grab a heavy object near my head and hurl it at my food bag. The noise continues, and I realize again: I'm inside. There can't be animals in here.

I turn on the light and sit up. The noise is someone in the room next door, using the bathroom. The thing I threw was the TV remote control.

Just to be sure there's no mouse or raccoon, I go over and slap my food bag and shake my pack.

"I'm in a motel," I say out loud. I sit on the bed and look around. I'm in the Howard Johnson's in Troutville, Virgina, and I'm sick. I have a cold or the flu and need rest.

The next morning I stay in bed until noon, then go out and walk along the strip of road where Interstate 81 and Virginia highway 816 intersect. It's a fast place, not built for human walkers. Cars roar past. There's no sidewalk, no trees, just a mushroomlike sprouting of fast-food places and stores full of things I don't need. I go to the post office and pick up my mail, then sit in a steakhouse reading it and eating plate after plate of food from the buffet.

It's 3 in the afternoon; no one else is here. The waitress refills my iced tea. I drink it and shiver; I'm not used to air conditioning or iced drinks. Is it possible to get hypothermia in a restaurant?

The waitress looks at my goose bumps and the mail spread out on the table, addressed to me in care of General Delivery. "Are you one of those hikers?"

"Yes, ma'am." I've walked through the South long enough to learn its polite ways.

"You aren't alone, are you?"

"Oh, no, ma'am," I lie. "All my friends are still sleeping."

"Well, just be careful. I heard two girls got themselves killed in Shenandoah park."

She brings me more bread, with motherly concern. I wonder why everyone says the women "got themselves killed." As if they willed it, did it to themselves, stepped into a plot, a web of circumstance, as if they were knowing victims.

Reading the mail, seeing the familiar handwriting of friends, makes me feel lonely. Although this trip has a flow of its own, a momentum I can feel, it's not really connected to the flow of other hikers' lives. On the way down the mountain to this road crossing, I was attacked by a pack of dogs and almost hit by lightning, which arced along a power line crossing the ridge. Dealing with these things alone is difficult; there's no one else to rely on, no one to laugh about it with later. It's tiring me out, emotionally and physically. And the constant warnings not to hike alone, reminders of the murdered women and rapists lurking on McAfee Knob, are wearing me down.

Some women, like Angie and Moira, have left the Trail because of the murders. I can't leave, even though I'm exhausted and depressed. I need this hike, as if it's food or air.

I hike down through the mountains, 12 miles by noon, in cool morning weather, and stop at Mott's Creek Shelter for a dip in the "natural Jacuzzi," where a stream pours through close-set stone walls. Another hiker has left a warning in the log. He saw a baby copperhead snake sunning itself on the warm stones, so I move cautiously.

The Trail is getting to me. In the past few days, since Troutville, I haven't been sleeping enough—too many bugs biting me at night, too many people who want to talk all night in the shelters. I'm getting cranky. Maybe it's the lack of sleep, but basically, I decide, I'm just bored with my own head.

I wash my clothes in the cold water and lay them out on the rocks to dry. There's no sign of the snake. Despite my intense boredom with myself, I feel a hopeful glow, as if something good is going to happen today.

Two other hikers, Spider Man and Georgia Dan, show up. Spider Man is burly, blond, and loud, an entomology student, only a dissertation away from getting his Ph.D. "I guess I'll have to finish it when I get back," he says. "But do I want to? Do I really want to look at bugs and spiders all my life? Yeah, it's a good excuse to get out in the woods. But do I want to teach? No. And with a Ph.D. you can't do much else."

Georgia Dan is thin and dark, and like me has had a series of low-paying jobs. He's studying English and wants to be a writer. "Hey," he says, "you wanna go to Glasgow with us? Some section hikers said they'd give us a ride."

Glasgow is a small town nearby. I hadn't planned to go, but it gives me a warm feeling: I'm included, someone wants to hang out with me. What a relief from my own stale and irritable mind.

The section hikers are a retired woman who thruhiked in 1984, a Quaker friend of hers, and two men. They take us to a diner, where we fill up on sweet iced tea and fried shrimp, and talk. The Quaker woman has one of those lit-up faces that lets you know she's really alive and awake. Just being around her makes me feel better; somehow she gives me faith that there are wider things out there, without saying so at all.

She gives me a Susan B. Anthony dollar. "Carry this and you'll always have another woman's company on your hike," she says. It's a nice change from people assuming I'd want to hike with a man. I put it in my pack, next to a big crystal that my friend Heather's friend Bea gave me back in Georgia, and my pebble from Springer Mountain.

When we're done resupplying and doing laundry, they shuttle us back to the Trail. "Happy trails," they say.

"I'll hold you in the light," the Quaker woman says, a beautiful way of saying goodbye. The silver dollar, in its pocket with the two stones, gives a little jingle as I step up on a rock, wave goodbye, and head into the woods.

That night I lie in the shelter, the remains of a fire scattering light around me, listening to the nearby creek, and feel happier than I've been in a while. A stranger's goodwill is helping me through; maybe someday her wish for me will come true.

The next day is filled with good tastes: blackberries, the last late strawberries from up on bald Cold Mountain, a wintergreen-tasting twig from a black birch. And beautiful things: the black-and-orange speckled inside of a nodding Canada lily, the sunlight-and-shade pattern of fritillary butterflies, columbines, purple phlox, yellow butter-and-eggs, golden ragwort, and yarrow. Big views of fields, forests, and mountains. The weather is cool, a joy to hike in.

I walk along the bald, on top of the world, and I couldn't be happier. I'm so lucky to be here. I don't know or care what time it is or what day it is. It's endless summer, the time zone I lived in during vacations from school as a child, when I walked all day, miles all over town, following the railroad tracks, picking berries, looking at flowers, listening to the hum of cicadas.

At The Priest Shelter, someone has left a doctor's bag with rubber gloves, ibuprofen, Band-Aids, thermometers, and other medical gear. We open the bag and play with its contents, like Stone Age people coming in contact with modern devices. We try on the stethoscope, listen to each other's hearts, look at the little numbers on the thermometer. We blow up the rubber gloves like balloons and laugh at the splayed fingers. Spider Man leans over and holds his balloon under his stomach, so the fingers hang down, like an udder.

"Maaaaaaaa!" he bleats. "I'm a goat. Milk me! Maaaaaa!!!"

We decide that we'll each tie a balloon to our pack, and whoever keeps the balloon "alive" the longest will be the "winner."

"What do we win?" I ask.

"We'll think of something," Spider Man says.

I take some of the ibuprofen, grateful for it. My feet are horribly swollen and painful. Later, as I'm dragging up a hill in the semigloom of twilight, Spider Man catches up with me. Our casual attitude about getting to camp late, so easy earlier in the day, is weighing on us now; we just wish we were there. We're both starving, so we wolf down some gorp.

"Do you have any extra snacks?" he asks.

"No, I'm running low."

"Me too. Damn, if I had a Little Debbie snack cake right now, I'd eat that bitch," he says. "Maaaaaaa!!!" We both burst out laughing. He goes ahead up the hill, and when I get up there, there's no sign of him on the Trail, but there is a side trail that goes downhill and is marked with a very different system of blazes. Assuming he has read them and taken the correct trail, I go on.

The shelter is difficult to find. It's supposed to be on the bank of a creek, but I cross the creek three times before finding it. Spider Man isn't there, although Georgia Dan and a hiker named Listener are.

"Have you seen Spider Man?" Listener asks.

"Yeah, a mile or so back," I say. "I think he went off on a side trail."

I fire up my stove. "Why don't you burn some leaves?" Listener suggests. "The smoke might keep these damn bugs away."

I do, and it works. We sit in our pall of smoke, blissfully secure. We decide that if Spider Man doesn't show up soon, one or all of us will go looking for him.

I ask Listener how he got his Trail name. He tells us he's a therapist who works in halfway houses for developmentally delayed and autistic people.

"What are they like?" Georgia Dan asks.

"Well, we had this one guy we called the Glad Man. He had this sexual fetish for garbage bags. He would blow them up, you know, like a big squashy balloon, then sort of roll around on them and get off on it. He got admitted because he was living with his parents and would go over to the neighbors' and pull their full garbage bags out of the trash, then roll around on the lawn with them. His parents couldn't deal with it, so they had him admitted to the halfway house."

"What did you guys do about it?"

"We just told him he had to do it in his room, that was what a private room was for."

After we've been talking for an hour Spider Man appears, cursing. Listener, who has recently gotten a mail drop, has saved him a bottle of Black Hook Ale, which cheers him up.

"Hey," I say, as we're all going to sleep, "my balloon is still alive and yours are all dead. What do I win?"

"A date with me," Spider Man says.

"No, thanks," I tell him. "Hey, what would you have done if Georgia Dan had won?"

According to the map, the side trail that swallowed up so much of Spider Man's time crosses several waterfalls and reconnects to the AT after a few miles. I backtrack to it and use it: the Mau-Har Trail. It's a lot of streamside walking, cascades of water, cool ravines, lots of chilled rocks—a welcome change from the heat on the ridges. I reach the next shelter for lunch long before the others, and even find an arrowhead as a reward for my unfaithfulness to the AT. I put it in the pouch with the crystal, the Springer pebble, and the Susan B. Anthony dollar, then fire up my stove to make lunch and fill the shelter with smoke to keep out the flies. I read the logbook; other hikers have also discovered the joys of blue-blazing on the Mau-Har Trail.

When Spider Man, Georgia Dan, and Listener arrive, I'm done with my lunchtime chores, taking a nap in my cloud of smoke. Spider Man eyes me suspiciously. "Did you hike here on the AT?"

"Nope. I blue-blazed."

"How could you do that? I had respect for you. I thought you were cool. Now you turn out to be a blue-blazer. What a stupid, wimpy thing to do."

"Enjoy your hike! I'm having a great one," I say. "I don't feel compelled to follow anyone's rules or earn your respect. A hiker I met down there in the ravine told me that trail used to be the AT, anyway. What's the difference if I'm hiking the AT from 1956 or the AT from 1996? It's a purely manmade distinction. I wanted to see waterfalls, so I hiked the Mau-Har Trail. If you want to stay on the AT, stay on the AT. I'm not going to ream you out about it, so don't ream me out about my hike."

I think what's really bothering him is my comment last night, when he said my prize for keeping my balloon alive was a date with him and I scoffed. He's said things like this before: Once he asked me if I had ever considered getting involved with anyone on the hike, and I said no, I didn't think the Trail was the place to meet anyone to have a serious relationship with; after all, we're all out here because we're confused, because we're in a time of deep change, so it's not likely that you'll meet anyone who's very stable. And then he said, "Well, how would you feel about a quick harmless fling?" and I said no to that too. There's only so much a guy can take before his pride is wounded, and apparently he's reached that point.

I roll over on my Ridgerest to complete my after-lunch snooze. I have no intention or desire to get involved with any guy, casual or not, serious or not, for any reason except friendship. Scraps of fights with Wade, old road trips we took, sudden mental snapshots of the disarray in his apartment still haunt me sometimes while I hike. I suppose all this stuff will continue to run through my mind and dreams until I've digested it and reached some kind of peace with it, and the only way to do that is to keep walking and not muddy the waters by adding another relationship on top of it. And besides, even if I didn't have this to deal with, I'm simply not interested in anyone out here. Or for that matter, any guy, period.

Another hiker shows up, this time from the Mau-Har Trail. It's Maine Event.

"Maine Event, you blue-blazing fool! Welcome to blue-blazer's heaven," I say.

"What, did you do this too?"

"You bet."

We slap palms and make triumphant motions with our fists. Spider Man isn't amused. Finally, I pack up and wander on, across the Blue Ridge Parkway, through fields, woods, over several rockslides, to a campsite on a cliff. Eventually all the guys show up, and we all camp there for the night.

From the cliff we can see a vast valley, and as the sun goes down, tiny lights of cars drive slowly and steadily, turning at precise right angles where the roads bend, slowing and stopping, pulling into farms and houses. It's like watching ants: mysterious. What are they doing? Where are they going? Those people have kitchens, showers, clean beds, and food. They also have work and routine. The valley, unlike this ridge, is filled with haze, so they can't even see the sky we see, filled with stars, and they probably don't know about the hikers, high on the ridge, watching.

Down below it's darker now, and people are getting ready for the Fourth of July, which is only a few days away: setting off small fireworks—lights winking on like fireflies, the tiny *pop!* of the explosions coming to us so much more slowly than the light.

I set up my sleeping bag in the open on the cliff, where the breeze will have a chance to blow the bugs away. If I were home right now—assuming I had a home—what would I be doing? I'd take a really long bath, lie down in a cool, breezy room, and talk with a friend or read. Maybe just sit outside watching the dark come down—just what I'm doing now.

When I get back to civilization, I want to enjoy its benefits without getting trapped and stagnated by it, without getting caught up in jobs and materialism and all the other isms. I don't ever want to be in a room where there's not an open door, or a window, to let the night breeze in.

In Waynesboro, Virginia, I run into a hiker named Little Cricket, who shaved her head earlier in the summer but left her bangs alone. This gave her a weird, patchy look, but now her bangs are missing; her head is completely bald.

"Hey, Cricket! Who cut your hair?"

"This guy down the street. It only cost a couple of bucks."

I don't want my hair shaved, but it's too long, heavy, and hot, and I want to cut at least some of it off.

The barbershop is down a steep flight of stairs, in a basement under a store, and has calendars from the 1950s on the wall, old-timey swivel chairs, and smells of grandfatherly hair pomade, leather, and cigarette smoke. A very large man is sitting in the chair chatting with the barber, and when I come in he gives me a dubious eye and leaves quickly, as if to clear the decks before things get dangerous.

The barber stands behind me and pats my head. "You want me to cut your hair?"

"Yeah, another hiker was in here and she recommended you."

"That little gal with the blond hair?"

"Yes, sir."

"Oh, I remember her. Well, I'll tell you, I ain't never scalped a woman before, and I'm not sure I like it. If my wife was here, she'd preach a sermon to that girl for having it done and to me for doing it. And another one to the girl for being in a man's barbershop."

I sit up. I had no idea there was a gender segregation rule in barbershops. "Oh, if you don't want me in here, I'll leave."

"No, that's OK. I just don't tell the wife. She don't approve. I get about one woman a week in here, and I just don't say nothing."

He lifts up my heavy braid. "You want me to cut this?" He fumbles with it, as if he doesn't know how to unbraid it, and picks up a heavy pair of shears. "You want me to just cut it off whole?"

"Uh, no. I thought you could just trim the bottom, you know, make it shorter all around."

He lifts the braid again, as if to test its weight. "I could just cut it off in one piece?"

"No." I untie it and loosen the hair. "Just cut around the bottom, a few inches."

He seems mighty peculiar, but I'm in too deep to walk out; he's already cut part of it. He seems disappointed, looking down at the two-inch-long snips falling to the floor.

"I saved that little gal's hunk of hair," he says, snipping. "You want to see it?" He opens a drawer. It's filled with hanks of hair; on top is Little Cricket's slender, bright-gold lock of shorn bangs, tied neatly together.

"I save other people's hair too. I had a colored feller come in with those long knotted locks of hair—what do they call 'em, dreadful locks? Well, he got a job over to the factory and they wanted him clean-cut, so he come in here and I did the job, and saved his hair. Then a few days later I had a feller who was one of them historical-reenactment buffs, and he wanted an Indian scalp as part of his costume, so I gave him that colored feller's hair. Looked just dandy, hanging from his belt. Very realistic."

He snips and clucks his tongue. "One day this long-haired Harley-riding biker feller come in and got all his long hair cut off. I saved it, and sure enough, the next day the undertaker come in for a shave. He said he had an awful job to do—some woman had shot herself in the head, and she was a right mess. He had to make her look nice for the funeral. Well, it turns out she had the same color hair as this biker, so I gave the biker's hair to the undertaker, and he dressed her up with it—covered the wound, you know—and she looked just wonderful at the funeral."

He fusses with the scissors. "You know," he says thoughtfully, "that hair was buried with her."

Now I know why he wanted to cut off my entire braid. I suspect he comes in here at night when his wife is sleeping, pets his chunks of hair, and plots what to do with them. I have no doubt that if I had let him cut off my braid, in a few weeks it would have had a more colorful life than I do—say, adorning a corpse, or sold to a backwoods voodoo operator, or maybe the local taxidermist would use it to fill in the rough spots on a stuffed raccoon.

The entire haircut, including the stories and the strange atmosphere, costs $2. He won't take a tip. I suspect he never takes tips from women; evidently he prefers to take their hair.

The next day I hitch back to the Trail. I'm heading for Shenandoah National Park, where Julianne and Lollie were killed, and it makes me nervous. I run into Sailor Dan, whom I last saw back in Tennessee, and we hike together to Calf Mountain Shelter.

He's a big guy; his pack is huge, but on him it looks like a daypack. He went to Yale on a football scholarship, and he could probably carry his pack, another hiker, and the other hiker's pack and never break a sweat. He's a good bodyguard for this foray into what hikers think of as the murder zone. After we trade information about our pasts, we run out of things to say, and walk in peaceful silence.

Somewhere, I've lost my pen—my only pen. I think about this, and about the fact that it may be several days before I can buy another one. Without a pen I won't be able to write in my journal. I could probably use another hiker's, but sometimes there are no other hikers, or they don't have anything to write with. I need a pen.

I come around a bend in the path, and there, lying in the dirt, is a brand-new, never-used pen with the cap still on. "Thanks!" I say out loud, and put it in my pocket. It's just another one of those mysterious Trail coincidences. You need something and it appears.

Maine Event is at the shelter when we arrive. We're all quiet, subdued by the thought that we're in Shenandoah. We go to sleep early, as the first drops of rain come down.

In the log at Pinefield Shelter, a hiker named Littlebear has written:

> Ever drive along in your car, singing at the top of your lungs to your favorite song, and then you come to a tunnel and as you are going through the tunnel, you continue to sing but the signal is getting weaker and weaker. Then at one point, the signal is almost indistinguishable and you lose the beat and stop singing. Just as you begin to reach for the seek button to find something else, the signal starts to come back and by the time you exit the tunnel you're back in concert singing at the top of your lungs again, having a ball.
>
> It seems lately I've been in the tunnel. Got all these schedules to meet and miles to make, but I can't find the beat. I'm listening close to make out the song so I can be singing at the top of my lungs again.
>
> What the hell, I can always pop a tape in!!
>
> Doctor doctor
> Give me the news
> I've got a bad case of
> Virginia blues!

Littlebear's journal entry sums things up for me—I feel the pressure of making the schedule to get to Katahdin, but if I adhere to it, I'll miss the point of being out here. I want to do the whole walk, the whole Trail, but I need to either get back into the rhythm I originally planned or else find new reasons for walking or new ways of being out here.

I haven't been happy with myself lately. As a friend wrote in a letter, "Out there, there's nothing separating you from yourself," and she's right. I'm no longer enjoying my own company. I'm deeply bored with my own head and irritated with all my small pettinesses and habits and annoying traits, my smallness of mind and spirit, and bad temper.

I've walked alone for three months, half the trip—long enough to run through all my mental material. I'm done with a lot of it, and need a new point of view. I'm ready to find a Trail buddy who shares my view of this trip as a pilgrimage. A friend, a good traveler, someone with humor and an open mind. And I want her to be female.

Is that a prayer? I write in my journal. *Yes, I guess it is.*

The first time I ever saw thruhikers was right here in Shenandoah, years ago. I came out for the weekend on an escape from D.C., and one summer afternoon I was driving along the Skyline Drive, nervously watching a thunderstorm in my rearview mirror. The storm caught up with me, and I was glad to be in a car as the lightning snapped at the ridge and the rain slammed down. I came around a curve and there, hiking along the side of the road, huge packs drenched, muddy legs corded with muscle, were four of the dirtiest, thinnest, most worn-out people I had ever seen. The lightning came closer, they flinched and ducked into the woods, and I went on around a curve, in the dry safety of my car. I didn't know about the Trail then, didn't know who they were or where they were going, but it was clear they had walked a long way and were headed even farther, that they accepted the weather they had to walk in. There was something about their eyes; they looked more alive than most people, more awake. I didn't just want to be like them; I wanted to *be* them. Whatever it was they were doing, I wanted to do it.

Later, when I learned about the Trail, I realized they were thruhikers. And now that I've reached the Shenandoahs, I realize they were blue-blazing, walking along the Drive, struggling with the blues, looking for the rhythm. And the way they were walking, I have every faith that they found it.

If they found it, so can I.

July 3
Pinefield Shelter, Va.

Chapter Seven

I look at my schedule, which seemed so sensible when I made it back in D.C. in the middle of winter. It looks ridiculous now. I'm about two weeks behind.

I lie on the hard wooden boards of the Pinefield Shelter floor and do the math. There are 94 days left until October 15, when Mount Katahdin is usually closed by snow. I've walked about 800 miles, and have 1,300 miles to go from here. If I hike every day, I'll have to do an average of 13.8 miles a day. If I take an occasional day off to resupply, say 14 days off between now and then (about one a week), I'll have 80 hiking days left. This means 16.25 miles a day, six days a week, then one day off.

Can I do that? I decide to try it for a while and see. If I skip a section—say, Pennsylvania—I could jump ahead, walk to Maine, and come back and do Pennsylvania later. I don't really want to do that, since it will cut the continuity of the trip as a whole.

I decide to just walk and see what happens.

The park is filled with deer. At night they lie in the grass outside the shelter, waiting for hikers to come out and pee, their delicate ears outlined by moonlight, eyes shining. When a hiker gets up and pees on the grass, the deer wait patiently, and as soon as the hiker is back in the shelter, they lick the grass and eat it. Salt. Most people, who think deer are so lovely, have no idea deer have this secret vice.

In daytime the deer come up to me on the Trail, looking for handouts. They've been fed too many times by foolish tourists, and now they're ridiculous. When I come upon them on the Trail I sing to them—the "Shenandoah Waltz"—and they listen raptly, big ears swiveling, deep brown eyes intent, only a few feet from me.

I cross Skyline Drive, and a herd of deer is standing in the middle of the road, in the path of oncoming cars.

I walk out among them and clap my hands. "Come on, let's get going, the road is no place for deer." I herd them across the blacktop, as the tourists sit in their stopped cars, video cameras whirring, filming this strange woman with the big pack and her personal herd of deer. The deer disappear into the woods, following the white blazes, and I follow them.

I'm sitting on the steps of the Mount Lewis campground store eating potato chips and microwave pizza and shivering in the expensive sweatshirt I've just bought when a woman ranger pulls up in a green pickup truck. "Thanks!" the passenger calls cheerfully and hops out. "Hey, Grace!"

It's Nomad. She hauls her pack out of the back of the truck and comes over, grinning. She looks refreshed and happy.

"Hey, Nomad, what are you up to?"

"I've been yellow-blazing, and damn, it feels good!"

"All right! What happened?"

"Oh, I left the shelter last, and I was in this dreamy, not-paying-attention kind of mood, and I turned right instead of left on the AT and walked like 10 miles, south. You know how things look totally different when you hike the other way? Then I ran into this thruhiker, and he goes, why are you hiking south? I said, I'm not hiking south, and he said, oh yes you are, and he was right, and there was *no way* I could catch up, so I just went to the nearest ranger station and explained the problem, and the ranger was cool, and she was happy to drop me off here. God, it feels great! I needed a break. From Dough Boy and his anal pure-white-blazing, and his damn *schedule*. I swear, he's getting on my nerves. I think unconsciously I backtracked on purpose, just to get away from him."

"I blue-blazed half the day today," I say. "It was great. Just for variety. You know how the Trail crosses Skyline Drive over and over again? I walked on the Trail until it hit the Drive, then I walked on the Drive until it crossed the Trail again. Back and forth. It was worth it. The Drive has much better views."

"You blue-blazed?"

"Yeah, I do it all the time. I'm a big blue-blazer. It's fun. Why not?"

"Wow. Whenever I suggest it, Dough Boy freaks out. He's like, absolutely not. He's so anal about hiking the pure-white AT that he won't even take the shortcuts to the shelters. He goes back and fills in the one-hundredth of a mile he missed. I wish I could hike with you."

"Why not? It'd be fun. I've been dying for someone fun to hike with. You can always meet him at the shelter at night and hike your own way during the day."

"Really? All right, I will. God, what a relief. It almost makes me want to hike again."

We talk some more. Both of us are exhausted. I've had a stomachache and diarrhea lately, and so has she.

"You know what's really sick?" she says. "When I thought I was getting sick I actually felt *relieved*. This part of me was like, all *right!* Maybe I'll even have to go to a hospital! Now I'll get to lie in a warm soft bed for a week and just sleep and be taken care of and not have to hike. Just rest."

"I know what you mean," I say. "I think everyone is feeling like that, but no one wants to admit it. I think Spider Man feels that way, and that's why he gets so mad at people for yellow-blazing or blue-blazing. He wishes he could do it too, but he's too stubborn to change his idea of the Trail, and he hates that we don't care and just take breaks and do it."

"Yeah, I think that's Dough Boy's problem too. God, he's so annoying about that schedule. He never has any fun or looks at anything, just ticks off the miles."

Right now, shivering on the porch, I just want to be warm and cozy and out of the wind, and I know I won't be. From hot and humid as hell to hypothermia, in a matter of days. The misery index has been rather high today, but things are looking up now that I have another woman to hang out with. And she's a writer too, so we have that in common.

The shelter that night is full: Nomad, Dough Boy, Spider Man, Georgia Dan, Maine Event, G.R.Dia, Zombie, and me. It's the Fourth of July, but the weather feels more like Halloween. We make a big bonfire and cook hot dogs. Zombie, who like all of us has worn the same shirt every day for three months, has just bought a new one and ceremoniously burns the old one, saving a piece to sew onto his bandanna as a sentimental trophy. We leap, laughing, around the 10-foot-high flames, and the light reflects on everyone's faces.

I sent my sleeping bag and winter gear home back in Waynesboro, and my new sleeping gear is a sheet I found in a thrift store there, which I sewed into a sleeping-bag shape with dental floss. Now it's 40 degrees, and I sleep wrapped in my tarp and the bunchy folds of Maine Event's tent, wearing my rain gear and all my other clothes, including the new sweatshirt. Every time I roll over, the slick materials rustle like dead leaves. My hips dig into the wooden floor. The hip belt on my pack is maxed out to the smallest possible setting; I wonder if it's possible for me to get any thinner, now that I'm down to bone. If it is, I'll have to get a new pack.

The best thing about today was running into Nomad and agreeing to hike together. I think about my prayer from the night before, for a good Trail buddy, a friend with a sense of humor and an open mind. My prayer has been answered.

In a loose pack, several of us hike through the rest of the Shenandoahs. Nomad and I hike separately from Dough Boy, who is, as Nomad warned, very rigid. He follows the white blazes, and we hike on side trails, the Skyline Drive, or the AT, whatever seems most interesting. We eat our way through the park, stopping at every lodge, restaurant, and roadside store. Hiking is a breeze, since we don't have to carry any food, and we can eat as many calories as we want, as long as we have the money to pay for them.

One morning we pass the site where the two women were murdered. We don't pass the actual spot, which is not on the AT, but we pass the side trail that leads to it. It's early in the morning, and it's spooky to think that the side trail, which seems so peaceful and looks like any other trail, was the last trail the women ever hiked.

We're subdued until we pass this, and relieved to have it behind us when we do. We relax a little as we get farther and farther away from it, though we're still paranoid. When Nomad and I enter the woods and two men follow us, we hurry ahead until we're around a curve in the Trail, then run down a side trail and lose them.

"Have you ever noticed on this trip," Nomad says, "how if you really need something, it just comes along?"

"That's how I met you. I asked for a fun hiking buddy, and the next day I ran into you. I've had other stuff like that happen too."

"I know, I've had that too. It's like someone oversees it or something, and just hands things out when you need 'em. Like some kind of Trail goddess. If she had a name, I wonder what it would be."

"Gladys," I say with certainty.

"Gladys? Why *Gladys*? That's a weird name. It sounds like some middle-aged telephone operator in the Bronx."

"I don't know. It just popped into my mind. But it's Gladys and nothing else." I lean back and look up at the trees. "Hey, Gladys!" I yell. "Thanks for the Trail magic!"

We're only 13 miles from Harpers Ferry, West Virginia, home of the headquarters of the Trail. Nomad and I run into a kind stranger who agrees to shuttle our packs ahead to town, and we run all the way there, leaping over roots and rocks, talking. It's amazing to be in such good shape, to move so effortlessly, to run up a hill and hardly feel it.

We skip along, singing "Johnny Appleseed," and tell each other stories. I tell her about the counselors singing at summer camp at night, and she tells me about her childhood camp. It turns out that we went to the same camp in Wisconsin. I loved that place. I knew every tree on the property intimately, and every trail in the woods. I often told the counselors I had a stomachache, got out of swimming, and as soon as the bus departed, taking everyone else to the Wisconsin River for a dip, I was off and running, straight into the woods. I'd run for miles along trails, exploring. I ate blackberries, chewed wild anise seeds, crushed handfuls of mint for the smell. I never felt lost or worried, but felt sustained, buoyant, carried along by a smooth current of life or love, the green fire of the living forest.

I'd almost forgotten about summer camp until Nomad brought it up, and I realize this is just like camp, this running through the woods—carefree. What a gift it is, to regain this feeling.

As we're going down a mountain, Nomad tells me about the Michigan Womyn's Music Festival, which she went to last year. "You're from Madison, right? Well, I met these women from

Madison at Michigan. You know how some people have those moles on their face that have, like, a million hairs hanging from them? Well, these women at the festival had these big moles, and they had all this hair spronging out of them that they had grown out to, like, six or eight inches long, and not only that, but they had *braided it* and wrapped it all with colored embroidery thread so it was, like, as thick as your little finger, and plus they had tied little ribbons and bells to the end. So all over the place you'd hear this little *tinkle linkle linkle ting!* and there would be one of these mole women. It was so weird. It was *gross.*"

For some reason this strikes me as hilarious, and I laugh uncontrollably. I stagger down the hill from tree to tree, leaning on them for support, stomach hurting, tears streaming from my eyes, until I can't even see the Trail and have to stop, leaning my full weight on a tree, just laughing. "Oh, stop it, stop it, my stomach is killing me," I tell her.

"Mole women," she says, sending me into a fresh seizure, and I weakly wave her away and clutch my tree. I laugh like this for 15 minutes, and Nomad laughs too, just watching. All the rest of the way into Harpers Ferry, as we go up and down the mountains and approach the Shenandoah River, I keep giggling, and all she has to do is say quietly, "Mole women," and I'm lost. I haven't laughed like this in a long time, and as I laugh, I feel things open up inside me, old fears and hurts slipping away, old clenched thoughts loosening and falling behind me.

We cross the Shenandoah River, a real marker—we've come almost 1,000 miles. Without packs, we skip along, waving at cars, holding our arms up like athletes in triumph, looking over the bridge at the beautiful view of water moving along between the forested bluffs. Water under the bridge: almost half the trip gone.

We come out of Harpers Ferry and cross the Potomac River on a railroad bridge, elated. The river is a great divide, and crossing it is a rite of passage, a physical reminder that we've walked a thousand miles. We're now officially on the second half of the trip; we've survived this far, and we'll keep going. We say it out loud: "A thousand miles! Waaaaah-hooooo!"

There's a loose pack of us all hiking together out of town: Nomad, Dough Boy, Spider Man, Listener, and me. Spider Man and Listener, always competitive, each try to walk faster than the other, and make grandiose estimates of their projected daily mileage. Dough Boy, like a kid embarrassed to be seen with his mother at the mall, edges away from us and joins them.

We turn right after the bridge and walk along the C & O Canal. It goes all the way to D.C.; if we kept walking along it, we'd end up in Georgetown.

We pass a giant teddy bear, facedown in the water. Bloated, swollen, it looks like a victim of mayhem in Toyland. Headlines flicker through my mind: ELVES INDICTED IN DROWNING. SANTA TO TESTIFY.

The three men walk faster, eventually disappearing up ahead.

"Well, thank God that's over," Nomad says. She wipes the sweat off her forehead. We slow down even more, just strolling. It's a typical resupply day: hot and humid as hell, and uphill. My pack weighs about a thousand pounds, and I mentally calculate the weight of the heaviest food items in it and wonder how soon I can eat them.

Relieved of the competitive energy of the men, we stop every hour for long breaks, sitting on logs or rocks, eating our heaviest snacks. We fall far behind.

And fall to talking. We talk all day, not even noticing the hills. We talk about our other travels, about first dates and first jobs, about why we're on the Trail. She tells me she's been wanting to ditch Dough Boy for several hundred miles because he's so sullen and morose, but she felt sorry for him so she didn't. Now she thinks, that's ridiculous, he's a grown man, he can hike on his own and be depressing on his own time. Enough is enough. Besides, he's such a mama's boy, he ought to be hiking with other men anyway. It'll be good for him.

"I'm not going to hike with him anymore," she says. "Tonight I'll tell him I want to hike separately, and then you and I can hike together."

"Good!"

We talk about people we've gone out with. I tell her I've been involved with women. I tell her about Wade. For the first time, this story I've been carrying for a thousand miles like a stone in my pack loses its weight and becomes just a story. Something to tell, something to laugh at. Like most bad relationships, it makes a great story: the tears, the lying, the peering through windows, the strange, obsessive habits. How upset I was. How remote it all seems now, how foolish. What was I thinking? As Nomad says, enough is enough.

The story pours out. Nomad laughs, egging me on for more details. "And then what did he do? You're kidding! What a freak! What other crazy shit did he do?"

I laugh and tell her everything I can think of, all the nervous nights and anxious days pouring out of me like sweat, evaporating in the summer air. She's a great audience, receptive, amused. She tells me about people she's gone out with, tells me stories of friends and their terrible relationships, and we both laugh. She's undisturbed by the news that I've been involved with women; she has a lot of gay friends. For the first time on the Trail the two different threads of my past have come together; the two conflicting stories are one. I feel strong and whole, grateful to her for being the kind of person whose world is big enough to take all of this in.

We talk all day, walking slowly, taking breaks, until we realize it's getting dark. We're supposed to meet Dough Boy at a campsite up ahead, since he and Nomad are sharing food, a stove, and other gear. We race the sun and get there at dusk. We stroll into the campsite, laughing.

Dough Boy is there, morose as ever. He grunts hello. The other men have apparently gone ahead somewhere without him. He radiates resentment and disapproval. "I need to talk to you," he says to Nomad.

The campsite has a bathroom with flush toilets and a hot shower; in front of this little building is a narrow cement porch with a light over it. I sit in this pool of light and cook supper; it's easier than trying to cook while holding a flashlight in my teeth. Nomad talks with him, then brings her food over and sits with me.

"He's in a pissy mood," she says. "He's annoyed because we had fun all day. And guess what? He said he doesn't want to hike with me anymore! So I didn't even have to be the one to tell him. I tried to act all serious and sad, but it makes me want to laugh! What a relief!"

We're ecstatic, though we try not to show it. Now we can do whatever we want—stop and pick berries, hike 20 miles a day or none at all, blue-blaze, yellow-blaze, or green-blaze, without him hectoring us about purity or a schedule or having to meet him somewhere at the end of the day. We'll hike with him as far as Boiling Springs, the next resupply stop, and then he and Nomad will divide their food drop and gear and go their separate ways.

It starts raining during supper, and instead of setting up my tarp in the wet grass, I go into the bathroom and unroll my mat on the cement floor. It's dry and cozy in here, safe from the rain. I've never slept in a bathroom; it's odd to look up and see the underside of a toilet, the dank bottom of a shower curtain. But it feels liberating; I can be at home anywhere.

Half-asleep, I hear a soft *slap! slap! slap!* on the cement floor, like someone doing a soft-shoe. Something hops onto me, light and springy and gentle, and bounces lightly from my hip to my shoulder, then slaps back onto the floor. I turn on my flashlight. It's a huge toad, as big as my two fists. It hops away into the shower stall, looking for bugs. *Good*, I think. *Eat them all.*

Coyotes howl outside. The toad's feet whisper past my ear. I smile into the dark, feeling free.

We cross the Mason-Dixon line, and the first person we see in Pennsylvania is an ax-wielding maniac. Actually, we hear him before we see him, as we pose and take photos of each other at the sign marking the division between North and South.

"Stand over there—no, move left so I can get the sign in."

Thunk... Thunk... Thunk...

"OK, your turn."

Thunk...

"What's that weird noise?"

We hike on and see a man, completely swathed in cloth, like the Invisible Man, slowly and repetitively whapping the flat side of an ax against a rotten log.

Thunk...thunk...thunk...

He's only about five feet from us, but he makes no sign to indicate he knows we're there. His motion is dull, machinelike, as if he's been there all day and will be there all night. His face is like a zombie's: nobody home.

Dough Boy is hiking with us, and although he and Nomad seem to be on good terms, he's as weighty as a pack full of bricks. We get to a road crossing, and even though there's a pizza place a half-mile away, he vetoes our suggestion to go there, saying it's a waste of time.

"The schedule won't allow it," he says. "If you go there, you won't catch up with me tonight, and we need to be in the same place because otherwise neither one of us can cook or filter water."

Later, as we sit on logs having a cold break in the rain, eating wet M&Ms, Nomad says, "How about if you give us the map? You can go ahead on the Trail, and we'll catch up later. Honestly, we will. I don't want to go without supper any more than you do. Just give me the map."

I look at maps as often as other people look at their watches; I love them. At night in the shelter, I can spend an hour or more just looking at the terrain. But my maps for Pennsylvania were lost in the mail, so I don't have one. Dough Boy never uses the map—you don't really need one if you stay on the AT—but until now, he's been reluctant to let Nomad have it. He has also hoarded most of their snacks, so she has to stay near him.

"You'll just use it to blue-blaze," he says. "I don't know if I want to give it to you."

"Oh, give me a break," Nomad says. "Just give it to me."

"I can't find it."

"It's in your pack."

"Yeah, but it's at the bottom. I can't reach it."

"That's a fine place for a map."

Eventually he breaks down, gives us the map, and leaves, stomping off through the rain.

"Wahoo!" Nomad says. "Now we'll have some fun. Thank Gladys for that."

At Caledonia State Park, we sit on the porch of the ranger station drinking sodas. Inside the station is a horrifying display: a stillborn fawn, preserved in some kind of solution, folded up and floating in a tank.

"Gross!" Nomad says. "Now I know why I'm a vegetarian."

We drink more sodas. It's hard to get moving; we're both exhausted.

"Do you think we have Lyme disease or something?" I ask. "I feel so tired all the time lately."

"How could you tell? What are the symptoms—being really tired, joint pain, weight loss, muscle aches? That sounds like every thruhiker on the Trail."

"It definitely sounds like me. I feel horrible."

"Me too. Like more horrible than just hiking would make you feel."

We drink big swigs of soda and take ibuprofen and contemplate the vacationers going in and out of the ranger station. My joints feel like they're all on fire. When I move my eyes, the muscles behind them hurt. I look at the map: How many more miles to the next shelter? Ten.

"Imagine," Nomad says, "if we got a ride, we could be in the shelter by like 1 or 2, and then just hang out all afternoon."

This is tempting. Lifting my hiking sticks is exhausting; my feet feel like lead.

"Maybe we can get some help." I look out at the trees.

"Hey, Gladys, could you help us out here?"

A man comes out of the ranger station, followed by his wife. Both are wearing Appalachian Trail T-shirts, and they're heading for a van that, though filled with four kids and gear, has enough room for two tired hikers and their packs.

"Hey, did you hike the Trail?" I ask them.

"We've hiked sections of it. Why, are you hikers?"

"We sure are, and we're trying to get down the road a little way to Birch Run Shelter. Are you going that way?"

"How far is it?"

"Ten miles."

"We're going the other way, but it won't be a problem to help a hiker. Hop in."

Just like that, we have a ride. As the miles slide by, the kids argue about who lost whose toothbrush. They're from Iowa, and they're all blond and have the same haircut, bowl-style. I know without asking that their mother has cut their hair at home.

One of the kids tells us about a barn fire they had. "We lost a lot of stuff, and I hurt my back," he says, "but we got all the animals out. That's the important thing."

He tells me about their animals, and I watch the yellow line on the road and consult the topo map so I can tell the man where to turn off. It's weird using a topo map to navigate on a road; I'm still using things like hills, streams, and the lay of the land to determine where we are. We get to the turnoff, and he drops us off at the Trail crossing, only a mile or so from the shelter.

I don't feel bad about yellow-blazing today. It's not what I expected to do, but that's probably a good thing. Until this trip, I'd never have considered hitchhiking. Now I've met people I'd never meet otherwise, and I've had a view of America and people's kindness to strangers that I wouldn't otherwise have had. Trust. It's more common than I knew.

When it starts getting dark, Dough Boy shows up and doesn't even ask if we've yellow-blazed; it's obvious we have, or we wouldn't be here ahead of him. Resigned, he starts making supper, and takes out a bag of stone-hard powdered cheese and bangs it on a rock to loosen some.

"Rock, paper, scissors—cheese!" Nomad calls out cheerfully. "I expect the rock will break."

❖❖❖

The next day Nomad and I hike together all day, singing in the rain. I teach her the song "In the Pines," and the harmony, so we can sing it together, wailing like the wind in between verses:

In the pines, in the pines,
Where the sun never shines,
And we shiver, when the cold wind blows.

Woooooo, hoo hoo, hoo hoooooo.

We sing other songs too, improvising harmonies, making up words when we can't remember the real ones.

After a long day of hiking and singing, Nomad and I sit on the porch of an insurance office in Boiling Springs, facing a pond, watching the rain. It's late afternoon, and a woman who works in the office is packing up her stuff and turning off the lights, getting ready to go home.

"Would you mind if we stayed here tonight, on the porch?" Nomad asks as the woman is locking the door.

"I can't give you official permission to stay," the woman says, "but if hikers stayed here I'd never know about it, and neither would my bosses." She winks, and drives away.

Nomad and I slap hands, jubilant. The other camping spot is a wet field at the edge of town, and it's already partly flooded, not a pleasant alternative.

It gets dark. Nomad gets the porch swing to sleep on, and I put my bag and bug net on the picnic table.

The night is peaceful, easy, timeless, with small-town sounds of barking dogs, the swish of quiet cars, the sound of a distant train.

The next morning we sit on the porch swing, eat leftover pizza and garlic bread for breakfast, and watch the ducks on the pond. "I think those two are an item," Nomad says, pointing at two ducks, one black, one white, that are inseparable.

It's still raining, and Dough Boy, who tented in the flooded field, comes huffing past the porch, on his way to a 22-mile day. Tomorrow he'll do five miles, then stop at Duncannon for a resupply. He and Nomad have split up their gear and food. Unlike me, she's not buying her food along the way; she spent months preparing, dehydrating, and boxing up complicated and tasty vegetarian meals, and someone back home is mailing them, in sequence, to post offices along the way. These boxes are intended for two people, Nomad and Dough Boy, and now, instead of buying all my food when I reach a town, I'll take Dough Boy's place and eat the food that was originally intended for him, in exchange for a copy of all the photos I take.

The rain pours down. Dough Boy stands in it; it runs down his beard and drips off his bent elbows. He leans on his hiking poles, surveys our dry domain on the porch, and looks miserable and sullen. It's not easy to hike in the rain; the Trail is a mudslick, and 22 miles, which is a hard day even when it's dry, will be a long, unpleasant hike.

"Why don't you hike 12 miles today, and 15 tomorrow?" I ask. "It'll be clear tomorrow, you'll have a better hike both days, and you'll still get to Duncannon the same day you originally intended."

"Can't. It's not in the schedule."

"What schedule? You made the schedule, you can change it. Anyway, what's the difference if you end up in Duncannon at the same time anyway?"

"It's not in the schedule."

Nomad rolls her eyes. I see what she was up against, hiking with him. But if he wants to hike that way, let him. Hike your own hike, as the hikers say.

He trudges off. We lean back on the porch swing, watch the

ducks, and study the sky. We have no plans. This is a day off, a rarity. It's been a long time since we had an open-ended day. Like Dough Boy, maybe we've been prisoners of the schedule.

Several hikers wander past, do a double take when they see us on the porch, then join us: H2O, Maine Event, Arkansas Traveler, G.R.Dia, Zombie, and Refrigerator, who looks like his name. The rain has sapped everyone's motivation.

"Where did you guys sleep?" Maine Event asks us.

"Right here."

"Wow, way to go. You were smart. We were in that flooded field. I didn't sleep at all."

Thunder rumbles from the west. Another wave of storms is coming in, and we all settle in to watch. The entire Spanish Armada of ducks and geese, including the devoted black-and-white couple, is on the lake. The clouds in the west are a massy, rounded pile of forms called mammatus, an ominous sign that a tornado was or is nearby, but it's relatively calm and clear blue right over our heads, as if the sky can't decide what extreme to go to. I wonder how Dough Boy is doing and what the weather is like over his head. He reminds me of those cartoon characters who have a small dark cloud that follows them everywhere.

We all talk about hikers we've seen lately. We mention those who've quit, like tribal people reciting a genealogy, as if naming the ones who are gone will keep us from becoming one of them.

"I saw Little Train the other day," Maine Event says. "She was really moving."

"She's cool, but what is it with all the hikers who call themselves Little?" Nomad asks. "None of them are. They're all just normal size. Whenever you meet someone who really is little, they just have a normal name."

"They're all women," I say. "Little Train, Little Cat, Little Star, Little Cricket. It's some kind of girly-girl thing: I may be out here looking like a big tough hiker, but I'm actually very little, so don't get threatened, guys, 'cause I'm *little*. Just a *little* girl. No man out here ever calls himself 'Little' anything."

"Ugh," Nomad says. "That's so gross. I'm gonna call myself Big Nomad from now on. In the logs, I'll write 'Big Nomad was here.'"

I mime writing in a logbook: "'BIG Amazin' Grace and BIG Nomad stopped by. Here comes trouble.'"

Maine Event laughs. One of the geese is interested in his breakfast, and he puts a bite of pancake between his lips and squats down. The goose gives him a quick pecking kiss, and the pancake is gone. I've seen him before, with squirrels and deer: He can turn any animal into an instant pet.

Nomad writes in her journal, Maine Event and the others run through the rain to a nearby gas station for snacks, and I watch the ducks and the changing sky. I've found something that was missing all my life. A deep sense of peace, of at-homeness, at-oneness, everywhere I go. Anywhere I lay my head, anyplace I even sit down, is home. I've slept in a feed shed, in a bathroom, on this porch, on cliffs, in the woods, in shelters, and in every one of them have felt more at home than any place I've ever lived. Somehow, in the midst of wandering, I've discovered how rooted I am; I'm no longer alienated. I'm home anywhere, everywhere, and will never feel rootless or homeless again.

I don't know if I would have found this feeling as quickly or easily if I had stayed on the official Trail. It's the contact with civilization that does it—that hobo feeling of being here now, then leaving, just passing through, sleeping where you can, talking to everyone, then moving on. It's the freedom I love: no rules, no set path to follow. Look at the map and choose your adventure. Everything is a challenge—living by your wits, carrying what you need, finding a place to sleep, scavenging, making do with what you have.

One of the men returns from the gas station and reports that according to the radio, there was a tornado touchdown somewhere west of here. We're all relieved that we're not hiking right now.

What do I need now? I wonder. To live and feel and sense deeply, to fill up on experiences and emotions and events, to be open to newness and to people, to lose any masks I wear, to lighten my load—physically, emotionally, and spiritually—to laugh, to sing, to commune.

Despite my feeling of emotional health, physically I'm still feeling ill, achy, and tired, even more fatigued than hiking would make me. At Duncannon I sit in the diner of the Clark's Ferry Plaza Motel, a truck stop at the edge of town where a bunch of us have gotten a room for the night, and drink glass after glass of orange juice.

The diner is a big, cheerful place, filled with the babble of truckers and families traveling across the state or the country. Above the swirl of conversation, I hear the word "scrapple" flung up like a flag, and think, that's how you know you're in Pennsylvania: They have scrapple. I'm not sure what it is, maybe some kind of sausage, but the name isn't very appetizing. I order eggs, home fries, and a chocolate milkshake.

A big Amish family walks in. Everyone else stares at them, and the Amish people all stare at me, at my bizarre, nearly naked (to them) appearance—tank top, shorts, and hiking boots—and my big pack, which takes up the seat next to me.

I ask the waitress how they got here; after all, this is a truck stop. Did they walk, since they don't drive cars?

"Nah, they have people who drive 'em, in vans. They get dropped off here, or they stop on the way to visiting their families out of state."

This seems ironic: The Amish people got a ride here, whereas I walked. And they may live the simple life, but right now mine is even simpler.

Nomad shows up, fresh from the shower, and slides into the booth. "I can't wait to get back to the woods," she says. "This morning I was walking across the parking lot and smelled wood smoke. It made me homesick for the Trail. I've had enough motel."

We both miss the Trail—our view of the Trail, the Southern Trail we've walked over so far. Here in Pennsylvania, the people are more wary than Southerners, less up-front friendly. Not rude, but reserved. The land seems scarred by too much human presence. Road crossings, views of towns and more roads, and power-line crossings are frequent, and you can hear the hum of cars at night. Maybe they should close the whole state, have everyone abandon it, and let the woods grow back and heal. I crave the cedary-mossy, more remote Trail; I miss whippoorwills and foxfire. I miss the Nantahalas.

Nomad picks up a tiny packet of jelly. "Mixed-fruit flavor? What's in that?"

"Mixed-fruit is the scrapple of jelly," I say. "Odds and ends, all together."

She spreads it on her toast. "Not bad. Do you have your notebook? Let's make a plan for the next section."

We're not allowed to use the word "schedule," because it's Dough Boy's word and he's given it a bad taste. We had to give Dough Boy's maps back, but we look at the *Data Book*, a thin volume that gives mileages between every landmark on the Trail. My copy is battered and torn, every page covered with scrawled math of distances and miles, and half of it is missing: I mailed the used pages home to save weight.

We peer through the forest of scribbled numbers and make our plan. It involves hikes of 11.8 miles, 17.7 miles, 17.9 miles, 14.2 miles, then 8.5 to a resupply stop in Port Clinton. Then 15.0, 17.9, and 18.1, ending at my friend Veronica's house—she lives near Allentown, so close to the Trail that from her living room, she can see the ridge top where the hikers walk. We'll stay with her for a couple of days, then hike on.

Satisfied with this plan, we finish eating and stand up—a painful process. My eyes feel like someone is hammering them, my joints are screaming, and my sinuses are about to explode. I think I have a fever. I lift my pack and put it on, and we head out, across a bridge over the Susquehanna River, and up the mountain on the other side, for our day's walk.

We meet a dayhiker and stop to chat. He lives nearby and often comes out here; someday he wants to thruhike, and he likes talking to any long-distance hikers he meets. When I ask how far the shelter is, he says, "Don't you have a map?"

"It was in my mail drop, but it got lost."

"Well, I have maps of all of Pennsylvania. Tell you what. I don't have them with me, but I'll give you this one, and later today I'll drive up and leave the rest under this bridge—see here, on the map?—and you can use them for the rest of the state."

"Do you want us to pay you?"

"Nah, I can always get more. It's a freebie."

"Write your name down, and we'll mail them back to you when we're done."

"OK." He writes his name in the margin, wishes us a happy hike, and we hike on.

"Thanks, Gladys, for the Trail magic!" we yell up at the trees. "We know you're watching!"

At Peters Mountain Shelter, the water source is far down a trail that leads almost all the way back down the side of the mountain, so steep that it's become a rockslide. I head down. The trail requires care and thought to negotiate, and this focus is grounding; it gets me back to the woods as I step (and sometimes slide) down, down, down. Beyond the trees, the sky appears in incredible colors: deep orange and fuchsia, shades of flame azalea and rhododendron.

The trail turns, going down, and I hear the spring water running down the hill. Far away, in the green distance, children are singing,

Amazing grace, how sweet the sound...

They're doing all the harmonies, and their clear voices blend with birdsong in the deepening dusk. There must be a camp nearby, and it reminds me of my camp days, the feeling of dusk coming down, the cozy squares of yellow light in the cabin windows, the campers singing together,

'Twas grace that brought me safe thus far
and grace will lead me home.

Silence. A wood pewee sings one last questioning note, and night is here.

I dip my water carrier into the spring and position a rolled-up leaf as a funnel to guide the water into it. Take a deep breath, hum the song, my song now, the song of my name, the song of this trip. Traveling home, trusting this pilgrimage to lead me there, wherever it may be. Take the heavy water carrier, turn, and climb back up the rocky slide, carrying the music with me. Carrying water, carrying life.

July 21
Peters Mountain Shelter, Pa.

CHAPTER EIGHT

Nomad and I study the map; we feel like blue-blazing today. A country road parallels the Trail and heads in the general direction we're going; later we can reconnect to the Trail, after a day of exploring off it. We reach a fork in the trail and head to the right, downhill, toward the road.

The road is lined with flowers, singing with crickets. Very few cars pass. We walk along, singing "In the Pines," refining our harmonies, feeling free. It's the usual blue-blaze feeling—the ultimate freedom from rules and expectations. If we're lucky, maybe we'll pass a general store and get some sodas.

A car passes, slows, backs up. "Hey, Nomad and Grace!"

It's Ron, the dayhiker we met the day before. "I didn't get a chance to drop off those maps yesterday, so I figured I'd do it this morning before you got there. I'm on my way to the bridge now. What are you doing? I never thought I'd see you on this road."

"Blue-blazing," we say, and explain.

"Well, I don't know if I should say this, but do you want a ride? I'm going toward that hiker hostel, the Bleu Blaze."

We look at each other. We were heading there anyway. What should we do?

"You know," Nomad says, "Gladys sent us this ride. We didn't even ask for it. I think we should take it."

We hop in. He hands us the maps, which are on the front seat. "I guess I won't have to leave these under the bridge now."

I ask him about himself.

"I used to be a smoke jumper—you know, fighting those fires out west—but I got laid off a couple of months ago when they had some budget cuts. You'd think they'd want to spend a little money to stop these fires, to prevent losing a lot of money when the fires burn everything up, but no, they gotta save those bucks. So I came back here. My family's here."

"Do you like it here?"

"No. It's beautiful and all, but the people are brutal. They call this area Pennsyltucky, because it's pretty backward. Just brutal. The people are tough, and they can be cold. A lot of them aren't very educated, and they don't have time for anything that doesn't make money. Like my friends—they don't understand why I would be a smoke jumper. They think it's a waste of time. They think I ought to have a normal job at a desk and make a lot of money. And forget trying to explain to them about hiking.

"I want to hike the whole AT, and I also want to do the Pacific Crest Trail and the Continental Divide Trail. I want to walk every step. I really feel like I need it. I need something, you know, that you only get in the woods."

We know what he means, even though right now we're happy to be in his car.

We speed along, gleeful at the acceleration. Going this fast—we're only going about 40, but compared to walking speed, it's like being in a rocket—is a novelty, partly frightening, partly exhilarating. I feel like hanging my head out the window and grinning like a dog, closing my eyes, and letting my hair flap in the wind. I look up ahead at the road. We cross the Trail again, and there are two hikers—

"Hey!" Nomad says. "It's Dough Boy and Spider Man!"

"You want me to see if they need a ride too?" Ron asks.

"No, they're purists. They won't want one."

We wave. They look up, startled, and scowl as we fly past. Yellow-blazers! We have no shame, no shame at all.

Ron drops us off at the hostel, which is a converted garage next to a spacious house. It's only about 11 A.M. No one's home; a note says they're all at a funeral, but we should make ourselves at home. There are ice cream sandwiches in the freezer: One per hiker, please.

Besides the refrigerator/freezer, the garage is equipped with big couches, bunk beds, shelves full of coverless paperbacks, and a shower. To us it's blissful luxury. Before the Trail, I had never thought a stranger's garage with a couple of couches in it would seem like a four-star hotel, but it does. It has everything we need.

"All right!" Nomad exults. "A whole afternoon to just chill."

It starts raining outside. We look at the books. At this point I'd read anything, and the selection makes it look like I might have to. The books are all odd—mostly offbeat "nonfiction," like a book about the Shroud of Turin, another about a man who does exorcisms for a living, and one about a Dutch psychic who helps solve crimes.

We lie on the couches, feeling deeply content not to be out in the rain, and read. I start an improbable book from the motley collection—stories by lesbian nuns—but I'm too tired to read. It's blissful lying there, listening to the rain, my sleeping bag warm around my shoulders. I still feel ill and achy, out of it, energyless, and rest is what I need.

Spider Man, Dough Boy, and a bunch of other hikers show up that afternoon. Most of them don't care how we got here, but Spider Man and Dough Boy are curt with us, offended at our yellow-blazing.

Ron shows up unexpectedly, this time with pizza and soda

for everyone. When someone makes another nasty comment about yellow-blazers, Nomad says, "This pizza was brought to you by Yellow-Blaze, Incorporated, and if you don't like yellow-blazing, hand me back your slice. Either that, or eat and shut up about it."

We don't hear any more comments after that.

The next morning we set out in drizzle, heading down the road to the AT. Despite my long nap yesterday, my legs feel like lead, my eyeballs feel hot, and my hands and feet seem very far away. We walk and walk, and still don't see the turnoff to the AT. I'm so tired I'm staggering; even lifting my hiking sticks seems like too much. The landscape bends and sways. My joints feel like they're lubricated with molten lead. Finally, we stop.

I lie down on the asphalt and feel a universe of inertia wash over me like a vast starry night, too big to ignore.

"I think I'm sick," I tell Nomad.

"I think you're right," she says.

We backtrack to the hostel and call my friend Veronica. Can she come get us? She can, but not until late tonight.

We spend another day on the couches, sleeping or reading. Mid afternoon, a hiker named Ramen shows up. Neither of us has seen him since Virginia.

"Hey, how are you? What happened? We heard you got off the Trail."

"I did, but I came back. It was weird. I couldn't relate to my family, and they couldn't understand what I'd been through out here or how it changed me. They sort of expected me to be the same person. I kept saying I was only home for a couple of weeks and then was going back to the Trail, but they kept distracting me: Do this, do that, trying to stuff me back into the same small mold I was in before. Finally, I just said, 'I'm going back to the Trail, because I need it,' and I left. I just got here yesterday. I saw a bunch of my old buddies, and they gave me all this B.S. about how they were my best buddies and would wait for me, but they didn't."

He sits down. "I think they were just happy to see me last night because I had pot."

"You may be right," Nomad says. "I've seen it happen before."

"I wish I could stop smoking it. It just feels, I don't know, like a kind of dead end. Like I'm not getting anywhere, you know? And then stuff like this happens, and it really makes me feel just sick. Like, who are your friends? And how can you tell? Are they your friends because they like you or because you have weed?"

"Probably both," Nomad says, "but they don't want to spend time waiting for anyone, especially if he doesn't have weed."

"I think I smoke it so I won't have to deal with stuff," he says. "I get upset, and then I smoke and forget about it. But I don't think it really goes away. I want to start dealing with stuff. I came out here to deal with stuff, and I haven't dealt with any of it."

We all make supper on our stoves and sit in the gravel driveway in front of the garage and have a potluck: two noodle dishes, powdered mashed potatoes and vegetarian gravy, Gummi Bears, green Kool-Aid, a hunk of cheese that Ramen brought. It's companionable, eating together. We feel like a family.

Veronica's husband Scott comes to get us late that night. Nomad and I spend a week at Veronica's house; I spend most of it with a fever, sleeping on the couch in her living room. The Olympics are on, and the announcers' voices fade in and out through my dreams. I open my eyes to see marathoners, emaciated but strong people who look like they can keep going forever, and for a minute I think they're hikers. I look like that, I think; it's a strange realization. When I get up to go to the bathroom, my joints are so stiff I can hardly move.

Veronica's daughter Ellen gets sick; she has the same symptoms I have, and they take her to the pediatrician, who says that a virus that mimics Lyme disease is going around. Since Ellen caught what I have, I must have that virus, and not Lyme, which isn't spread by direct contact. It's a relief. Now I won't have to wait around for a week to see the doctor and get antibiotics.

A few days later I feel much better. The rest has worked; it's time to move on. We've lost a lot of time while I was lying here; now there's no way we can make it to Katahdin before snow if we start walking from where we are. We'll jump ahead, to where we would be if we had kept walking, and resume the hike from there.

At Gren Anderson Shelter in New Jersey, Nomad and I make dinner and read *Tricycle*, a Buddhist magazine Nomad got at a bookstore back in Veronica's town.

There's an article on walking meditation, a form of meditation-in-motion: You simply walk, being very conscious while you do so. Achaan Chah, a Thai teacher, advises: "Walk at a normal pace from one end of the path to the other, knowing yourself all the way. Stop and return."

This makes us laugh. If only we could be conscious for a mile, let alone 2,000.

Thich Nhat Hanh, a Buddhist monk, writes about the great variety of paths there are, but how people can't enjoy them because they don't have peace in their hearts.

"He's a big old blue-blazer," Nomad says. "Walking those many paths. If it's good enough for Thich Nhat Hanh, it's good enough for me."

Thich Nhat Hanh also advises that when you're doing walking meditation it's the walk itself that matters, not the destination.

This is how I want to hike: living fully, every step. Not hurrying. Not hiking only to get to Katahdin, only to see the end.

Hiking for life, for the fullness.

A group of 4H kids shows up. They've never camped before and don't have very good gear, and we make room for as many of them as possible in the shelter and rig up my tarp to make a roof for some of the others. We show the ones with tents how to lay their ground cloth so that none of it hangs out beyond the bottom of the tent. If it hangs out, all it will do is funnel rainwater under them, and they'll wake up in a puddle.

I'm happy to be back in the woods—I've missed them, and wish we could get into the groove of a good long week's walk, the rhythm of it, the peace. I look at my hands. My fingernails, so clean at Veronica's, are already black and grimy. I'm home.

Rain in the night. I wake to it, so light it sounds like wind, and get up to pee before it starts to pour. I finish and stand there, looking out at the dark fog-and-mist-filled forest, listening to the rain, feeling its coolness on my skin. The forest smells clean and alive.

Something in me has shifted, a tide has turned; I can feel the inner motion. Until now I've often felt blocked, weighed down, as if I don't have full access to my emotions or creative energy. It's been underground a long time, like a root in winter, healing and slowly gathering energy again after the fiasco with Wade. Now I feel the change, as if some burden has fallen off me, and I'm open all the way, no longer root but flower. The trip will be different from now on.

The rain feels good, and I stand in it, letting the forest wet me, breathing, a tree among other trees, an animal among the other animals, one with the woods, in motion with the journey.

I go back to the shelter: everyone sleeping, peaceful breathing. I get into my bag, hear a haiku, and write it down. It's the first creative writing I've done since Wade, not counting my journal. I'm back: here in the present, no longer weighed down by the past.

Nomad has caught the same virus I had. We walk very slowly, stopping often for breaks, and don't get to High Point Shelter until 7:30 at night. Our breaks are shortened by the mosquitoes, which have suddenly undergone a population explosion. When we reach swampy areas, our slow walk is abruptly interrupted. Leaping, slapping, and cursing, we skip down the Trail, then throw down our packs and claw frantically in them for repellent. The packs are still warm and sweaty, and clouds of mosquitoes swarm over them, poking their proboscises into the fabric, looking for blood.

"That is *so* frightening," Nomad says, looking at the insects crawling over her pack and stabbing it. She leaps and slaps her shin. "Bastards!"

As we hike, sweat runs down our arms, washing a thin line of skin, dripping off our elbows and leaving them free of repellent. Mosquitoes bite me repeatedly in that same spot, until both my elbows are swollen and stinging.

H2O and a hiker named Rainiac are at the shelter. Rainiac, like Nomad, is interested in Buddhism, and the two of them happily discuss the *Tricycle* articles.

I read the log. A hiker named Porkchop has written:

> Two paths diverged in a yellow wood.
> One was grassy and flat.
> The other was rocky and uphill.
> I took the uphill one because it had white blazes,
> But I don't think it made any difference.

H2O is a purist—white blazes all the way. He's at peace with his hike, though, and is unbothered by the hiking philosophies of others. He trades me a couple of Clif Bars, which he receives in every mail drop and is heartily sick of, for a couple of Snickers. I buy Snickers in every town, purely for the calories, and am heartily sick of them, so it's a good trade.

H2O's background as a scientist is always obvious on the Trail. He's not a neat freak, but his pack is orderly. He keeps drink mix powder and condiments in tiny plastic vials, unlike the rest of us, who use messy and leaky zip-lock bags. When he mixes lemonade or pudding, he carefully pours powder from a vial to make an exactly measured, double-strength batch first in one water bottle, then pours half of that into his other bottle, and adds enough water to each bottle to fill it to the top. According to him, this results in a more uniform, evenly mixed, and precise-tasting drink.

He mixes lemonade now, his motions economical and neat. The mosquitoes hardly touch him, as if they know he wouldn't be so lax as to allow them any of his blood; after all, he has the exact quantity he needs.

The next day's walk is beautiful, through woods and agricultural land; fields singing with crickets, pastures, and flower-filled fields. We pass the first paper birches I've seen on the Trail, which is a sign that we're closing in on New England, making progress. We pass wetlands filled with purple loosestrife, an invasive but gorgeous weed, ditches full of black-eyed Susans and goldenrod, woods full of Solomon's seal and false Solomon's seal. The berries on mountain-ash trees—which as a child I called "Back-to-School Trees," because they ripen when school is imminent—are turning orange. We pass beeches, their smooth bark unsullied by lovers' initials, and swamps full of cattails. I pull up a cattail shoot and eat it; the white part at the base tastes exactly like a cucumber.

Nomad is definitely sick. We walk more and more slowly, and she's pale and miserable. After we've walked about six miles, I check the map and the hiker handbook. "There's a hostel in the next town," I tell her. "We can go there and you can sleep the night in a bed, and tomorrow if you still feel bad we can take the day off and you can sleep."

She nods. We come to the road that leads to town and walk down it. There are ghost blazes on the telephone poles; this road used to be the Trail.

We walk, envisioning comfortable bunk beds, pizza, hiker camaraderie, friendly hostelkeepers, a quiet place to rest.

The "hostel" turns out to be a 5-by-12-foot storeroom next to a bar. The "bunk beds" are the shelves where they used to keep things; they're two-and-a-half feet wide. The floor is a heaving sea of rolled and wadded-up old carpet that someone has slung in here, difficult to stand on, and a stained mattress standing on edge takes up half the room. In a corner is a cardboard box with a forlorn selection of things past hikers have left: a packet of noodle entrée, a zip-lock bag full of clumps of powdered milk, a leaky plastic bag of oatmeal.

I climb up on a shelf and lie down, experimentally. I can touch both walls, and the shelf above is a foot from my face; I feel like I'm in a coffin. It reminds me of diagrams of old slave ships, or a submarine. It's incredibly hot, even though we've opened the window.

There's a shower out back, a plywood hut. I stay in it a long time, scrubbing, stepping carefully around the poison ivy shooting up through cracks in the floor, using an assortment of shampoos hikers have left. Someone has also left a sports bra behind, and it's my size. I wash all my clothes in the shower and then wash the bra; it's mine now.

Nomad reluctantly leaves her shelf and takes her turn in the shower, then we lay out our clothes to dry and go looking for something to eat.

In the town's only restaurant, a sign warns customers not to drink the water but doesn't say why. I wonder, if I use my filter, can I drink it? After all, we've been drinking water from streams and rivers. It's ironic that stream water is apparently safer than drinking water in this town.

The menu is all meat, and Nomad is a vegetarian. The waitress gives us the once-over and stands with her arms folded, as if she expects trouble.

"Do you have any grilled cheese?" Nomad asks the waitress.

"No."

"Do you have bread?"

"Yes."

"It says here you have roast beef and Swiss cheese. Could you please just give me the bread with the cheese, without the meat?"

The waitress looks at her as if she's a smart-ass. "No."

We shrug and leave. "This town reminds me of Elk Park in Tennessee," Nomad says. "Did you go there? It was weird. People were really unfriendly."

"I didn't go there, but I remember other hikers saying that. Maybe they should have some kind of sport where they decide who's the toughest and unfriendliest town on the Trail. Towns that want to try can get together every year for a mass brawl and see who can kick the other's ass."

We buy supplies at the store, then head back to our closet. It's so hot that our clothes are already dry. A southbound hiker we don't know has come and gone, leaving a note:

> I came and looked it over.
> I'm heading for the woods. Good luck.

That night, country music bounces from the bar, the bass line like a heartbeat. Cars crunch and pop on the gravel, truck doors slam. Couples walk unsteadily across the lot, fighting in narrow New Jersey accents:

"You were looking at him—"

"I was not! I was looking at the jukebox."

"BullSHIT! You were looking at him. You bitch—"

Slam! Slam! Doors close, and they squeal out of the lot, spraying pebbles.

Guys come out of the bar.

"So I said he could just go fuck himself and fuck his goddamn job. He thinks he can just bust my chops all day. Not anymore."

"He's a fuckin' asshole. I hate that guy. My brother used to work for him when he had that landscaping business. He quit too."

"What's all that shit over there? Boots and shit."

"They let those hikers stay in there. I heard it's a couple of girls."

"Girls! Hey, hiker girls! Come on out and play! Hiker girls!"

Another guy comes out, drunker than the first two. "Whassup?"

"Hiker girls in there."

"Heeeeeeyyyyyy, hiker girls! I know you're in there! Hey, hey, heeeeeeeeyyyyy, hiiiiiiiikeeeeeer giiiiiiirrls!!!"

He pounds on the window. Nomad groans. We hunch in our sleeping bags, playing dead, hoping that the lock on the door will hold and he won't break the window.

Eventually they get bored with our possum act and leave. More couples come, go, drink, and fight. Finally, things quiet down, but it's almost sunrise. Time to get up.

"I have to pee," Nomad says.

"Me too. We can use the bathroom in the bar, but guess what? It's closed now."

I go outside and look around. The bar is on a busy street in a residential area; there are no nice big bushes anywhere. At one house a woman in a bathrobe is sweeping her steps; she gives me a disapproving stare, as if she knows what I'm thinking as I scan her yard.

"We'll have to use containers and just toss them in the dumpster. Don't look."

I use an empty milk carton, and hope I don't forget about it and kick it over before we go out and toss it.

"I never thought zip-lock bags would be so handy," Nomad says of her chosen container. "Just zip it, toss it in the dumpster, and go."

"How are you feeling today?"

"Like shit."

She looks it: pale, her face puffy. I feel her forehead; she has a fever.

"Listen, the guidebook says there's a bed and breakfast place near here. It has real beds, I swear! I'll call them and see if they can come and get us, since there's no way you can hike there. We can just stay there until you get better."

Graymoor Friary, the home of the Friars of the Atonement, is right on the Trail, east of the Hudson River in the tiny town of Garrison, New York. The friars have been giving hospitality to hikers for years, and we've heard this is a stop we shouldn't miss.

When Nomad and I reach the friary, we find a few other hikers who are also seeking shelter for the night. A brother meets us and tells us we must wait for the guest master. He shows us to the library, where we wait in unaccustomed comfort on chairs—no rocks or logs, or bare earth!—and read. We shiver in the air conditioning and breathe deeply of the scent of paper and ink, and savor the cool stillness of the library. It reminds me of medieval times, when all the books were kept in monasteries and pilgrims like us would stop for a break from hard traveling. We sit on the soft chairs and read about Mother Teresa, current world events, and the Native American saint Kateri Tekakwitha, until Father Fred, the guest master, comes and shows us to our cells.

The cells are tiny dormer rooms on the top floor of the Old Friary building, which was built in 1926 and until recently was crumbling, with a leaking roof. The problem was so bad that in 1995 the friars had to close the rooms. The Appalachian Long Distance Hikers Association offered to do the repairs, in thanks for past hospitality, and many hikers volunteered to help. Now the hiker hostel is open again.

The other hikers are all assigned private cells, but Nomad and I share one: It's one less room the brothers will have to clean. The room is tiny, cozy, with warm yellow walls and a slanted ceiling, and simply furnished with two beds, a desk, and a chair. To us, this simplicity is luxury.

Down the hall, two novice friars are practicing a hymn. Their clear voices resonate smoothly, with stops and starts as they repeat a line, then go on.

Father Fred tells us the story of how the friary began taking in hikers. The Trail, which was completed in the 1930s, passed by the friary, and one day a thirsty hiker stopped to ask for water. The friars realized that treating all strangers or guests as they would treat Christ was part of their mission, and they began not only giving hikers water, but offering a bed for the night, and dinner. This is part of their ministry, which also includes a shelter for homeless men, an outreach for people suffering from alcoholism and drug abuse, and more recently, support for people with AIDS and HIV.

We shower and put our clothes in the wash—another gift not to be taken lightly!—and Father Fred takes us on a tour of the friary and its grounds. In one of the chapels, a stained-glass window shows Saint Therese of Lisieux walking at night as a girl, with her hand in her father's, looking at the stars.

This image, unexpectedly, makes me weep. My dad and I spent more nights than I can count lying on the grass on summer nights, looking at stars, watching meteor showers.

Father Fred joins us for supper in the friary dining room. There are seven of us; at times, he says, there have been more hikers than the friary had beds for, so we're lucky we don't have to camp outside on the brothers' baseball field.

After supper, we go to our cells. I sit in the small yellow and white room and read the guest book, where hikers have signed in. Okeepa, a hiker who's a day or two ahead of us, has written:

> The yellow soothes—and the white cools—and I hear the sounds of quiet conversation. Echoes of deep sleep from those with tired feet as they dream of the long walk to Katahdin. Nothing pulls so hard as the truth in one's heart—carrying us all over our mountains. So walk on, my brothers and sisters—spread your wings and fly. The world, it waits to greet you.
>
> In peace at Graymoor,
> Okeepa

The next morning, we rise early. I go to the chapel to look at the stained glass again, and when I come back, Nomad has her clean clothes on and is rearranging the gear in her pack. I write a quick letter to a friend and put my pack on. Down the hall the novice friars are singing again, and I wonder how many other wanderers have heard this same music over the centuries. We'll hike 18 miles today; our clothes won't stay clean for long. But the peace and renewal we've found here will go with us, a lasting gift to carry us through the miles.

At Morgan Stewart Shelter, near Shenandoah, New York, we sort through our packs. A hiker named Marmalade Cat has appointed herself the official Ruthless Gear Remover, and she paws through our stuff. Another hiker, Trekker, has a bandanna with a chessboard pattern and a set of pieces, and he sits nearby, playing a game of solitaire chess.

"What's this?" Marmalade Cat asks Nomad scornfully. "Vitamins in the original bottles? Put 'em in a plastic bag. And why do you have so many? You have enough to get all the way to Maine. Take a week's worth out and mail the rest to your mail drops up the Trail. You don't need to carry them all."

She pulls out Nomad's office supplies—tape, paper clips, scissors, colored pencils, paper. "What's this? You running a kindergarten? Toss it."

Nomad ends up with 10 pounds of extra stuff to mail home at the next town. I can't believe she's walked this far with all that excess on her back, but then she's taller and stronger than I am.

Marmalade Cat looks suspiciously at my pack. It's pretty clean and light, except for my sleeping gear, which now consists of a thin fleece blanket and the sheet I got at a thrift store back in Virginia.

"Ditch the sheet. It must weigh a whole eight ounces."

Reluctantly I leave the sheet in the "Hiker Box"—the cardboard box full of things people leave behind, which invariably are picked up by others behind them. It's been hot lately; maybe I won't need it.

"You have *how* many pairs of underwear?" Marmalade Cat pulls them out. "Six? You don't need *any*."

"I'm keeping them all," I say. "The only parts of me that are as clean as they are in civilization are my teeth and my underwear."

"Well, everyone's entitled to one nonnegotiable luxury item. Although I think that notebook of yours qualifies as that. What's up with you writers? You and Nomad both have enough paper to stock an office-supply store."

"Checkmate!" Trekker yells.

"Nonnegotiable!" we both call out, before Marmalade Cat can start ripping pages out of our journals.

Gear sorting over, we relax. The shelter is in one of the stranger locations on the Trail—a suburban neighborhood. Big signs around the perimeter of the shelter, like signs in a zoo, warn:

DO NOT UNDER ANY CIRCUMSTANCES BOTHER THE NEIGHBORS! THEY RESPECT THEIR PRIVACY AS MUCH AS YOU RESPECT YOURS! PLEASE CONTACT THE CARETAKER IN THE EVENT OF AN EMERGENCY! THANK YOU!

I look out at the late-afternoon sun slanting down and feel like a kid again, as if every day is one of those endless summer days when you have no appointments or plans, the light seems like it will never end, and whatever you're doing at the moment is all that matters. We walk a mile down the road to the Shenandoah General Store, a classic old-time store with a wooden floor and that general-store smell—crackers, old wood, soda, and chocolate. We buy mint-chocolate-chip ice cream and talk with the store's owner, who asks if we're hikers and then shows us photos of his family's trip to Maine.

"This is the last year the store will be open," he tells us sadly.

I'm sorry about this: The store is a thruhiker tradition; everyone stops here for a snack.

We take a photo of him standing on the steps of his store, take our ice cream outside, and sit on the steps of the Baptist church next door, eating and talking to the friendly preacher.

This area is as calm, laid-back, and rural as any part of the South, but a sign behind the shelter reminds us that we're far from the South now. We've come 1,429 miles from Georgia. Only 743 left.

I've gotten really good at just sitting—anytime, anywhere, for any reason—and being perfectly content, needing nothing, and not caring what time it is or what day it is or what mile it is, just enjoying the breeze and the chance to rest and see whatever there is to see. At the moment, it's the Poughquag, New York, post office parking lot and the people of Poughquag making their last-minute attempts to mail things before noon, since it's apparently Saturday. Peacefully I watch mothers with children, three giggling teenage girls, an elderly woman, and a man in work clothes. Nomad stands in line with them, patiently waiting to mail her extra gear home or ahead. Like me, she's gotten very good at waiting.

When she's done, we ask the man in work clothes, who has a pickup truck, if he would mind giving us, Marmalade Cat, and another hiker named Mellow Man a ride back to the Trail.

"Hop in," he says. The others jump in the back, and I end up getting in front with him. Instead of pulling out right away, we sit for a while. He looks at a magazine he has in the front seat, and I glance surreptitiously at it. It's a mountaineering magazine, open to an article about Everest. He's not reading it, just sitting with his head down, looking fixedly at the page. We sit so long that I become nervous: What's going on? Is this guy OK? The atmosphere in the cab is strangely heavy, something I can't put my finger on. I look at the others, in the bed of the truck, and try to catch their eye and signal that something is wrong. They're all laughing, carrying on, oblivious.

The man and I sit, in silence.

"My son was like you," he says finally. "He loved the outdoors. Mountain climbing, hiking. He died on Everest."

He tells me about it. His son hiked all over the world, climbed several famous mountains, and hardly ever sat still. His death was a shock—not even a body to bring home. It's still out there somewhere, frozen on the mountainside, too expensive to reach. It's hard to mourn when you don't have a body; it always seems as if the person is still out there somewhere and will come home someday.

I know what he means. When my father died, none of us saw him after he was dead. By tacit agreement, avoiders all, we chose not to see him in his coffin, and it was probably the worst decision I have ever made. After the funeral, I went straight back to D.C., where I had been working, and couldn't mourn. I hadn't seen him dead. In D.C. I never saw him anyway, so it seemed like nothing had changed, as if when I went back to Wisconsin for a visit he'd still be there. It took me much longer to get over his death than it would have if I had seen the physical evidence of it: just a body, my father gone.

"You know," I say, "your son lived a really full life. He got more living in his short time than most people do in an entire lifetime. He didn't waste time. And I bet he was the kind of guy who would say that if you have to go, you should go doing something you love."

The man nods; it's true. I feel strange, open, like a hollow tube, as if I'm just transmitting this message, as if something larger than I know is going on here.

He reaches down and closes the magazine, and we drive, past fields and rivers and old farmhouses. He's not going as far as the Trail; we'll have to walk from here.

"Thanks," he says when we get out, as if we're the ones who have done him a favor, not the other way around. "You all have a good trip. And be safe."

There's a nice blue-blaze that follows the Housatonic River, and Nomad and I follow it. The trail is beautiful and flat and leads us to Cornwall Bridge, where we resupply and stop at the "package store"—New Englandese for "liquor store"—for a free drink. The owners give one free beverage to each thruhiker, and several other hikers are there, laboring to put up a new sign for the store in exchange for more free beer.

A woman from the package store offers to drop us off at a side trail we've found on the map, which leads back to the AT. When she lets us out at this dirt road we walk into the woods, happy to be back. Ahead of us there's a barely audible rustle, like that of a woman in old-fashioned skirts sweeping down the hallway of a plantation. A score of turkey vultures lofts into the air.

"Hey, look, a feather." It's longer than my forearm.

We keep walking and find a scrap of shredded cloth that was once red but is now a grayish salmon.

There's something uneasy about old clothes lying around in the woods: beaten down by rain, faded, collapsed into the ground. Several times during the hike I've found old clothes or the remnants of someone's abandoned camp. It spooks me every time, as if something bad has happened and all that's left of a person is some flattened pieces of dirty cloth and corroded gear. Anyone could disappear, in the woods. Hypothermia, accidents. Or the city person's bogeyman: a homicidal maniac.

Murder has already happened once this summer. It could happen again.

There are hard things in the grass, like stones. Long, thin hard things. Bones. More vulture feathers. We're in a clearing. Ahead of us gapes a pit.

It's too deep for us to see the bottom from where we stand, and I'm glad for that. Bones are scattered around its lip, and more tattered shirts and shreds of cloth. Some of them are stained with blood.

Nomad kicks something. It's a spine. "Are these…human?"

"I don't know. What's with the clothes? I'm not looking in that pit."

"You couldn't pay me to look down there. No way. I'm glad

we can't see the bottom. Let's hope they're only animal. Let's go."

We walk on, skirting the pit so we can't see what's in it. The bones look animal to me, but who am I to know? Some are long but thin, like the leg bones of a child. Above us, in the window between the trees, the vultures glide in calm circles, waiting for us to leave. I imagine that people come here and throw dead things into the pit, then the vultures come and pull them out, piece by piece, and scatter them around.

"I don't think these are human," I say. "This looks like part of a deer or some big animal. See, it's a pelvis."

"What about the clothes? Deer don't wear clothes."

"I don't know. I don't want to know."

We come out into another clearing, this one ringed by defunct cars: rusty old De Sotos, broken-down 1950s cars with bulging fenders. An entire skeleton of a deer, minus the head, lies in the exact center of the clearing, like some kind of symbol: nature, sacrificed to the soul-sick cult of the automobile.

"This is *not* the dirt road that leads us back to the Trail, I bet."

We check the map. After minute inspection and comparison of compass, sun, and the road we drove in on, we determine it's not. On the map, the trail we're on is marked by an almost invisible dotted line that disappears into unmarked space. The dirt road we thought we were on is a mile or so farther down the asphalt road. The helpful driver has let us off at the wrong place.

"Let's get the hell out of here before the deer killers come back."

We don't want to go past the pit again, so we follow the defunct trail, which is soon swallowed up in underbrush. We can tell where it once was because it follows the course of an old stone wall. This hill was apparently cleared in the early part of the century; since then the trees have reclaimed it.

We bushwhack back to the main road. It's late afternoon. By the time we get back up to the AT, it will be nearly dark. We hurry along the shoulder, and when we reach the dirt road we need, we go up it gratefully. We're almost home.

The road leads uphill past houses, past a secluded alcohol treatment center, past a graveyard. We stop in the graveyard to slather on more insect repellent and eat some snacks.

"Another boneyard," Nomad says, gleefully spraying Yard Gard, which she got back in town, over the headstones. "Perimeter secured. We can eat in peace."

"At least here the bones are buried."

"At least here we don't have to see their dead clothes."

It's getting dark. Gradually the Yard Gard wears off and the mosquitoes start moving in.

"Let's go."

We walk in silence for a while. Then Nomad says, "I'm more freaked out about the clothes. Why would there be all those clothes scattered around?"

"Maybe the guy who killed the deer or whatever had blood all over his clothes after butchering it and just tossed the clothes in there instead of washing them."

"Gross."

"Yeah, well."

"Maybe there's some freak who lives in the woods who sets traps for hikers, and when he catches them, he kills them and throws them in the pit. With a few deer bones for camouflage."

"Shut up! Why do we always start telling these stories when it's getting dark? Let's talk about something nice."

"Like pizza."

"Roast deer meat, yum yum."

"Ugh. Meat. Hurry up, it's going to rain."

"I hope there's someone else at the shelter. Someone normal. Where do you think H2O is?"

"He ought to be catching up to us. And so should Maine Event and those other guys."

"I wonder where they all went. They were right behind us, then they just disappeared. Do you think they could have passed us somehow?"

"Maybe the pit people got them."

It's true, the Trail has been lonely lately. We've seen few of our old friends, but it's starting to feel like there's no one behind us, that we're the last thruhikers of the season, migrating late, like slow geese. Will we make it to Maine in time? I think so. But it will be cold.

"There's a white blaze," Nomad says.

We're home again, on the Trail. We enter the woods with relief. As we climb up the rocky Trail, past occasional views of idyllic-looking farmland, I can see the clouds coming in. Tomorrow it will rain.

To our surprise, H2O is at the shelter when we get there.

"I was sick," he says when we ask him where he's been lately. "I got food poisoning, and I was all alone a couple of shelters back. I had a really high fever and started hallucinating. I kept thinking there was someone in the shelter with me, and I kept yelling at him, asking why he wouldn't go get me some water, but he'd just sit there, and I'd get angrier and angrier. I even cried. Then he'd disappear. I was so dehydrated, I passed out whenever I started to get up. I was really scared. I had this tiny bit of rationality left, and I realized I couldn't walk out, and if I stayed up there, I could die of dehydration."

"What did you do?" Nomad asked.

"I sort of staggered and crawled down to the spring. I kept falling. I drank some water and threw up. I kept drinking little sips, and eventually I could keep it down. I fell asleep and felt better the next day, but hiking lately has been a bitch. I'm kind of uneasy about hiking alone now. I didn't realize it could be that dangerous."

It's unusual to see him so down. Until now, he's been indestructible, cheerful and positive. He's small and thin but one of the most mentally and emotionally strong and balanced men on the Trail.

"I was even thinking of quitting once I got to Massachusetts," he says, "since I'm from there."

"Are you going to?"

"If I quit, I'd just have to go back to work, and I'm not ready for that. I didn't like what I was doing before, but I haven't decided what I want to do next. So I'll stay out here for now. I'm really burned out, though."

"You ought to blue-blaze," Nomad says. "It'll make your hike fun again. When Grace and I started feeling burnt-out back in Virginia, we changed our whole view of the trip. We looked at where the joy was, and it was in that burst of energy you get when you go off on a blue-blaze, all the people you meet, and adventures you never have if you stick to the white. We're having a blast."

He shakes his head. "I see your point. But I want to do the white blazes. I'll have to find a way to make them more fun."

I respect him. He chooses what he wants, but unlike some other hikers, he doesn't judge us for hiking differently.

Two young women show up and set up a tent nearby.

"Are you thruhiking?" I ask.

"I hope so!" one says. We have several moments of confusion until we figure out that she thought I said, "Are you through hiking?" She and her friend have been out for three days. They're already sick of walking.

Just as I predicted yesterday, it's raining today—a cold, steady, hypothermic rain. Like H2O, I'm feeling queasy, with chills and nausea, and don't want to go anywhere. Nomad still has her colored pencils and the paper that Marmalade Cat couldn't convince her to part with, so she's happy to spend the day drawing.

After a few hours, the rain slows. Nomad gets bored with sitting still and goes off without her pack to reconnoiter. I poke around near the shelter; the hiking stick I got back in Pearisburg, Virginia, has grown too short, worn down by grinding on the rocks, and I need a new one. I find a dead maple sapling with just the right size, strength, and straightness, and spend the afternoon cutting it to the right length and peeling off the bark. It's the stick

I've been looking for since the beginning of the Trail: the stick that fits my hand perfectly, as if it knows me.

I write a note on a piece of birch bark:

> This stick was found in Pearisburg, Virginia, and I've carried it for over 800 miles. It's too short for me now, but if it's right for you, take it and enjoy it—it has a lot of good hiking karma in it. Happy trails—Amazin' Grace.

I attach the note to my old stick with a piece of dental floss and leave it in the shelter for someone to find. I hope whoever finds it is a kid, or someone else who's excited by the idea of an 800-mile hiking stick.

I still have the bamboo stick I got when I was with Wade. I could get rid of it anytime and get a new one, but I don't want to. I have to carry it all the way to the end of the Trail. At the end I'll leave it behind: a symbol of something I thought I needed, but that I've walked away from during the trip. And I'll keep the new stick, the one I found and cut myself, the one that knows my hand, to represent all the new things I've gained.

The water source here is a brook flowing from a swamp, supplemented by springs. I get water and see, in the brook, the mysterious swirling places where the water bubbles up. The woods are very quiet today: no birds, nothing moving. I touch the water; it feels like a baptism, though into what I'm not sure.

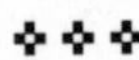

Nomad's boyfriend, Ian, is coming for a visit. He'll meet us in Salisbury, the next town, and there's some question about whether he'll hike the rest of the way to Maine with us, or whether she may even go home with him after he hikes with us for a few days. I hope she doesn't. If she does go home, the end of my trip will be like a mirror image of the beginning—

walking alone. She's so much fun; I'll really miss her company if she leaves.

Salisbury, like many towns in New England, is too wealthy for hikers. There's no place where we can afford to spend the night, and no restaurant we can afford to eat in, even if they did let us in with our hiking clothes. And there's no legal place to camp, but this is hardly an obstacle.

As soon as twilight comes we go behind the library, where it's dark and secluded, enclosed by bushes, out of sight of the road, and set up our sleeping mats and bags on the grass. The lawn is clean, green, and flat, the best campsite in the world, and across the road is a public spring where water flows endlessly into a stone basin. According to locals, the water is clean, tested, and reliable, and, indeed, a steady stream of people in cars stop there to fill up jug after jug.

Ian shows up about midnight, with two friends who are dropping him off. They set up next to us.

It's a peaceful spot. Katydids sing in the old trees overhead, cars slide past on the road in front of the library. We talk, just small talk about their trip and ours. I feel completely content, right at home.

The library clock, in a tower over our heads, bongs ponderously: midnight.

The clock will ring every hour, I tell the watchful part of myself. *You don't have to wake up. You only have to wake up if there's an animal in your food, in your pack, or within two feet of your head, or if strangers are near. Got that?*

Got it.

The grass is soft. Ian and Nomad whisper together, then sleep. The two friends are still awake, and I fall asleep to the murmur of their voices.

On the way out of town we pass the Salisbury graveyard and wander in to look at the stones. Ian and Nomad disappear; they haven't seen each other in a while and have a lot of catching up to do. Although it's early, it's already hot, sweltering, and none of us is in a hurry to hike, although the later we wait, the hotter the day gets. I drink green Gatorade, walk among the stones, and read:

SARAH NORTON DIED SEPT. 3, 1904
AGED 64 YEARS
SHE HATH DONE WHAT SHE COULD.

This inscription has a faintly mocking and exasperated tone, as if this is something Sarah said too often in life when her family disappointed her, so in revenge they put it on her tombstone: "Well, I've done what I could. If you want to go out without gloves, let it be on your head." "I've done what I could—if you never get married, don't blame me."

I walk farther, and read:

THE TRUMPET SHALL SOUND
AND THE DEAD SHALL WAKE

The third line is obliterated, and the fourth line can't be what it looks like:

BUT NEVER AGAIN MY BED I SHALL MAKE.

My father's grave, on a hillside in upstate New York, is a quiet place. There's no poem on his headstone, just an engraving of a mountain scene showing a cabin set among forested slopes, and his name. My mother and I visit periodically to plant flowers, eat a picnic, and reminisce. I've had some stormy years with her, but in this we're united. It's a bond, going there, digging in the dirt, removing weeds, planting flowers; even if we don't talk at all, the work and our memories unite us.

We finally get around to hiking, just three miles up the humid hillside to Riga Shelter. It's only the middle of August, but the woods have begun to smell and look like fall. All around are oak trees, and the fat acorns fall and smack into the metal roof of the shelter with a heavy *whock!* that makes me jump.

I'm alone in the shelter; Nomad and Ian are tenting nearby. It's peaceful, with a beautiful view of farms and fields, and I stretch out, lying so I can see night come down over the valley.

Whock!

I set my night alarm: *You don't have to wake up when you hear that,* I tell the "noise sentinel" part of myself. *Animals near your head or in your food or gear, or strangers nearby, are what matters. You can sleep through everything else.*

Peace. I'm feeling it. There are few things more restful than sitting on a mountaintop and seeing black dots of cattle on a green field slowly coalesce and disperse. Like watching fish in a tank, but much slower. Faster than clouds, slower than fish.

"Thanks, Gladys," I say out loud.

The trees rustle and hush. I plan to lie here and look at stars, but after I see the first one, I'm asleep.

I hike alone the next day, for the first time since Nomad and I began hiking together. Nomad and Ian are having a reunion honeymoon, with lots of giggling and kissing, and they need time alone.

It's a treat to be alone again. I feel free, spacious, relaxed, at peace.

Someone has left a bag of apples at the Connecticut/Massachusetts state line, and a note:

> Thruhikers: Help yourself to the apples.
> —AMC Ridgerunners

There's only one apple left. I take it, leave a note saying thanks, and walk on. Fresh fruit is the most delicious treat on the Trail, because it's too heavy to carry. The apple's flavor mingles with the pine scent in Sages Ravine, a dark hollow with big trees and a series of clear pools connected by cascades.

On the cliff along the spine of Race Mountain, I stop and sit, admiring the view, eat a big snack, and write in my journal. It's breezy up here, no bugs, with the trees rustling for miles below, making a waterfall sound.

I came out here because I wanted my life to change, and by now I have some ideas about what I want to change. I want to go home and get rid of things. According to my friends, I owned almost nothing when I left for the Trail, but now I'm thinking, *What's all that stuff in storage at Mom's? Who needs it?* The first thing I'll do is get rid of it.

I'll go back to Wisconsin, where I have friends, and stay there for a while, transitioning back to civilization, readjusting. Then I'll move elsewhere. Where, I'm not sure, but I feel changes coming.

In the meantime, I'll cross-country ski, walk, or run every day. I'll live near water, in a place with a wood stove. I'll enjoy times with friends, and I'll write. Every day.

I think about Gladys, this Trail goddess we've invented, and all the stories we've told about her, all the treats she's supposedly provided. How mysterious it is. You need something and it appears. A candy bar. An apple. A pen. A friend.

The Trail is like a river, and if you swim with the current, everything seems easy. There's a flow to life out here, a sense of connection, of convergences. Things come to you, or you come to them. It reminds me of canoeing with my dad when I was young, and him teaching me to read the river, to know where the rocks are, and the smooth passages through them, even if you can't see them. How to tell from the surface what deeper things there are, beyond what you can see. How to move, seamlessly, easily.

Finally, on this trip, I'm moving with the current, not even reading the river, not having to—just one with it.

I've spent a lot of time on this trip thinking about what I don't want: I don't want to go back to some meaningless job, I don't want to ever be involved in a wrong relationship with anyone, I don't want this, I don't want that. From now on, I decide, I'll drop these negatives and think about the kind of life I do want.

I want to do what I love—write. I want to make enough money doing it to live a simple, peaceful life in a beautiful place. I want love, connection, spiritual kinship with a good partner. I want to be as happy and whole off the Trail as I am on it. It does no good to go on a pilgrimage if you can't carry it home inside you. I want to carry it home.

Coincidences, convergences. Trail magic. Gladys. It would be funny if I ever ran into anyone who was actually named that, out here on the Trail. It would be the ultimate Trail magic, the ultimate synchronicity, some kind of sign that I really will carry it home, that all these dreams are true.

I close my notebook, put it in my pack, hoist the pack, and start walking, balancing on the rocks and cliffs, admiring the view, as the day grows warmer.

A few miles later I'm heading up the dry, rocky south slope of Mount Everett. Above me, two hikers are on their way down: a man and a woman, dayhikers with small packs. The man is stocky, dark haired; the woman is small and strong but feminine-looking, with a mass of reddish-brown curls.

"Hi," I say. "How's your hike going?"

"Great," the woman says. "We're just out for the day. Are you going far?"

"Yeah," I say, "to Maine."

She lights up. "We were just talking about that! About how there are people who hike the whole Trail, and we were wondering if we'd meet any. That's so cool, that you're a woman."

She has a deep, sultry voice with a hint of an exotic accent. I wonder where she's from. Her eyes are a deep, rich, warm brown, like mahogany. I stare at her, and it feels strange, as if I'm falling into her, as if I can see all the way inside her. She looks away, embarrassed, but immediately looks back at me. We stare some more. I have a feeling of deep kinship and recognition, as if we've met before: She's one of my tribe, whatever that tribe may be.

"Yeah," the man says, "and I was just telling Gladys here that we might not meet any, because—"

"Your name is Gladys? Your name is *Gladys*?! No way! I can't believe this! This is so weird!"

Before they can say anything, I babble out the whole story, about Trail magic, about all the coincidences and gifts, about how we've been making up stories about a Trail spirit named Gladys for hundreds of miles, about how I had just been up on a cliff thinking how mysterious and funny it would be if I met someone with that name on the Trail, how it would be a sign about the whole future of my life and happiness. Amazingly, they believe me.

"Where are you from?" I ask Gladys.

"New York."

"No, before that, where were you from? You have an interesting accent."

"See if you can guess."

I study her. She has gold earrings on, little cascades of dangles among her curls. They look familiar: I saw earrings like that in college, when I spent a year abroad studying in Egypt. Her accent is familiar too, but she looks more European than Arab; her hair and eyes are light, and her skin is very fair. And then there's her name: Who ever heard of an Arab named Gladys?

"You're from the Middle East," I say.

"Wow! No one's ever guessed before. They always think I'm Hungarian or Israeli or Russian. I'm Lebanese."

She tells me how her family came over here when she was a teenager, to escape the war in Beirut, and how she lives in New York now; she's a doctor. She and her hiking friend, Michael, work together and just came up here for the day. I wonder if they're involved, but they seem more like friends. For some reason, too, she seems like she would love to camp overnight, whereas he seems like he would only dayhike. *Forget about him! Come camping with me!* I wish I could say.

"I'd love to hike the Trail, like you're doing," she says. "Have you hiked other parts of it, besides this?"

"No, this is the first time I've ever been on it!"

"You've never been on the Trail before, you live five hours away in New York, and you just randomly ended up on this piece of Trail? Why didn't you hike closer to home?"

"I don't know. Michael was here before, and he told me it was beautiful, and I've been meaning to hike up here for years but never got around to it until this weekend. We just came up here on a whim."

I shake my head, and so does she. I feel like laughing, as if the universe has just played a big trick on me and somewhere all the animals and trees are laughing. In civilization this meeting would amaze me even more, but in the context of the Trail, it seems almost normal or inevitable.

I get her to write her address and phone number in my journal, then give her my mother's address on a piece of paper. "If you ever want to know about the Trail or get hiking advice or just talk, give me a call," I say. "I should be back in civilization by the end of October, and I don't know where I'll be living, but you can reach me through my mom."

We talk for about 20 minutes, standing on the mountainside. I take her picture; she smiles at the camera as if she knows me, as if we're both up to something. Whole encyclopedias of information are flowing between us, without words. It's like I know all about her without even asking. I know we'll meet again; we'll always be friends.

Big clouds are building in the hot, humid sky. "We'd better get going," she says. "There are supposed to be big dangerous storms this afternoon, and we have to get back to our car. Sixty-mile-an-hour winds and hail, I heard. Be careful."

I look at the sky. "It won't rain until really late, like midnight. You'll be fine."

"How do you know?" Gladys asks.

"I just know. I look at the sky a lot, walking out here. You just get to know after a while, from experience."

We talk some more. Finally, we both have to go. It's easy to say goodbye, because I know we'll meet again.

"Have a great hike—I'll get in touch with you afterward," she says.

"I'll send you a card when I get to Maine, and let you know how the hike went."

They go on down the mountain, and I go up happily, heading for the summit.

Yes, I think, *and thank you. I'll carry these gifts home from the Trail, I know.*

No one else is at Glen Brook Shelter, which is in a pine grove, fragrant and carpeted with needles. There's a stream nearby and I go over to it, to a secluded pool, and get water to wash with. The water is cold and clean, and there's a mat of soft moss to stand on while I dry myself with my bandanna.

The afternoon sun slants down through the trees, touching the trunks with gold, highlighting needles, making some spots look special, as if, when you stand there, you'll be filled with light.

When I go back to the shelter, Nomad and Ian are there. "Hey, how was your hike?" Nomad asks.

"Great! I met Gladys!"

She stares at me as if I said I've just met Elvis. "Who?"

"Gladys." I tell her the story and show her Gladys's handwritten address in my journal.

"Well, damn, we missed her! What a rip-off. We had a great hike, though. What a great day."

Big storms come in around midnight, soaking the ground. Hailstones fall on the metal shelter roof like thousands of acorns striking at terminal velocity. The wind blows sideways, bringing in waves of rain. I get up and tie my tarp across the entrance, and so does another hiker, so we're sealed in. Tomorrow, when the front passes, it will be cool and clear.

Lightning flashes, and I think about Gladys: if the storm will reach her in New York and if she'll remember our conversation about it. Where is she tonight? I know I'll see her after the Trail. Meeting her was more than a coincidence, and when I get back to civilization I'll find out why it happened, why I knew her name, why we felt such kinship and connection, standing there on the mountainside, looking into each other's eyes as if we've known each other a lifetime.

August 17
Great Barrington, Mass.

CHAPTER NINE

In a Mexican restaurant in Great Barrington, Massachusetts, Nomad and Ian and I eat burrito after burrito and wonder how we'll get back to the Trail, and if we don't, where we can sleep without being caught by the police. We were lucky to get a hitch into town from a man who does volunteer maintenance on the Trail. Now it's getting dark, and it doesn't seem likely that we'll get a ride back to the woods tonight. Great Barrington is a town of expensive black cars, antique shops, and country club members. These people don't usually let dirty hikers into their lives or onto the leather seats of their fine automobiles.

A couple comes in and sits at the next table. The man is wearing pastel plaid seersucker pants, loafers without socks, and a knit shirt with a small logo on the pocket. The woman is carrying one of those hideous vinyl-looking Louis Vuitton purses that cost several hundred dollars, has an extremely fussy hairdo, and is wearing a sleeveless shell dress and pearls. She gives us a long, disapproving stare.

"Betcha they won't give us a ride," Nomad says. We start laughing. The people are caricatures of themselves. I get out my camera and hold it in my lap.

"What are you doing?" Nomad asks.

"Taking a picture."

"They'll see you!"

"So? Besides, they won't. They're the kind of people who think it's unseemly to notice anything."

I raise the camera, focus, and take a great point-blank shot of the two of them over wine. They don't even blink.

"I'm going to call this photo 'The Kind of People Who Don't Give You Rides in Great Barrington.' "

We leave and start hitching. No one stops. Most of the drivers avert their eyes, as if even seeing us will taint them. The man who gave us a ride into town said he has a friend who owns a greenhouse near the Trail and if we get desperate we can sleep there.

As we walk, we calculate how far it is to the greenhouse and the Trail: at least seven miles. We passed a graveyard on the way to the restaurant and it's not far, maybe a couple of miles. We can always sleep there. So far, I've been unsuccessful in convincing other hikers that graveyards are ideal in-town illicit campsites: They're secluded, full of flat sleeping areas, often have faucets providing clean water, and are usually safe from curious locals, since no one goes there after dark. Maybe this will be my chance.

Loud, head-banging music cascades out of a run-down building as we pass.

"Hey, let's go in here," Nomad says. "I have an idea."

It's a skateboarding place. Inside, teenagers in black T-shirts pendulum up and down on a huge U-shaped wooden track. The music and the thunder of their wheels are so loud that Nomad has to shout as she schmoozes the owner, who would be happy to give us a ride except he can't leave the store. Most of the customers are too young to drive or have paid for an hour or more of time on the track. No one is leaving soon.

"Nice try," I say as we leave. "It was a good idea."

More teenagers drive by in a BMW. Nomad waves, and they pull over. "Need a ride?"

They're a girl and two guys, dressed in black, wearing spiked collars and wristbands, decked with heavy chains. The girl is strikingly beautiful; her face, as serene and perfect as a Renaissance Madonna's, glows in its setting of black leather. She has a wreath of daisies in her hair, and she's clearly in charge.

"We're giving these people a ride. Dog, get in the backseat. Move that stuff over. Just kick it around, I don't care if you put your feet on it. Brian, take her pack and put it in the trunk, then get up front. Dog, move over."

She turns and looks at us, crammed into the backseat with Nomad's pack across our laps and Dog, who needs a bath as much as we do, next to us. "Where are you guys going?"

We tell her. As she drives, Nomad asks how they like living here.

"It's a shithole. Nothing to do. Picking up you guys is like the high point of our whole summer. There's nothing here but rich assholes."

Nomad asks if they have any dreams, if they know what they want to do when they get out of here. No one has any idea. No one cares. They're all going to expensive colleges in the fall because their parents insist on it and their parents will pay for it. It's a way to get out of town. They have no idea what they'll do when they get there, and don't care.

"We'll probably meet more rich assholes. They're everywhere."

They drop us off at the greenhouse, and I take their picture. They slouch, not looking at the camera, resplendent in their chains.

"I'm going to mount this next to the last photo," I say.

"What's this one going to be called?"

"'The Kind of People Who *Do* Give You Rides in Great Barrington.'"

Nomad is annoyed by their boredom, their aimlessness, the waste of their wealth, since they don't appreciate it and aren't using it or their time wisely. I grew up in a wealthy suburb and know them well. They're exactly like many of the kids in my high school. I was lucky: My parents, especially my dad, spent a lot of time with me, taught me self-reliance, and enjoyed my company. You can tell that these kids' parents don't know what to do with them and throw *things* at them—nice cars, expensive clothes—instead of time. I think of Vampire, the "poor little rich girl" back in North Carolina, who did anything she could for attention, good or bad. She was an extreme example but not an isolated one. If rich assholes are everywhere, so are their confused and dispossessed kids.

The greenhouse is at the edge of a swamp, and it's not enclosed. Clouds of mosquitoes swirl in through the open windows and doors; going to the bathroom involves running into the weedy wasteland out back, behind piles of muddy buckets, old plastic plant flats, and random lumber—and a lot of jumping and fanning.

Nomad and Ian set up their tent on the ground in the greenhouse and get in to escape the bugs. I go into the next room and set up my sleeping bag and bug net on a long trestle table, between flats of flowers, and get into it immediately, although I'm not yet tired. The whole place has that green, exotic, blossomy smell you only find at flower stores and funerals. Through the glass overhead, stars gleam. It's peaceful, spacious, and fun to be here, sleeping in a greenhouse—the kind of thing any adventurous kid would love. I wonder if it's too late for the Madonna in the car and her two friends to find this feeling. I hope not. They're bored, jaded, asleep. Hopefully someday they'll escape, and awake.

I look at the darkening sky through the glass of the roof and think about how this town, which is an adventure to us, is the most boring place in the world to the kids who live here. I wonder how many places I've driven by at home that would have been interesting if only I'd come from somewhere else. It makes me want to go back to my own hometown, sleep in the graveyard, pee behind the greenhouse, set up an illegal campsite behind the library, and talk to every stranger I meet.

Ian decides to go home, and his friends pick him up. Nomad and I return to the Trail. At Mount Wilcox North Shelter, we meet Kankakee and Speedy Slug, two hikers Nomad knows but hasn't seen since Tennessee. We all fill each other in on Trail gossip—who's ahead, who's behind, who's gone home.

"Did you guys know that guy Popsicle?" Speedy Slug asks. "The mooch? He borrowed 10 bucks from me, and I never saw him again. Anyway, I heard he showed up at a shelter in Delaware Water Gap and there were about eight hikers in it and it was raining. You know how when it's raining people try to make room even if it's crowded? Well, he had ripped off every single hiker there somewhere on the Trail. Like he borrowed money, or smoked someone's weed, or whatever, and never paid them back. So he walked up to the shelter at night, in the rain, and they were all like, 'Get lost, man, go sleep in the woods, you parasite, you loser, you're not a hiker, you're a mooch.' And I heard after that he left the Trail."

He tells me that GI Joe, whom I last saw in Georgia with blisters covering the entire soles of his feet, spent a week in the hospital, got back on the Trail, and is now somewhere ahead of us. I hope he makes it.

Chocolate Chip is long gone: The word is that he left after his run-in with me in Pearisburg.

Speedy Slug tells us the names of more hikers who are gone, and we tell him what we've heard. None of us knows if there are any more hikers walking behind us; unless someone catches up to us, we have no way of finding out about them. It's a strange feeling, this apparent void behind us, the fear that we may be the last hikers of the year.

Kankakee says, "I hate these people you run into in towns who go, 'Gee, you're walking pretty slow. Most of the hikers have been through already. You're not gonna make it to Maine before the snow.' What the hell do they know? They won't even walk a block from their car to the store. Actually, I don't hate them. I've walked too far for that. But I really hate it when they *say* that. Like, why not be encouraging?"

I think we'll all make it to Katahdin before October 15, as long as there are no more major delays, like sickness or bad weather. We just have to walk steadily, with not many days off.

Speedy Slug and I discuss books, and then I spend a long time trying to retrieve my flashlight, which has fallen through the wide cracks between the boards of the shelter floor. The floor is full of big holes chewed by porcupines, who like the taste of wood seasoned with salty hiker sweat. After unsuccessfully trying to hook the light with a stick, I put my arm in a hole and feel around down there, hoping the porcupines are elsewhere, and finally find the light.

Nomad and I get out our map and study the terrain, looking for alternative routes. There's an interesting possibility: If we hike down to Hop Creek, we can then bushwhack across a meadow, reach a country road, and have a pleasant four-mile hike up to Upper Goose Pond. The shelter there is actually an enclosed cabin, complete with bunk beds, a kitchen, and a canoe that hikers can use. If we take the shortcut we can spend the afternoon lounging around, canoeing, and looking at the view, instead of hiking, sweating, and getting there late in the day, too late to enjoy anything.

The hike down to the creek is easy, but the meadow—which looked so innocent and easy to traverse on the map and from the mountainside above (we imagined the scene from *The Sound of Music,* with us running gloriously through grass and flowers)—is filled with thorny briars, stinging nettles, and cleavers, a plant covered with recurved spines that scratch as viciously as an angry cat. The plants grow far over our heads, so densely that once we've wormed our way into the meadow, we can lean sideways and not fall down; to go forward, we grunt and lunge like linebackers, taking turns going first, getting a brief running start and breaking the tangles with the combined weight of our bodies and our packs.

"Which way are we going?" Nomad asks.

"I don't know. Lemme check my compass. OK, we want to go north. It's that way."

Sweat, mingled with blood, runs down our legs and arms. As we rip our way forward, a bramble bush tears the sleeping bag off my pack, and I crawl back, reclaim it, and tie it back on. Somewhere in the meadow, to this day, is a pink bandanna the briars tore off my head and never returned.

"This was a bad idea," Nomad says.

"You're right." By this time I'm so whipped, scratched, and stung, my skin so overstimulated with pain, that I'm trembling uncontrollably. Nomad's legs and arms are a mass of long thin cuts. We can't sit down and rest, because the ground under us is swampy.

We lean on the springy, spiny, stinging wall of plants and consider our situation.

"Well, it's too late to go back," Nomad says. "We must be halfway across by now, and if we go back, it'll be the same amount of work, because all the plants behind us have closed up, so it's not like it'll be easier to backtrack. Besides, then we'd still have to hike all that way on the Trail."

"I vote to keep going," I say.

"Me too."

We push on, swearing, and distract ourselves by fantasizing about our afternoon. I'll put up my hammock and rest, we'll take out the canoe, we'll make the best dinner in our food bags, we'll sleep on soft beds. We'll write in our journals and read whatever half-books other hikers have left at the cabin. If we keep going, we might get time for these pleasures; if we turn back, we definitely won't.

We go on. There seems to be a clearing coming up; we can see a piece of sky. Is it the road we're heading for? We don't hear any cars.

It's a river, which isn't on the map. We stare at it in dismay, although we're relieved to be temporarily free of the whips and thorns. We'll have to ford it.

The water is muddy and comes up to our waists, and as we cross we sink deep into the ooze at the bottom. The cool water feels wonderful on my scratches and cuts. On the other side the bank is six feet high, so we flounder around in the mud and slog downstream for a while until we find a place where it's possible to take off our packs and hurl them up onto the bank, then struggle up and out.

On the other side, the dense thorns and masses of stinging plants continue. We push and swear our way through, walking backward and letting our packs take the worst of it. Finally, we come to a track, worn by vehicles, where the nettle thickets are crushed down.

"Let's follow it. If trucks were here, it has to lead to a road."

It does. We sit at the side of the road, dazed and still trembling from our endorphin overdose, and eat dried bananas and energy bars. It's so peaceful here, in the yard of someone's expensive vacation home. They probably have no idea what a hell exists in their very own backyard. Or maybe they do know, and they count on it to keep out lazy, shortcutting hikers.

We consult the map and turn right on the road, looking for another dirt road that leads up toward the lake and the cabin.

"Turn left at the yellow house," a woman working in a nearby yard says. "Don't mind the dogs. They won't hurt you."

This is usually what people say right before their dogs sink their teeth into you. Warily, we spot the yellow house and turn left onto the dirt road. The dogs are in the house, and they leap and slaver at the windows, but we resist making faces at them and walk on. The washed-out dirt road, marked with ghost blazes that show that it was once the official Trail (Ha! Take that, white-blazers!), is pleasant after our ordeal in the meadow, and as we walk several miles up the mountain we fantasize out loud about how wonderful it will be to swim in the pond, take the canoe out, and rest for the afternoon.

At the top of the mountain, the road is paved and leads past large houses on a beautiful lake. Lower Goose Pond. According to the map, this road leads east along the edge of the pond, then dwindles to a trail that crosses a narrow channel between Lower and Upper Goose Ponds and leads to the cabin, which is on the upper pond.

We follow the road around the pond, which is huge, actually a lake. We're almost there.

The channel is too deep to ford—over our heads. We go in as deep as we can, and spend some time standing there in water up to our shoulders, balancing our packs on our heads and discussing our options.

"We could leave our packs on this side, swim over, walk to the hiker cabin, get the canoe, paddle back around the point and into this channel, get the packs, and canoe back to the cabin," I say.

"Good plan."

We hear the soft splash of a paddle in the water. A man in a canoe is coming down the channel toward us. When he sees us he stops, backpaddling.

"Hi! You startled me. I canoe this stretch every afternoon, and I've never yet seen anyone standing there. It was a sudden vertical in an expanse that's usually all horizontal. What are you doing?"

We explain about the Trail, our trek from Georgia to Maine, and our ill-fated blue-blaze.

"We're trying to ford here, but it's too deep for us to get across without getting everything we own soaking wet. Hey, could you ferry our packs across for us? We can swim over and meet you on the other side."

"Why don't you just get in, and I'll take you *and* your packs. You're going to that hiker cabin on the other lake, aren't you? I'll take you right to it."

"Thanks!"

I take his photo, and he says, "Do you have any paper?"

I get out my journal. He takes it and draws a quick, perfect sketch of the two of us standing in the water, then introduces himself. He's an artist and lives on the lower lake, and he and his wife are having a barbecue that evening. "Why don't you come? We'd love to have you. It will be just what the party needs.

"Everyone else is city people," he explains. "They'll love to hear about your adventure. They're mostly musicians and artists, and some of their patrons. City people. You're just what we need."

Nomad shoots me a look. I know what she's thinking. This man has to be rich to live up here. Maybe he's somebody famous. When we get back to civilization, we'll have to look him up. The little sketch in my journal is probably priceless.

"We have plenty of food. Lots of steak, marinated portabello mushrooms, corn, salad, and beer. Is that all right? Come around 7. I can pick you up in the canoe. There's no way to walk there from the hiker cabin because there's too much private land in the way."

"The cabin has a canoe—we can take that."

He gives us directions to his house. We're jubilant. What an adventure! We're going to the millionaires' barbecue. Steak! Corn! Marinated mushrooms! Music! Interesting people! What will we wear?

He paddles us over to the cabin, and as we arrive, someone says, "Hey, blue-blazers!"

"Not blue-blazers," Nomad says, "*aqua*-blazers, since we came across the water. And we're going to a party!"

We swim in the lake in lieu of a bath and wear our "dry" clothes, because that's all we have, and they're relatively clean, although not pristine. There's nothing we can do about all the slashes on our arms and legs, but we figure they make us look more rugged.

The other hikers, gathered at the cabin, grumble at our luck. Steak and beer! Some people have all the luck! It doesn't help that our luck is (as usual) the result of blue-blazing.

At the appointed hour, Speedy Slug and Kankakee give us a ride to the party. They want to use the canoe, and if we take it for the evening they can't, so they'll drop us off and come back later.

The food at the party lives up to our expectations—delicious and plentiful. The other guests are named things like Biff and Kip and talk about their children's boarding schools, about summers on Martha's Vineyard, investment opportunities, and music. One woman is an artist from the Southwest, and several others are musicians from Tanglewood. They all ask about the trip, and we tell them stories about lightning and bears, about sleeping on porches and in feed sheds, about Southern hospitality and our night in the monastery. I feel grateful for my life, for its invisible wealth of experience.

After supper one of the musicians gets out her cello, and we all sit on the deck, facing out over the starry lake, while she plays. The music drifts out over the water, mingled with the sound of waves, the light rustle of wind. Our "taxi" arrives—the two guys in the canoe—and they stay for music and a beer, until eventually we all have to leave. It's late, and we have to get up early.

We paddle home, using the stars to guide our way to the channel that leads to the other lake, where the hiker cabin is. The music follows us, curving across the water, lifting up to starry space, and a vast sweep of stars is reflected in the lake, as if we're canoeing across the sky.

I dip my hands into the water, wet my face, and look out at the humped hills, the stars marking the way.

"Home," someone says, when we see a candle lantern shining through the trees up ahead. "There's the cabin. We're almost home."

At dawn, while everyone's still asleep, I get up and skinny-dip in the pond. The water is very cold and clear; on the bottom is a tumble of polished glacial boulders, fish nibbling at my toes—that funny dull-edged bite, like someone gumming you. It's so calm that every tree is reflected in the water; a small island in the middle is doubled, upside down. The water is soft and caressing, and I swim, feeling free.

Later, Nomad and I hike past more lakes, through dense woods. We pass a southbound hiker, who's thin and ill-looking.

"I got giardia," he says. "It's hell. I got medicine, but it's taking a while to work. Don't ever drink unfiltered water. You'll be sorry."

He's the first hiker I've met who has giardia, though I've heard of others. This disease, which one can get from drinking untreated water, results in horrendous diarrhea. I think I must be immune, but you never know. We have water from the spring at Upper Goose Pond, but all the other water we've seen today is mud or swamp and doesn't look very appetizing, even if it's filtered. My filter is, once again, broken, so all we have to purify the water is iodine, which doesn't change the appearance of the water, it just kills the cooties—so you still drink brown sludge. It's clean brown sludge, but not very appetizing. We decide to wait and see if we can find a clearer source.

We walk contentedly. "Do you think there's anyone behind us anymore?" Nomad asks, reviving the topic we all discussed back at Mount Wilcox North Shelter. "Are we the last hikers of the year?"

"I think we're the last women, anyway," I say.

We talk about how nice it would be to run into other women hikers and hike with them.

"Maybe someone will catch up," Nomad says. "Hey, Gladys!" she calls out. "We could use some girl power out here, please!"

A bear crashes across the Trail just ahead of us, in a hurry to get somewhere. I only hear it, but Nomad sees it, and she says it's big. We walk more warily for a while. The woods smell like fall, mingled with the last green flush of summer: fruity scent of berries, rich musk of rotting leaves, mixed with a green tang of grass.

We come to a road and decide to walk on it for a while. We pass a sign that says:

ANGER

ROAD CLOSED

We laugh at it: It's like a road sign for a bad relationship.

Our water is gone; we're thirsty and need more. According to hiker lore, the "Cookie Lady" lives on this road, and hands out cookies to hikers who pass. Maybe she'll give us water.

She's not home, but her husband is. We find him splitting wood, and he's happy to stop and chat. They have a blueberry farm, but he's also an inventor and a pilot, with his own private grass airstrip out back. Their house is heated completely with solar and wood energy. His mailbox, which he made, looks like an airplane.

Their two Siamese cats wind in and out through our ankles as we fill up with water and listen to him talk about his experiences as a pilot. By the time we leave, it's late afternoon, and it's still 12 miles to Dalton, where we're headed. We walk along the road, and when we hear a car purring along behind us, our thumbs fly up in unison.

"It's a VW van," Nomad says jubilantly, watching it approach. "Hippie time. I bet you a million dollars this guy stops."

Sure enough, the guy stops. He drops us off in Dalton, at the home of a man who lets hikers tent in his yard. Several other hikers are there: a guy named Ishmael; Blister, whom I haven't seen since Waynesboro, Virginia; her friend Anna Banana; Anna Banana's dog, Alice B. Toklas; and H2O.

I thought we would simply sleep in the Trail angel's yard, but within minutes of our arrival he brings out a huge vat of chili, and pasta, cheese, bread, fresh tomatoes, cola, ice water, and pickles. It's a great kindness, and he doesn't have to do it.

We eat and talk. I ask Blister what happened to her friend Red Hot.

"Red Hot went home," Blister says. "She got really sick of hiking, but she said she knew how much it meant to me, and she totally supports the idea of me finishing. She's gonna come up to Maine and pick me up at Katahdin, and we're gonna drive home together."

Anna Banana, a friend of Blister and Red Hot's, came up with her dog and met Blister on the Trail, and they've been hiking together ever since. Anna Banana is a small, boyish-looking woman. She punches me and Nomad in the arm and says, "Hey, there!"

Blister has changed since I last saw her in Virginia. Back then she was tense and angry, and I never saw her smile. Now she's relaxed, open, happier.

We decide to hike together for a while: four women and a dog.

"Gladys comes through again," Nomad says. "More Trail magic. Just ask and it comes. You want to hike with women? You get to hike with women."

❖❖❖

We hike slowly, steadily, keeping an even pace, heading up Mount Greylock, the tallest mountain in Massachusetts. There's a meditative space and peace about this; we're in no hurry, we'll be going up for eight miles, for most of the day. We walk through fields of yellow flowers, through pastures, and gradually enter the balsamy woods, carpeted with needles. There's a loose group of us, strung out up the mountainside: me, Nomad, Blister, Anna Banana and her dog, H2O, Ishmael, and a guy named Happy Hatter. Through the day we lose each other, then catch up, then lose each other again, stop for breaks, and greet the hikers catching up from behind.

We zigzag up and up, pacing along the switchbacks. It's occasionally steep, mostly steady, easy to enjoy. Birch trees lean over the path, and there are sheets of birch paper on the ground. I pick them up to write letters home on later. The earth is deep black, boggy, balsam needles embedded in the mud.

As we approach the top of the mountain, it grows dark. Clouds roll in, and I feel thunder in my bones. When we reach a place where a tree has fallen, opening a view to the sky, we see the storm coming fast.

We move faster, hurrying. There's a stone lodge on top of the mountain, and if we hurry maybe we can reach it before the storm.

We make it, running inside just as lightning hits the tower on top of the mountain. We stand in the lobby, looking out the wide windows at the clouds, still breathing hard from running the last few hundred yards.

We were planning to hike up and over the mountain, not stay here, but the longer the storm goes on and the more we sit in the comfortable lobby chairs, the less inclined we are to move. We make a deal with the staff: If we help with their work, we'll only have to pay a few dollars to stay in the lodge, and we'll get supper and breakfast too.

Anna Banana's dog isn't allowed in the lodge, and Anna Banana doesn't want to leave her outside alone, so when the storm passes she takes the dog and heads for the nearest shelter, three miles away. We'll meet her there tomorrow.

We go to the kitchen and get a snack—leftover stew, bread, and salad—take showers, and begin working. Nomad does laundry—washing the paying guests' sheets—and I set the tables in the dining room for the 36 guests who will be here for dinner. The staff, called "the croo," are all college-age, friendly and energetic, and as we work they blast music, mostly tunes from the '70s.

I sweep the dining room floor, wipe the tables, set out the chairs, put out plates, cups, bowls, salt, and pepper, and fill pitchers with water. The tables and chairs are all wooden, all cheerfully mismatched and slightly rickety; the plates are heavy, white, and sometimes chipped, and the silverware is industrial stainless steel. The lodge is for outdoor people and has a carefree, casual, rugged air, much more pleasant than being in a place where everything is perfectly matched.

During dinner all the guests file in, the croo blasts Beethoven's Ninth, and we all eat mountains of turkey, mashed potatoes and gravy, salad, and bread. Someone's baby screams and bangs a bottle on the table, everyone shouts to be heard over the music, and a croo member, Badger, comes out and sits at our table with his girlfriend. They flirt, and you can tell from the conversation that they haven't known each other long:

"You always have food jobs. How come you always get the cushy food jobs? You had that job in Cheshire, right? The one where you never had to work?"

"Well, yeah, tell me about *your* jobs. That one where you were working in the camera store, and the manager was never there. You didn't have to work much there, now did you? You just sat around looking pretty. Like you are now."

The next morning, it's a steep, rocky, slippery downhill to Wilbur Clearing Shelter. Anna Banana isn't there, although she signed her name in the shelter log.

I eat snacks and wait for Nomad and Blister. You can tell we're in New England; instead of the usual scrawled-in-charcoal shelter graffiti about "Troop 206 was here" or "I miss you Patty," this shelter has graffiti that says:

YALE SUCKS

Underneath, someone else has added:

AMHERST SWALLOWS

Nomad and Blister catch up, and Blister is annoyed that Anna Banana has walked on without leaving a note telling where we're supposed to meet her. "She's playing some kind of game," Blister says. "I bet she's mad we stayed in the lodge without her."

We go down, down, down, through balsam woods, through black mud, and after this long downhill, get to the town of North Adams, stop for pizza, then hike on. Now we're going uphill again, and I get into a very calm state, just flowing along, probably high on endorphins after the knee-killing descent down Mount Greylock.

After 11 miles, we cross the Vermont border—another state!—and two miles later, reach Seth Warner Shelter, footsore and tired. It's very quiet and peaceful here. H2O was here and left a hello in the log for all of us. Anna Banana was also here and left another note in the logbook saying she has gone on to the next shelter, which annoys Blister again.

Happy Hatter and Ishmael eventually show up, and set up tents behind the shelter. They make a fire, and the purr of the flames is soothing. Owls sing back and forth. It's cold, the first night since spring that I wear long underwear and a scarf over my head to sleep. I sink deep into my sleeping bag, light my candle lantern, and read the shelter logbook.

My friend Elizabeth from D.C. was here earlier in the summer, and I find her entry in the log. It's comforting to see evidence of someone I know from the outside world. It makes this trip seem more real, not just the dream it sometimes feels like.

After resupplying in Bennington, we head for Goddard Shelter on Glastonbury Mountain. Anna Banana is with us again—she and Blister have reconciled.

We hike through the humid afternoon as clouds pile up overhead. Between birch and balsam boughs, dark gray billows of clouds rise. The wind sweeps in and thunder rumbles. We hurry, climbing up through the green darkness. The birds have all stopped singing.

We pass a spring, and I stop to get water for the night, as lightning strikes nearby. I grab the full water bag and run—there's the shelter—leap up the steps and under the roof just as the rain comes down in a wall.

The shelter is full of hikers. Lightning flashes on everyone's face like a strobe, freezing moments—everyone grinning, laughing—taking pictures of everyone sitting on their bags watching the storm as if it's a suspenseful movie.

Slam! The air around us explodes. We jump. We smell singed wood, the ozone tang of lightning. A hit! We cheer, hoping it's not the shelter. It turns out to be the privy, which now has a big hole burned in one wall. "Better ventilation," someone says. "And now you can see all the spiders on the wall, not just assume they're there."

The storm calms down. I change into my dry clothes and hang my candle lantern from the ceiling with the usual assortment of stuffsacks, wet socks, shorts, shirts, bandannas, boots, and packs. There are hiking sticks slung into every corner, and suspended food bags to duck around whenever you move. Maine Event is cooking next to me, someone else is cooking on the porch, and other hikers' candles are flickering. Nomad and I light incense we bought in Bennington to repel the bugs, and write in our journals.

The moon sails out from behind the clouds, and I look out over the pointed tops of the fir forest. Far away, through the mist, is a dim light—the beacon on top of Mount Greylock, 38 miles away. The air smells like Christmas.

"I saw moose tracks today," someone says. "They were huge."

It's good to be back on the Trail, back with the storm and the moose and the Christmas-tree forest, back in our little cabin filled with wet gear, the wooden ceiling lit by candlelight. It's good to be here in the shelter, feeling the pain in my feet, drinking water from the spring.

Anna Banana lays out her bag and eats Nutter Butters from the same zip-lock bag she keeps dog biscuits for Alice B. Toklas in.

Another hiker, named Boots, is here. He's a small, thin man with hair so short it's nearly shaved; he's one of the few male hikers I've seen who shaves every time he reaches town. He and Anna Banana share an uncanny resemblance, not just in the face but also in the body, like twin brothers, and they give each other the once-over, like skeptical mirror images.

Boots does a handstand. "You ought to try this," he says, from his upside-down position. "It reverses the flow of gravity on your body. It makes your back feel great."

He drops his feet down and makes a U with his body, stomach side up.

"Look at this guy," Blister says. "You could have sex with him all kinds of ways."

Boots's U abruptly collapses, and he lies on the floor, laughing, then rolls from side to side.

Nomad writes in the log, "Sister Love's Traveling Salvation Show was here," naming us after the Neil Diamond song "Dr. Love's Traveling Salvation Show." We must be the biggest group of women hikers on the Trail, and when we tell Boots he's lucky to have our company, he laughs and says he'll be honored to travel with us for a while.

❖ ❖ ❖

Owls sing through the night woods. I'm standing barefoot in a shallow stream near Clarendon Shelter, pouring potfuls of cold water over my body. The icy chill is always a revelation, shocking me awake, so that even if I'm already fully awake, I move to a higher level of awareness. I can hear and feel the water and the stream but can't see it in the dark. Pebbles dig into my tired feet, and leafy branches stroke my arms as I bend and scoop and pour.

I feel around for my clothes and can't find them, so I light my candle lantern and hold it high. On the bank of the stream, an orb weaver spider is making her web. She tumbles and runs along the threads, spinning out line, making it fast, each turn around the spiral tight and perfect, as she measures it, checks it, and runs on. I blow out the light and close my eyes, feeling the forest filled with these intricate processes, everything in nature connected by invisible threads, everything moving: water, spider, owls, leaves. Us. We're souls in motion. People are made to move.

Dressed, I walk back to the shelter in the dark, light my candle lantern and hang it from a nail, and write in my journal. Blister has made a fire, and the other hikers are sitting at it, not talking, just happy to be here. It's an old scene, one people have witnessed for thousands of years, and one that's on the verge of being lost forever: your tribe sitting at the fire after a long, nomadic day. I write:

> This journal, which is mostly a recording of daily activities, rarely touches what's really going on in my mind and heart. I hardly know myself; it's hard to talk about the journey while you're in it. All I know is the pleasurable pain of pebbles under my sore feet as I stand naked in a cold stream, washing the sweat and dirt off; the smell of pines, the moss I step out onto, the branch of a birch I hang my clean clothes over. The spider weaving nearby is a holy mystery.

I know the feel of a canoe's side gripped in my hand as we cross a night lake, watching stars to find the way home; holding up the flashlight so that Kankakee, who's steering, can see the rock that marks the Goose Pond cabin. I know the cold water on my palms, sliding past; shadows of stones and weed below; fish nibbling my feet when I swim.

I know breath and exhaustion and hunger, moments when I must eat or pass out; I know birches in sunlight, pieces of bark dropped on the ground like notes from someone who writes in a horizontal code. I know fire, the warmth of a sleeping bag, the furtive rustle of animals after my food, owls singing the night awake. I know the weight of my pack, which my body is so used to that when I take it off, I can't balance without it, and stagger like a drunk, unused to weightlessness.

I'm not sure how I've changed on this trip, but I know I have. Right now I feel as if I've shed a skin, the remnants of my old life that didn't fit; so I'll scatter it to the wind, and walk on.

A crane fly, drawn by the light of the candle, is brushing my forehead with long legs and wings—as if I were the light. Wish I were.

Rocks and roots and the cold, rich scent of wet stone and damp earth. Evergreen. Ferns. The sound of water running, and your own breath. Killington Peak is a long climb, a jungle gym of roots and stones, and in some places we have to lever ourselves up, hanging on tight to young trees, which feel like strong girls' wrists. I feel high, like I've felt so often lately: all the colors brighter, saturated as if after rain, all the smells more intense, my body one with the mountain.

Nomad and I talk as we climb; we've saved stories for this all-day uphill. We talk about how we want to change. We talk about Trail magic and the mystery of my meeting Gladys, about the lesson that teaches about trust, about Nomad's boyfriend and whether she wants to be with him forever. She'll make some changes when she goes home, even if she doesn't yet know what they are.

We climb. We finish our stories and walk, in the flow, the forest all colors and shapes and textures, spots of sunlight on green moss, lichen on rocks, the smooth slide of mud underfoot. We find a spring and drink the water straight from the mountain's heart.

Up on top, we can see all the way to Canada. The other hikers in our group are there, waiting. We all sit, looking north, toward Katahdin. The White Mountains loom high on the horizon, ready to test us.

We all hike down together, flying past weekenders, rushing down to the pass, where we'll camp in a clearing across the road from an inn. We'll let them do the cooking tonight. Irish stew. Hot bread and butter. Applejack and ice cream. And in the morning, another mountain to climb.

We come to the "Maine Junction," where the Long Trail, which crosses Vermont and has been concurrent with the AT for the past 100 miles, branches off, leading left to Canada. To the right, the AT leads to Maine. Katahdin is getting closer all the time.

A few miles later, just outside the small town of Sherburne, Nomad and I stop to study the map. There are several apparent routes to our destination, and we consider them all. Boots looks at us scornfully.

"Are you two going to blue-blaze in the Whites too?" he asks, as if the White Mountains are somehow sacred and there's only one way to hike them.

"If we feel like it, yeah," I say. "Who died and made you Trail King? We're not making you blue-blaze, so get off our case."

Despite his talk, for once he doesn't want to hike any more than the rest of us, and we stand in the road debating what to do. The town pool is nearby, and we swim for an hour, then resume hiking. It's hot and humid, and our motivation, so easy to come by when it's cool, has evaporated.

"Where's that blue-blazed trail again?" Boots asks. "Lemme see the map."

We don't even say anything about hypocrisy, but when we all walk up and down the road looking for the blue-blazed trail, we find it's completely overgrown, gone. We head back to the white blazes and begin hiking steeply, up and up. We pass Zombie, who's sitting exhausted and demoralized under a tree. He waves his hand weakly. "I'm taking a break. If you see G.R.Dia up there, tell him I'll be along soon."

Everyone else is energetic. I drag along behind, not wanting to hike today. I'm tempted to go back and sit with Zombie, except then I'd have to hike up this steep section again. The others all seem like they're running, and trying to keep up makes me anxious. I come up around turns just in time to see their disappearing feet and hear their cheerful laughter as they round yet another switchback. Finally, they're far ahead and I'm hiking alone. It's both a relief and a letdown.

I slog along, feeling depressed and out of it, worn out, filled with the awareness of all my faults, selfishness, and flaws. A five-mile section feels like an eternity. I keep checking the map, just like I used to check the office clock when I had a job, wishing I was farther along. Finally, I reach Stony Brook Shelter.

We have a "hiker's potluck" supper—we each cook our own meal, then trade. We all have similar food, but somehow someone else's mac and cheese always tastes much better than your own.

I go to sleep early, feeling as if my shadow has grown huge and is hanging over me. I dream of an evil sea captain who has a change of heart and becomes good. It reminds me of a story someone told me early on the Trail, that the man who wrote the song "Amazing Grace" was a slave ship captain who repented. Well, if he can do it, so can I.

The next morning I'm sitting at the edge of the shelter looking at the dawn above the treetops, still depressed and lonely, when Anna Banana wakes up. She raises up on an elbow and asks, "Are you always so happy in the morning?"

"What?"

"You always seem so peaceful and content," she says. "Especially in the morning. I don't know how you do it. I hate getting up."

I laugh. "Actually, I'm horribly depressed today. I feel like I've been such a bitch to everyone."

"I hate to burst your bubble, but you're filling the whole shelter with happy vibes. I don't think you've been a bitch. What are you talking about?"

This cheers me up, but I still feel the need for a change. I write an apology in the shelter log to anyone I may have offended in the past. I'm grateful to the Trail, to Gladys or God or whatever it is that seems to be watching over me. Every time I've asked to learn on this trip, I've been taught.

Nomad and I slip back to our old blue-blazing ways, and Blister joins us. We attempt to follow an old trail through the woods, but the way is overgrown, filled with springy, spiky, complicated blowdowns, which we climb over, under, and through, like jungle gyms. Doing this with a big pack isn't easy. The first blowdown is entertaining, the second one is an obstacle, the third is a pain in the ass, and by the fourth one, we're ready to backtrack.

In addition to the blowdowns, we keep finding forks in the "path," with no indication of which would be better.

"If we keep taking the leftmost fork, we'll eventually intersect the Trail again," I say.

"I need to get to the post office in South Pomfret," Nomad says. "I can't fart around all day like this."

Blister's back gets stiff. "I'm not farting around," she says. "I'm doing my best to get where we want to go."

We finally decide that, whether we're farting around or seriously wayfinding, this is taking too much time, and we hike back the way we've come, back to the shelter, which is near a logging road.

As we reach the road, along comes a logging truck with FRENCHY written across the cab in swirly writing. We hold up our arms for the big red-bearded driver to stop, and he tells us, in a strong French accent, that the road goes through remote forests all the way back to Killington. If we take the road in the other direction, in five or so miles we'll reach a paved, well-traveled road where we can hitch a ride to Woodstock, and from there, go to South Pomfret.

He rumbles off toward Killington, and we head in the other direction, down the dirt road. We pass a cabin where an old man is sitting on a porch festooned with shed deer antlers—one has a bird's nest in it—and ask for directions. He tells us we're on the right road, and we walk on.

"What a bastard," Blister says irritably. "In the South, anyone would have invited us to set a spell on his porch, or at least given us water. These Yankees don't know hospitality."

"We have hospitality," I say. "It's just different from the Southern kind."

"Yeah, like more rude."

We pass another house, where two very large people tell us the walk is "easy and downhill," then get into their car and drive that way.

"If it's so easy," Blister mutters through her teeth, "why don't they take their big old selves out and walk it?"

We keep walking. Finally, Blister says, "Maybe I'm giving us bad trip karma because I have a bad attitude today and I'm bad-mouthing people. I'm sorry. I'm going to change my attitude."

She looks up at the sky and says, "I apologize to everyone

for my bad attitude," then picks some asters that are growing beside the road and attaches them to her pack. A minute later a vehicle comes down the hill, raising a cloud of dust. It's the old Yankee man, the one with the deer-antler porch, in a pickup truck.

"I got to thinking," he says, "that you might like a ride."

We hop in and rattle along past farmhouses, stone walls, and the shallow rapids of Stony Brook, and onto paved roads. He lets us out at a diner at an intersection of paved roads, and as soon as we hop out, a woman in a VW van offers us another ride.

In back, it's as soft as a couch, and I fall half-asleep back there as Nomad chats with the driver. The woman drops us off two miles from South Pomfret and we walk the rest of the way to pick up Nomad's and my food at the post office. I drag behind, feeling weepy, worn out, and exhausted.

I need rest, and time alone. I want to just curl up somewhere clean and quiet and get my head together. It's been hard for me to keep up with the other members of the Traveling Show lately—my knees are hurting badly, forcing me to walk more and more slowly, while they run ahead. I feel pressure to keep up and feel panicked at the thought that I can't. Our recent high-mileage days and high hills have taken their toll on my body, and high introspection has taken its toll on my spirit.

I need a break, and I need it so badly that if I don't take one, my body will give it to me in the form of sickness or injury. My mother has a friend who lives nearby in Hanover, who's expecting me to stay with her for a night, so I give her a call.

She comes and gets me, and meanwhile the other members of the Traveling Show regroup and hike on; we'll all meet in Hanover in a day or so.

I spend the night at Anne's house on Lake Sunapee, enjoying her Yankee hospitality: hamburgers, and fresh corn and tomatoes from her garden. She's very down-to-earth and matter-of-fact, but I detect an initial hesitancy in her, as if my mother has led her to expect me to be a lot weirder than I actually am. This wears off after a while.

I sleep in a room with a lake view, and wake to bagels and coffee and writing in my journal on the sunporch overlooking the lake. It's not a long break, but it's a good one.

In Hanover, New Hampshire, the home of Dartmouth College, we stay at a frat house that has offered hospitality to hikers while the members are away for the summer. Only two members are there, and the rest of the house is empty. Hikers colonize the cavernous public rooms, laying out sleeping mats all over the beer-soaked red carpet. The house is old and elegant, but trashed—every surface has a sticky patina of dried beer. Group photos of young men from past years hang high on the walls, and the glass covering them has dried rivulets of beer, as if the brothers only open cans after vigorously shaking them. The house smells like a bar, and after we've been there a while, our sweat-and-old-boots aroma blends with the beer to make it smell like a bowling alley.

One of the frat brothers plays reggae on his stereo, and from the other common room comes the click and thump of polished wooden balls on a felt pool table.

The Traveling Show has two new members: Skywalker and Macaroni. Skywalker, a high-mileage hiker we ran into in town and convinced to walk more slowly, is with us. He's a purist and will remain one, but he likes our company. Macaroni is a woman who's been hiking alone until now. Despite this, she seems shy and innocent, and her most notable trait is gullibility; you can tell her anything and she'll believe it. We test her by telling her increasingly unlikely stories, all of which she accepts. Because she's such an easy mark, the fun doesn't last long, and we soon stop teasing and quietly accept her.

Skywalker has an electric razor, which he uses to shave his head and then mails ahead to the next town. Anna Banana looks at Boots, who also has a shaved head, and asks to borrow it. We go outside and help her shave her short hair, and she emerges grinning, looking even more like Boots's twin. At a glance, I can't tell them apart, and neither can anyone else. They slap hands and grin, amused at themselves.

We all lounge on the cushy, beer-smelling couches and talk about reentering civilization. "I came out here to figure it out," Skywalker says, "but I don't know if I'm any closer to doing that than I was back in Georgia."

"What did you do before?" I ask.

"Inventory. It was horrible. I worked for this company that sends you to other companies to count things. It was mind-numbing. But I'm not sure what to do instead."

"All I know is, it won't be easy," Nomad says. "We have the most perfect life, we're all happy and free, and I for one don't miss that bullshit at all. Malls, 9 to 5. Yuck. Any job would seem like such a trap after this."

"Yeah," Boots says. "I love hiking. I love being a hobo. I love that we can just walk around and sleep anywhere."

We talk about the mountains ahead: the Whites. On the profile map, the Whites look like shark teeth. Huge, steep climbs, with jagged ups and downs. They're said to have terrible, dangerous weather and to be one of the toughest sections on the Trail; doing 10 miles a day is equivalent to doing 20 anywhere else. The weather is so bad, in fact, that instead of shelters they have "huts," little enclosed lodges where you can buy dinner and sleep in a bed.

I have a postcard I bought in town, the kind of photo you look at and want to walk right into. It shows Lakes of the Clouds hut in the foreground, looking tiny against the vast ridgeline. The Trail meanders up and down this ridge, then down into a deep valley and up again, and behind it mountain after mountain rises up, immeasurably blue and remote and wild. There are no trees because it's above tree line. I look at this picture and feel myself leaning into the wind, and smell the wet rocks and the air coming straight from Canada. It's a landscape so exaggerated and archetypal it doesn't seem real, but here it is, and soon we'll be walking there.

Macaroni's parents live nearby and offer to shuttle our packs ahead to a place where the Trail crosses a road and meet us there later. We hand over our packs and head out of town, toward Trapper John Shelter, named after the character from *M*A*S*H*, who was supposed to be from Dartmouth. When Nomad and I cross a country road, we take it and meet a man who's standing in the yard of his neat white farmhouse. He offers us water and tells us his family has lived on this spot for seven generations. He's a classic old-time Yankee farmer and has a lot to say about the government, all of it cynical but lucid. We could listen to him all day, and clearly he wishes we would, but we have to get moving. He tells us about a shortcut back to the Trail, and we plan to take it.

The walk is filled with cicadas yelling up in the trees, yellow flowers, and blue sky. We pose, holding out our hiking staffs, and I take a picture of our shadows, black against the road. They look like the outlines of muscular goddesses on an ancient Greek pot.

We get to the shortcut, which is a dirt road that eventually leads to a lot of forks, then to a network of deer trails, and then completely disappears. By now we're deep in the woods—not lost, but I for one don't want to backtrack all that way.

"Never listen to locals who think they know the mountains," Nomad says. "They never do. We should have asked him when was the last time he was back here."

"Probably 1922," I say. "Let's just use the sun and the lay of the land and head for this road." I show it to her on the map. "We're in here somewhere, in this empty space. If we go downhill and east, in a couple of miles we'll hit this road, and then we can walk along the road and find where the Trail crosses it."

"Oh, right," Nomad says.

"Well, do you want to walk back the whole way we came, and go back down the road we came up, and end up where we started on the Trail?"

"No way!"

We follow a deer trail as long as it goes the same way we

want to go, then bushwhack a while, then find another meandering deer trail. It's lonely back here, swampy and spooky, with mysterious clearings. Every now and then we find a rose bush or a gnarled apple tree, remnants of a long-gone farm.

We come into a tiny valley. Six deer trails lead out of it in six different directions.

"I really think we're lost," Nomad says.

"No, we're not. See how the sun is still behind our left shoulders? And we're going generally downhill. We'll come out by a road, and then we can take a right to the Trail."

"Yeah, right."

We go on. We thrash through a meadow and come to a place where all the trees have been cut down.

"If we follow the trail of human destruction," I say, "it'll lead us to a road. People don't do stuff like this unless they can come in on a road."

We follow the trail of wood chips and ruined trees and sure enough, it leads to a dirt road that has been chewed out of the woods by Caterpillar machines. The dirt road leads to Goose Pond Road, just as the map shows.

"I never would have thought it," Nomad says.

We turn right and eventually find the Trail and Macaroni's father, who's waiting with our packs. We sit with him and eat potato chips, and he goes back and forth to the road, looking for his daughter.

Seeing him, and seeing Macaroni with him, reminds me how much I miss my dad. How I wish he could visit me on the Trail, hike some of it with me, share this experience. He would be just like her dad—involved, amused, plotting ways to help.

When the others show up he takes us to a store, where we buy a strawberry cheesecake, wine, French bread, real butter, and a lot of other things, which we shove into and tie onto our packs. He takes us back to the Trail, and we hike up, steeply up, to the shelter. Nomad, who has the cheesecake tied to the top of her pack, is jubilant, full of smiles. All I can think about is the butter: pure calories.

We make a bonfire and have a party, and I eat a whole stick of butter. Back in civilized life this would have disgusted me, but now it tastes delicious, and every cell in my body seems to relax and open up, thrilled with calorie infusion. The cheesecake is gone in minutes, and while we're eating we talk about every other food in the world: cake, pizza, ice cream, pie.

It's a cold hike, but it feels good to be cold. Low clouds scrape along, threatening rain, keeping us cool even on the uphills. Mount Cube is wild—wind so fierce it blows us sideways, spruce and fir forests twisted by the wind, rocks to climb, lots of roots and fog and the roaring wind. The air is filled with the smell of fir, clean and cold.

Blister needs to go to town to get a mail drop, so eventually we get to a road and decide to hitch into Warren for lunch, and from there we'll go on to Glencliff, where the mail drop is.

It's a long hitch; not many people come down this road. There are four of us now: Nomad, Anna Banana, Blister, and me. The others are going ahead on the Trail, and we'll meet them later. Still, not many people are prepared to pick up four hitchhikers, even if they are all women. We stand by the road a long time and invent a game, road hockey, to pass the time. This involves finding pebbles and either tossing or kicking them into the road, with the goal of getting them into the inch-wide black space between the two yellow lines in the middle of the road. It's a challenge; in an hour we fill the road with pebbles but only score twice. Whoever scores gets to eat one of Blister's jelly beans, but the score is so low and we're so hungry that eventually we give up and eat the jelly beans anyway.

We finally get a ride in the back of a pickup truck and cruise happily to Warren, which has its own missile, inexplicably planted in the center of town, looming over the small white frame houses like a scene from a Cold War–era sci-fi movie. Any minute now, I expect, a giant ant or a slug as big as a car will come galumphing out from behind one of the houses, and the townspeople, women with carefully set hair and pointy bras and men in narrow slacks with black-framed glasses and neatly combed hair, will flee, screaming, off into the hills.

In a small restaurant we order the greasiest food on the menu. While we're eating, two other hikers come in: a couple named Rice and Beans. They look at us, then sit down at a distant table without saying anything.

I've met them several times before, and each time they've acted as if they've never met me. When I've passed them on the Trail and said hello, they've never said hello back, just ignored me, and when I've seen them in shelters they've always been aloof.

"What's with those two?" Blister hisses, leaning over the table to whisper between clenched teeth. "They're *so* unfriendly. I've seen them off and on ever since Georgia, but they won't even say hello to me."

"I thought it was just me," I say. "I've met them over and over, but they never even say hi."

"Me too," Nomad says.

"Me too," Anna Banana says. "How can hikers do that? It's stupid. What if you needed help? If you act like that, no one will ever want to help you."

This seems prophetic, because shortly after, Rice comes over and asks if we have a map of the area.

"*No,*" we all say in unison. We all have maps; mine is in my pocket as usual, folded up and digging into my leg.

"You want to be alone, you get alone," Blister says after he's gone. "One strategic hello in the last few months would have gotten him a map today."

I feel like a member of some tribe or strict religious sect. They've broken the hospitality rules, so now they're ostracized, like Popsicle at the Delaware Water Gap or like Fullabeans back in North Carolina.

We move on, hitching another ride to Glencliff, where we're due to meet the others at the post office, which is now closed. These towns are so small and northern—tall, narrow frame houses dressed in clapboards, painted white, looking beleaguered, as if even in summer they whisper to one another about their dread of the oncoming winter. The yards look sparse, as if the summer is too short for anything to really grow, as if the trees and bushes never need pruning; they're whipped into line by the relentless weather.

Right next to the post office is a wooden building with a wooden sign:

WILLING WORKERS HALL

I take a photo of Blister sitting there on the steps, doing nothing.

The others show up, having hiked all the way here, and we salute their perseverance and move on to Jeffers Brook Shelter. Our mood is changing; we're expecting heavy rain and wind tonight, and tomorrow we'll officially enter the White Mountains, and all this playing around will be over.

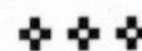

"The Whites are our final exam," Nomad says. The rain and wind have arrived, and we're all so nervous about the Whites that none of us can sleep. We lie in our bags and try to relax.

"And maybe the rest of the Trail is Senior Week," she adds hopefully, "when you get to slack off and have parties."

None of us buy it; we've all seen the maps, with their jagged teeth, and we've all heard the southbound hikers telling stories about their frightening weather and harsh terrain. We only have about 380 miles left, which no longer seems far, but a week or so of those miles involves getting over the Whites, and it won't be easy.

Macaroni's parents are going to give us a slackpack over Mount Moosilauke. Slackpacking is hiking without a pack, when some helpful person with a car carries your pack forward and meets you up ahead. We're going to hike over Moosilauke backward—shuttling around to the northern side, hiking over the summit without packs, meeting Macaroni's parents at the southern side, then shuttling around to begin hiking again, with packs, at the northern side.

At 7 A.M. they arrive, with huge bags of hot, greasy fast-food breakfast sandwiches. It's still raining, still cold, and the hot food is a godsend. Then we pack, with a mixture of skill and haste—like students cramming at the last minute—hike to the road crossing where they've parked their van, and load our gear and ourselves into it.

"OK," Boots says, "we have to be up and over Moosilauke by 1:30, so we can do another nine miles by dark."

"All *right*!" Anna Banana says. She leans forward like a sprinter, as if, even in the car, she wants to get there before he does. No one else says anything, but I personally don't want my hike to be shadowed by some clock, especially if it's someone else's clock and they've decided this without asking me. I'll hike as slowly as I need to, and if I finish after 1:30, good. I have no intention of hiking over Moosilauke and then doing nine more miles today; the terrain is too difficult.

Because the weather seems risky, I don't slackpack, but carry my pack and everything in it, which will make me much safer.

They drop us off, and up from Kinsman Notch we go, up a climb so steep that there are metal handholds set into the rock for us to haul ourselves up by. The climb parallels a long cascade of waterfalls over Beaver Brook for a mile, and it's beautiful, straight up through mist and fog, fragrant evergreen trees, the rich, grounding smell of wet stone and roots.

My mind and heart love this mountain, but my knees, which hurt more and more lately, are screaming. They don't care how much ibuprofen I take. I hike stiffly, wincing with every step, as endorphins—naturally produced drugs that the body makes when it's in pain—race through my system. They're chemically similar to morphine, leading to a strange combination of pain and a very good mood. My knees scream, but I'm blissfully happy.

Alpine forest—spruce and fir. Christmas trees. Moss. Mist. Good clean smells. Alive smells. We hike up again, then down, then up, not so steeply now. The trees get smaller and more stunted, then stop: We're above tree line, and we're in a cloud.

I look at the ground and follow the narrow footpath others have worn through the boulders, through lichen, moss, and tiny flowers. Because there are no trees up here to paint blazes on, the Trail maintainers have built cairns, rock piles as tall as a person, to mark the way.

It's so foggy we can barely see one cairn from the next. We walk slowly, peering ahead, and the next cairn looms up like a slow ghost. When I get ahead, I look back and wait for Macaroni and her mother, and can't see them until they appear suddenly out of the mist, as if they're walking themselves into existence.

This mountain, like all the Whites, is said to have awe-inspiring views, but white is all we see. Maybe that's how these mountains got their name.

Eventually we meet trees again, and walk down and down and down—more knee agony—so far down that we come to a zone where broadleaf trees dominate the woods, and it's actually warm. In one day we've gone from summer to winter and back.

We pile into the van, and my knees scream all the way as we drive to the far side of the mountain, back to Kinsman Notch, where we started hiking over it. As we drive, I see the mountain, looming over the road. We were up there, in the clouds; it's like a dream. And secretly I'm glad it's late, too late to hike nine more miles.

That night I lie in Boots's tent in Kinsman Notch, writing in my journal by the light of my candle lantern. The candle is almost burned out and I hope it will last until I'm done writing. Rain pats the sides of the tent like a thousand soft hands, and I'm happy to be relatively dry and clean after the hike over Mount Moosilauke.

Nearby, Beaver Brook washes its collection of stones. The rivers here are like misers who hoard stones instead of money. They wash their stones, they count them, they lovingly polish them, and now the rain is adding to this music. It's going to rain all night, and we're all doubling up—those without tents, like me and Nomad, sharing with those who have them.

A bird shrieks outside, sounding like something from the jungle. Boots, who's also writing, looks up and says, "I don't know what bird that is, but whenever I hear it, I think of this book I once read, *The Obscene Bird of Night*. Have you ever read it? It's good."

I write the title down in the margin of my journal. "No, but I'm always looking for recommendations. What else have you read that you like?"

"This book called *The Alchemist*, by Coelho. I like those South American writers."

The rain intensifies. My feet feel damp, and the tent is stuffy, filled with our combined aromas of sweat and unwashed clothes and stale breath, but I don't care. It's better than being outside in the pouring rain.

"I want to do a lot of miles tomorrow," Boots says. "We've been traveling too slowly. Tomorrow we really need to move."

I think, *Fine, then move*, but don't say anything. I like Boots, and I'm too tired to start a fight. It's not his fault that I'm exhausted.

We fall asleep, but in the middle of the night we hear a horrendous, cracking crash. The ground trembles.

"What was that?"

From the other tents, everyone yells.

"Macaroni, is that you?"

"What the hell was that?"

"It was right by me," Macaroni yells. "It made the ground shake!"

"Get a flashlight!"

"I bet it's a bear," Boots says. "It probably knocked all our bags down."

We all run outside into the rain. There are the food bags, still hanging high in a tree.

"What the hell was it?"

"Look at this!"

A birch tree, about 10 inches in diameter, has fallen and landed on the ground about a foot away from Macaroni's tent and her head.

"Holy shit! It's a good thing you didn't put your tent a couple of feet farther west."

In the morning it's still pouring, and I scrounge around under fallen trees to find enough semidry wood to cook oatmeal. I've eaten oatmeal for breakfast almost every day for five months, and I'm so sick of it that it makes me gag. Every morning it's a contest of wills between the gag reflex and the swallowing reflex. I've worn the same clothes every day for the last five months too. We all have—if Nomad didn't wear her blue shorts and pink tank top, I might not recognize her.

I put on my own uniform—khaki nylon shorts and blue tank top, both soaking wet and cold—and choke down the oatmeal.

"Come on, let's go. I'm freezing."

We jump around and rub our arms, waiting for the others to finish packing. As soon as we begin I'm behind, as the others race off up the mountain. Their voices trail behind them. "Betcha can't..." "How many miles..." "Fastest..." "Let's do 20!"

The first half of the day is peaceful, meditative, though it's cold and rains constantly. I can't walk any faster, and if the others want to race ahead, let them. I vow to enjoy the walk and not be stressed by the pressure to keep up. I can't keep up. My knees ache, and I'm limping on both legs.

The Trail up and over Mount Wolf is mossy and damp, deeply green, smelling of wet birch bark and rocks, sometimes muddy. I cross small streams, look at views, but mostly just hike, up and down, through rich forest. It's peaceful, being alone, but also frightening at times because my boots, which I've worn for more than 800 miles, through the last eight states, ever since I replaced my first pair in Virginia, are so worn that they have no traction. I'm walking stiffly because of my sore knees, and more than once I slip and fall off a cliff.

The cliffs are short—only a few feet—and I land on my pack, which cushions me, but every time there's a split second of *whoops!* and a brief free fall during which I don't know how far I have to fall or if I'll be OK when I hit the bottom. Then *whump!* I land, and lie there, dazed and trembling, thinking, *Oh, shit, this could have been a much higher cliff. I could have been killed.*

Each time this happens I get an adrenaline rush, then I crash, and each time the crash is lower. I'm trembly and anxious and tired.

I finally get to Eliza Brook Shelter. The others are all there.

"We've been here an hour," Nomad says. "Where have you been?" They're all rested and relaxed.

I eat snacks and debate what to do. Should I stay here? I'm exhausted. I don't have much food, and I'm not in good shape to hike. But if I do hike, I'll get to town, and food, that much faster.

It's late afternoon and still drizzling. I'm cold, tired, and hungry.

"Come on, hike," they say.

If I stay here, Nomad will have to stay too, since we're sharing gear. Like the others, she's full of energy, impatient, not in the mood to stay here.

"OK," I say.

We set out. The others all run ahead. Macaroni says, "I think I'll just hike with you."

The hike up the south and north peaks of Kinsman Mountain seems straight up. The mountain is a rock pile, seemingly miles and miles of climbing hand over hand, gripping rocks and roots to pull myself up, teetering dangerously on edges with my slippery boots, crawling on hands and knees. When I climb, I can't hold my hiking sticks, so I hurl them overhead like javelins and hope they'll get stuck up there long enough for me to crawl up to them. Sometimes they do, but more often than not they come slithering back down through the rocks like arthritic snakes, slamming me in the head.

The rain is cold and getting colder. As we ascend, it gets windy. I try to climb stiff-legged, without bending my knees—an impossibility.

Macaroni climbs patiently behind me. As we climb I think of her father and how nice he is, and how I miss my own father, and begin to weep. Waves of sadness mingled with anger sweep over me. The mountain seems to continue forever, and each time we creep around a turn and I see more slick, slanted rock faces to climb, a fresh burst of misery overtakes me.

The mountain is wrapped in clouds, a realm of cold ghosts.

We come to a boggy lake rimmed by stunted trees, eerie in the clouds, in the fading light, the penetrating rain.

This mountain wants me dead, I think, shivering. *This is some kind of lake of the Underworld, and I'm going to die up here. Dad, I miss you, I wish you could be here, please help me make it through.*

"Are we at the top yet?" I ask Macaroni. She doesn't know. The Trail continues up and up. More rock climbing, more roots, more muddy slides.

Finally, we start down, and now it's rock-climbing in reverse, even more agonizing to the knees. And it's dark now, fully dark, windy, freezing. The rain bites through my jacket to my soaked body and whips my face, and my hands are so cold I can no longer feel my sticks. My flashlight has burned out, and when Macaroni tries hers it flickers for a moment and dies.

After several dangerous falls, I slide down one rock face after another, on purpose. A controlled fall is better than an uncontrolled one. I hurl my sticks down the cliffs and jump or slide after them. I'm talking, not making sense, cursing the mountain and crying and weeping about my dad and my knees and my hunger. Macaroni, climbing steadily down behind me, is relentlessly cheerful, warm, and capable, and I alternately thank God for her and curse her for not understanding: I'm going to die, and here you are being bubbly.

"I have hypothermia," I tell her.

"No, you don't," she says. "You're just a little cold."

I feel lost and alone, even though she's right there; she won't listen to me, and I'm facing this fear all by myself, because she won't acknowledge it.

We can barely see the blazes in the rain, and I roll and leap down cliffs, not even caring where I land. She climbs down carefully, hand over hand. We're a mile from the shelter, and if I go down the mountain slowly and carefully, I'll never make it. It's better to take risks—just get down the mountain, as quickly as possible, and get to shelter.

My mind is sludgy, slow. I can't feel my hands. Or my feet. I'm clumsy, grabbing trees, my hands slipping, dropping my sticks, my feet flying out from under me, sliding down until I hit a sapling and come to a stop, the breath knocked out of me. I slide with my arms over my face, head down, protecting my eyes. My knees are like bright lightning bolts of pain, lighting up the dark. I lever myself down, my pack slewing sideways, weeping without words. I'm going to die up here. We won't get to the shelter in time, without a light.

We come to a place where we must inch around a corner, holding on tight to wet rocks. Suddenly a light explodes in my eyes. "Hey!" I yell involuntarily. "Hey!"

"Grace? Is that you?"

"Boots?"

"Yeah, it's me. Are you OK? We got to the shelter, and we got really worried when you didn't show up. I said I'd come back and get you. Just follow me. It's only a quarter of a mile away."

He leads me and Macaroni, pointing the flashlight down so we can see our feet. We traverse another quarter-mile of slanted rocks and wooden bog bridges, then come to the blue-blazed trail that leads to the shelter. I cry all the way, frightened, relieved, grateful, unable to express any of it. I'm shivering with spiritual cold, not just physical cold.

We get to the shelter. I put my pack down and think, *Dry clothes*. Then the thought disappears, and I sit unmoving. My thoughts are frozen, like my hands. *Dry clothes*. I move slightly closer to my pack, then forget what I was doing. I need something, I can't remember what.

"Grace, change your clothes," Nomad says. "I'm making mac and cheese."

Get dressed. Dry clothes. I claw open my pack and sit, looking at the warm dry clothes, without moving.

The shelter caretaker shows up, an officious young woman with a clipboard. "Hello," she says. "This shelter costs $5 a night. Please pay me now."

I look at her stupidly, unable to move my lips to speak. *What was I doing? Something about clothes.*

"Leave her alone," Nomad says. "Come back later. She's hypothermic, for God's sake. Give her a break. You'll get your money."

She hands me a mug of hot chocolate, and I drink it, then slowly, slowly fumble out my camp clothes and change into them, then get into my bag and lie there, shivering. Nomad stirs her mac and cheese and looks at me with an expression of mixed compassion and annoyance. I know I'm not pulling my weight, I ought to be helping with the chores. I can't. I fold up small and shiver. When the mac and cheese is done she gives me some, with rough grace. I eat, and warmth seeps through me. I understand Nomad's annoyance—I've been slow lately and must be a drag—and I'm so grateful to her and the others for helping me. Without them, without her and Boots and Macaroni, I would have died up on that mountain. Although, come to think about it, without them I would have stayed at Eliza Brook Shelter instead of hiking over Kinsman in late afternoon in the cold rain.

I vow that from now on I'll follow my instincts, despite what other hikers want to do. I put myself in danger by letting myself be swayed by everyone else. No more. If I have to hike alone, I will, but I'll do what's right for me.

I hike down six miles to a road, sliding down a few rock faces and fording a couple of streams on the way. Most of the hike is easy, and it's no longer raining, but I hike slowly, partly because of my knees and partly because of the slipperiness of my tractionless boots. Once again I'm alone, limping along, the others far ahead. When I reach the road to the towns of Lincoln and North Woodstock, everyone else is already there.

"I'm hitching in with Blister and Anna Banana," Nomad says curtly. "You can hitch in with Macaroni and Boots."

They get a ride immediately and disappear in the back of a pickup, not looking back. Our hitch takes longer, but eventually we all meet in the Laundromat in North Woodstock.

I want to wash all my clothes, which means I'll have to find something else to wear. I rummage through the lost-and-found box and find a pair of kids' sweatpants and a torn Bon Jovi T-shirt, strip, put them on, and toss my filthy clothes into the washer. It's one of those front-loading ones with a clear glass window; as the water fills up, it turns deep brown. The sweatpants are skintight and barely reach below my knees. Nomad puts on a slightly larger pair of boys' sweatpants and a tiny sweatshirt.

"Listen," she says. "I have to talk to you. You're not pulling your weight. I feel like I get to camp and do all the work, and then you show up and just eat and go to sleep."

"I know," I say. "I'm sorry. It's not just last night, but it's been going on for a while. See, the thing is, my knees are screwed up, and you guys are all hiking a lot faster than I can. I can't get to camp when you do. So either you're gonna have to stop during the day and wait for me to catch up, or you're gonna have to get to camp and wait for me then, because I can't help with chores if I'm not there. And I'm hiking as fast as I can. If you want, I can get my stove back, and you can get your own water filter, and we can each cook our own food and filter our own water, and then you won't feel burdened."

"Well, we'll see," she says. "I hope it works out."

We take turns washing our hair and bodies in the Laundromat sink. It feels good to be alive, on flat ground, and warm; it's almost orgasmic to be clean. There's nothing like a little near-death hypothermia to brighten your day.

We go outside to comb our hair in the sun. Alice B. Toklas is guarding our packs, and the others have spread out their wet gear in the vacant lot next door. Someone nearby is listening to a football game on the radio, and I realize how long we've been walking. When we started, it was still basketball season.

Boots does handstands over his drying tent while tourists watch from the outdoor café across the street. "We have to hike out soon," he says, his words distorted by his upside-down position. "What time is it? We should meet here in an hour, and be ready to move."

"I don't want to be ready to move," Nomad says. "I have things to do, and they won't be done in an hour."

"Like what?"

"Like the rest of my laundry. Like food shopping. Like calling home, checking mail, and fixing my stove. And Grace has to get new boots. Plus, look at the weather up on the mountains. It's nice down here, but up there it sucks."

Boots flips upright, distressed, but before he can argue, a man walks by and gives our wet gear and bizarre clothes the once-over. "Hey, you guys need work for the weekend?"

Nomad and I look at each other. "Maybe. What kind of work?"

"Scottish festival. Up at Lone Wolf Mountain Resort. I run food service. We need people to sell hot dogs, things like that."

"We have to hike."

"It's gonna storm up in the mountains. Bad. There's a hurricane coming. You think about it. Under the table. Seven bucks an hour. Cash, no questions asked. If you want work, come ask at the café across the street. I'll be over there."

I desperately need money for new boots, and we're all tired. The hypothermia incident scared me. I don't want to hike out this afternoon, straight up the side of yet another mountain in the wind and rain. I need a rest.

We tell the man we'll think about it, and hustle around town doing errands. Boots keeps looking at the angle of the sun over the mountains and asking people who have watches what time it is. "We have to leave by 4," he keeps saying. We all pretend we're going to leave town by 4, but by 4 all of us, except Boots, are still doing errands, buying food, repacking food, calling filter manufacturers, calling home, looking for boots. I don't want to hike one more step without new boots; I've endangered my life enough.

At 6, we finally agree to leave the next morning, but the next day, after breakfast, we all stand in the street, looking at the clouds and the mountains. Up on the summits, black storm clouds boil. I don't see the point of hiking up above tree line to be exposed to freezing rain, wind, fog, and no view; if we wait a day or so, maybe we can avoid hypothermia, experience the Whites in all their glory, and see the views we've heard about for more than 1,800 miles.

Boots and Anna Banana eye each other like uneasy twins. "You gonna hike?"

"Are you gonna?"

"I don't know. What are you gonna do?"

They both decide to hike on, each unable to back down and let the other possibly get ahead. Nomad, Blister, and I decide to stay, work at the festival, and if we can, meet up with them later.

We stay in the employee housing at the resort, a cross between a dorm and a cheap motel. There are few workers around now because the ski season doesn't start for another couple of months, and the place is mostly deserted; it's kept locked most of the time, and we use our ATM cards to slip the lock and get in when we come back from work.

I lie in the bathtub, scrubbing off the festival's bearbait reek of grease, fried dough, sugar, and hot dogs, reading a book I've found, but not really paying attention to it. I have things on my mind. I'm thinking of hiking on my own again. Our group has undergone a sort of meiosis and mitosis, swelling and then dividing like a cell. Now maybe it's time to divide again. I don't like the pressure of having to keep up with people when I can't or don't want to, and I'm sure they don't like sitting around waiting for me to come limping over the hill. I've lost my happiness and freedom, trying to keep up, worrying that I'm not pulling my weight, and endangering myself by trying to.

Blister is also tired of Boots's pushing. She and Nomad are talking about yellow-blazing ahead, skipping much of Maine, and doing the last hundred miles of the Trail—called the 100-Mile Wilderness—hiking up Katahdin, calling it quits, then going home. They both have relationships back home, and being away from their loved ones is wearing thin for them and the people they've left behind.

I don't have any compelling reason to leave, have no home to go back to, and don't want to skip any of Maine. I've hiked all this way, and I want to hike Maine. All of it.

I call my mother and ask her to send my stove to Gorham, New Hampshire, the next town. From Gorham, I'll be hiking on my own.

Alone

Anything we fully do is an alone journey.

—Natalie Goldberg, *Writing Down the Bones*

September 17
Gorham, N.H.

Chapter Ten

The weather continues unchanged, as one horrible storm after another marches through the Whites. I decide I'd rather skip the Whites for now and come back sometime in the future, when I can actually see them as I hike over them. It seems pointless to hike up there and see nothing but a freezing whiteout—maybe that's how they got their name, but I've had enough of it for now.

Blister and Nomad agree, and the three of us get a ride around the mountains to Gorham, where we stay at the Hiker's Paradise, a cozy hostel behind a motel.

The hostel is full of frazzled, frightened hikers who have the shell-shocked look of people who've been through a war.

"We were, like, lying down, holding onto boulders so we wouldn't be blown off the mountain," one says. "The wind was 90 miles an hour. God, it was fuckin' *scary.* We had to lie like that for hours. We both just panicked. Finally, the wind slacked off and we just ran for it and made an escape run down Pinkham Notch. I'm like, 'Fuck the Whites.' We just yellow-blazed here from the Notch, and we're gonna chill out a while and then restart from here."

"I'm leaving," says another guy. "I've had it with this shit. You guys were smart to go around. It's too dangerous up there. It's *stupid* to hike in this weather. I've had enough."

The weather improves and Nomad and Blister leave the next day, heading out to look for a hitchhike across Maine to Monson, near the start of the 100-Mile Wilderness. I have to stay in town until my stove arrives, so I'm looking forward to at least one day off.

As soon as they're gone I miss them but also feel relieved not to be living on someone else's schedule. I hope they have a good hike, and I plan to get in touch with Nomad after the hike, but for now I'm looking forward to taking it slowly, enjoying the last 300 miles at my own speed.

My stove arrives the next day, but my winter gear has been lost in the mail. At a thrift store I buy a parka, rain pants, gloves, and a hat, all for $10. This gear is not outdoor-stylish, but it does the job. I amass food for the next section of the Trail and make plans:

- Gorham--->Gentian Pond Shelter: 12 miles
- Gentian Pond--->Full Goose Shelter: 9 miles
- Full Goose--->Speck Pond Shelter (via Mahoosuc Notch): 5 miles
- Speck Pond--->Frye Notch Lean-to: 10.6 miles (hitch out and resupply in Andover, Maine)

Mahoosuc Notch is reputedly the hardest mile of the Trail: a crack between two mountains, formed in glacial times, filled with house- and car-sized boulders. The Trail winds over, under, around, and through these; hikers must crawl, climb, and slide, sometimes taking off their packs and pushing them ahead. In the caves and crevices below the rocks there's always ice, even in summer. People say it can take three hours to traverse this single mile.

I get all the money I have left in the world, $200, out of the bank and turn it into travelers' checks. There are no convenient ATMs or banks near the Trail in Maine, so this is my last chance to get money. It will have to last until I get back to civilization.

I buy a cheap watch. I've never even owned a watch until now, but lately it's been so cloudy and stormy, and darkness is coming earlier each day as fall approaches. Because of the clouds, I often can't tell how many hours of daylight are left. The experience on Kinsman Mountain left me fearful of being caught on some mountain after dark. Now I'll know how much time is left in the day and take precautions.

I'm sitting on a big flat rock at the edge of Gentian Pond, in the cold woods near the Gentian Pond Shelter. On the other side of the pond, cliffs rise up, covered with spruce and fir. There's a bog on the other side of the pond, and I'm hoping that if I get up early tomorrow and come to this rock, maybe I'll see a moose. I saw a lot of their tracks today as I hiked up here from Gorham.

Maine Event, Zombie, and G.R.Dia are tenting nearby. In the shelter is a German guy who's either shy or doesn't speak much English and two hikers who speak enough of it to fill in for his silence. They're called Yikes and Sunny Delight, and as I go back to the shelter and make supper, they keep up a continual running patter of stream-of-consciousness updates:

What flavor is that? It could be anything. It could be two flavors mixed together. It's hot. It's a combination, that's for sure. Good question. You know what the answer is? Oh, well—who cares? Rock on. Oh, yeah. Hey, we're almost there. That pat feels good on my leg, right there. It's like a heating pad. You never slept with a hot water bottle? Warm, it's warm...

They remind me of a bird I've often heard on the Trail, the red-eyed vireo, which sings all day, never stopping, singing short questioning phrases over and over. Not a second passes without this banter in the background:

Yeah, this zipper. Well, once it got stuck. You ever have that? Oh, yeah. A problem. But zippers are good, you know? A good thing. It's all good, all of it. Everything's good. That's a rock. Whose rock is it? Is the rock mine, or am I the rock's? Here's this floor, it's all boards. Gotta sleep on boards, except I got a Thermarest. It's all good. Oh, yeah...

I get out the big quartz crystal my friend Heather's friend Bea gave me, back in Georgia when I began, and lay it next to my candle lantern, where it reflects and magnifies the light on my journal page. Outside the shelter all the nearby rocks are filled with mica, and they shine like a field of stars laid out on the ground. The near ridge is black, with silhouettes of pointed trees, and across the valley the far mountain is gray, mysterious. In the valley, a few warm house lights shine, like the bits of mica, like the stars.

I hear the stream-overflow of the pond falling down a cliff, the purr of H2O's stove as he cooks pasta, and smell the noodles and the clear Christmas-tree air. I love this life.

It's a long, hard, but beautiful day. I'm thrilled to be walking by myself, at my own speed, which is incredibly slow. My knees are in agony, and there are a lot of 45-degree rock faces to climb, which I'm very slow at. Some sections are so vertical they make me laugh: "You've got to be kidding," I say out loud when I come to Goose Eye Mountain, where there's a climb up a cliff so impossible that a log ladder has been placed there.

Up on the mountaintops there are incredible views, and I can look back to see Mount Washington and the other Whites, snowy in the sunshine. The wind here is so strong that it threatens to blow me over, and I walk in a kind of crouch, gripping rocks, grabbing roots, staying low.

The north side of Goose Eye Mountain is a series of slanted, bare rock faces, easy to slip and fall on, since I can barely bend my knees. I put on my slick rain pants, then sit down and slide on my rear, easier and faster than inching down. From these slanted rocks I can see a vista of treeless, high areas filled with bog and shrubs—and the Trail, traversing them on rickety log walkways.

I walk through the lonely bogs, keeping a wary eye on the sun, which is setting. I'm walking slowly because of my knees, wincing with every step. I walk and walk. No sign of the shelter. I check and recheck the map. Could I have passed it?

I could camp anywhere, but I need water. The land here is boggy, but the water is all underground; none of it is standing, available for my filter.

It grows darker.

I pass a puddle left from the last rainstorm and think about camping right there on the Trail, filtering water from the puddle. I'll go 100 more yards and, if there's no sign of the shelter, turn back and camp there. I need water to drink and cook with. I'm starving.

A spruce grouse, eerily tame, watches me from the deep shade of a nearby tree. These birds don't fly away, and sometimes they'll let you touch them. "Fool hens," early settlers called them, because they'd sit still to be killed. The bird watches me with a measured, meaningful gaze, as if it has a message for me. *You're in trouble,* this one seems to be saying. *You'd better camp somewhere before dark.*

Voices drift through the woods: men. Hikers I know or strangers?

Cautiously I advance along the Trail. It leads to a small rise, so steep that a rough ladder hewn from young trees has been fastened there.

I climb stiffly, almost falling because my hands are cold and my knees won't bend. At the top, on a little plateau, is the shelter.

It's fully dark now. Dimly, I can see the humped shapes of people snoring in their bags on the sleeping platform of the shelter. Nearby, blue domes of tents glow, and the shadows of hikers I know, backlit by flashlights, pantomime sorting gear.

Thank God. My stomach feels like it's touching my backbone. I can't find my candle lantern or my flashlight, so in the dark I stumble down to the spring, finding it more by the sound and smell of running water than by sight. The water is so cold it makes my hands ache. In the dark I fill my cooking pot with water; in the dark, gather twigs to make a fire; pour macaroni into the pot, cook it, and add the cheese powder, powdered milk, and a little oil. I dig in my spoon—the only utensil I have, apart from a Swiss Army knife—and take a bite.

The mac and cheese is full of foreign objects. Crunchy, hard, shivering into glassy bits when I chew. Insects? Ashes? Twigs?

Who cares? It tastes wonderful: hot, cheesy, salty, greasy, filling. I eat it all, then use my finger to get the last sauce out of the pot. Nothing has ever tasted better. I make instant oatmeal for dessert and follow this with a quart of instant lemonade. It's the best meal I've ever eaten.

As I crawl into my bag and fall asleep, I wonder dreamily what the foreign objects were. Probably bugs—that suspicious glassy crunch of chitinous wings. Well, at least they were cooked. And they're a good source of protein.

I sit in the shelter the next morning, waiting for my water to boil, wearing shorts, a long-sleeved polypropylene undershirt and a wool shirt, with my hair in a braid, a bandanna tied over it, with wool socks and Teva sandals, my in-camp shoes, on my feet. I'm heading through Mahoosuc Notch today, and since it's supposed to take three hours, it'll probably take me five.

I eat my oatmeal—the daily contest of swallowing versus gagging—and through sheer willpower, choke it down. I swap hiking boots for the sandals and get moving. It's very cold today, wintry cold. My water was frozen when I got up, but as soon as I'm underway I'm warm.

I fall down several times before even getting to the Notch, despite the new boots I bought in New Hampshire. The problem is my knees, which are torture to bend. I wince and gasp with every step but keep going anyway. It's the same strange hypnosis I had when I was hypothermic: Must—Keep—Going. Forward motion has a momentum all its own.

I finally reach the Notch, a snack and several ibuprofens later. I enter it—an amazing, out-of-scale jumble of fallen trees, boulders the size of cars and houses, and sparse white blazes showing the best (or only) way through. I creep from rock to rock, nervous because of my lack of depth perception, and almost immediately slip and fall into a crack between boulders, a dim and icy cave. I squirm around and take off my pack, which I've landed on as usual, and hurl it up overhead, to the top of the boulder, then hurl my hiking sticks up too, and attempt to climb out without bending my knees. I slew my legs sideways, grip with my arms, and haul myself up. Then it's down, over and across to the next boulder, and again I slip and fall, this time ending up wedged into a hole like a cork.

I begin to weep, hanging there, legs dangling into some unknowably deep and dark space that has been deep and dark and icy ever since the glaciers melted. Who knows what's down there. If I fall far enough, will I ever be able to get out?

I toss my poles up, wiggle my shoulders, swing my legs. I grip a knob on a rock and once again pull myself up with my arms. My pack is more than a burden—it's a menace, unbalancing me. The Trail leads through a hole between boulders, and I take my pack off and shove it through first.

When I fall the third time, I lie in the little cave, study the great mass of stone hanging over my head, and curse. This is clearly not a good idea.

I haul out and sit on a boulder, breathing hard, feeling inherently unstable. My knees scream. My right hand, which is holding both of my hiking sticks, ascends of its own volition, opens, and I see the sticks fall down into oblivion, down into the dark ice caves, farther down than I've fallen. I see them both down there, the bamboo one I got with Wade, and the one I got back at Pine Swamp Brook Shelter in Connecticut and have carried ever since, the one that knows my hand, the one that has supported me all this way. I don't care about the bamboo one—I was planning to toss it off Katahdin anyway—but I'm sorrowful about dropping the new one, which has become an old friend.

Now, why did I do that? I wonder. I need those sticks. But it's too late now. No way am I going down there to get them.

Maybe, I think, *someone else who's more agile will see them, know they're mine, and carry them forward.* Hikers do this all the time. At various points on the Trail I've carried a bandanna, a notebook, and a $20 bill that were lost by people ahead of me, until I caught up with them. It's not impossible. *Gladys, are you listening?*

Carefully I backtrack to the entrance to the Notch. A blue-blazed trail meets the AT there, and by studying the map I determine that if I walk on it 12 miles out of my way, I can go around the one mile of Notch.

Along come some clean, cheerful weekenders, two men and a woman. "Whatcha doing?" they ask.

"I'm trying to decide if I should go through the Notch or go around," I say.

"Oh, just go through with us," they say. "We'll help you."

The two men take turns carrying my pack ahead, and I clamber awkwardly through the boulders, deeply grateful. One of them turns and watches me.

"I'm a chiropractor," he says, "and I can tell by the way you move that you're in some kind of serious knee pain."

"That's an understatement," I say.

"Where are you headed?"

"Speck Pond."

"Well, we're going there too, and tonight I'll do some adjustments on them, and I'll show you a way to tape them that will help you hike with a little less pain."

"Thanks."

I fall twice more, and they patiently haul me out. I've put on my rain pants to make it easier for me to slide down the rocks instead of climbing down, and this saves me from losing all the skin on my legs.

We reach the end of the Notch, and they hand me my pack and hike on. "We'll see you up at Speck Pond."

Mahoosuc Arm, the mountain after the Notch, is very steep. I grab roots and trees and lever myself up the incline, swearing. With each step, I grit my teeth and wince. I'm moving slower than a mile an hour. At this rate I won't get to the shelter until dark.

By that time I can barely walk. Stiffly, painfully, I hobble over to the shelter. Several thruhikers, as well as the friendly weekenders, are there. The chiropractor, John, massages my knees, then shows me how to tape them to keep the kneecaps more stable, so they won't rub the bone beneath them.

"The cartilage is probably worn," he says. "You'll have to be careful."

My knees feel slightly better when he's done, but I think it's a good idea to take tomorrow off and rest so I can heal enough to get off this mountaintop.

Canada jays come down and check out what we're cooking for supper, and steal my ramen noodles, one by one, from the boiling pot. I don't mind; I have enough, and it's worth it to see their aerial display. I hold up a peanut, and a bird lights briefly on my hand—a startling, sudden grip of strong claws, a brief peck, then my hand is empty and the bird's flying away. The weekenders have rice cakes, but the birds spurn them—like hikers, they scorn any food that doesn't have enough calories to make it worth eating.

The next morning the weekenders bounce up, happy to be eating oatmeal, happy to be hiking; they can't wait to get out there and up that next mountain. The thruhikers huddle in their bags, cursing, tired and sore. I'm not going anywhere. I watch the weekenders and think I'd much rather be like them, all enthusiastic, than like the thruhikers, worn out and depressed. These mountains aren't going anywhere. Someday I can come back and hike them when I'm uninjured, when I'm fresh, when every mountain is new, not just another obstacle on the way to Katahdin. When I go to Katahdin I want it to be for the right reason: because I want to go there, not because I said I'd go there and if I don't now I'll lose face.

Eventually everyone reluctantly packs up and hikes on. I stay at the pond, trying unsuccessfully to get the jays to eat rice cake crumbs, looking at my maps of Maine, writing in my journal, looking at the trees. It's silent up here, and I'm glad to have a whole day to rest and enjoy it. For some reason, I feel like I could end the trip right now and be happy with it.

Is this just the voice of fatigue and pain? I wonder. *Or something real? Am I really done?*

I think about this.

I think for a long time.

I lie on the wooden shelter floor, looking at the interlocking pieces of wood in the ceiling, thinking. When I threw my sticks into the crevasse in the Notch, it was like some kind of decision point or turning point or growth-mark or letting go, even though I didn't know it at the time.

I'm done.

My body is wiser than I am. I vowed long ago that I would leave the bamboo stick, the Wade-stick, on Katahdin when I finished the trip, and now I've gotten rid of it early. And it doesn't represent just Wade and all the confusion and turmoil surrounding him, but many more things, much bigger things. The need to be what others expect me to be, the need to be straight, to be "normal," to be what other people expect a woman to be, with all the limitations that implies. The idea that I have to have a normal job, the idea that I'm limited. All of that is gone, disappeared. Like the stick, these are things I carried for far too long, leaning on them, when they were really more of a hindrance and a burden than a help in my life.

I think about Wade. Why was I with him? It's almost like I chose the most inappropriate man in the world, just to teach myself a lesson: Enough is enough. If I had chosen someone different, someone less over-the-top strange, a truly nice guy like some of the guys I've met on the Trail, then conceivably things could have dragged on a lot longer. We could have lasted for years in a relationship based on friendship, mutual respect, and my desire for a normal life at any cost. I could have ended up in a stale but pleasant marriage, and my longings—for adventure, for a relationship with a woman, for truth above all else—might have been muted by the comfort of our friendship and my respect for my partner. It might have been years before I woke up and took a long, long walk and asked myself what I really wanted.

As it was, the experience with Wade sharpened things in a hurry and sent me straight out on the quest for a new life. And for that, I'm grateful. Now I can move on and live it.

I'm crying now—that must be it, I'm done. I've released the final burden. I've reached the "place," the place I vowed to go, the goal of the pilgrimage. Wherever that is, I'm there. It's a shock to realize this so suddenly, but I feel the completeness deep down, in my bones.

I feel huge, as if every mountain I've walked over is inside me, and no one can ever take it away or make me feel small again.

There's no better place to cry than beside a high mountain lake when there is no wind. Absolute hush. If I wailed, the sound would carry all across the lake and up to the top of Mahoosuc Arm. The birches up there are turning yellow, mixed with the deep green of spruce and fir. These boreal forests always seem so old, as if they've been here forever—older than other kinds of forests, darker and deeper.

I look at my maps. I want to be certain that leaving is the right thing to do, so I want to make sure I know what I'm missing. I follow every inch of the Trail across Maine, look at the 100-Mile Wilderness and all its lakes, and the sudden five-mile-straight-up of Katahdin. I feel peaceful about it. I don't need to continue.

I'm done.

In the afternoon, other hikers show up: Hurler, Speedy Slug, Marmalade Cat and Mellow Man, a couple named Pam and Arthur and their dog Oliver, the German guy who was at Gentian Pond, and some others.

Arthur is carrying my hiking stick: the one I wanted, not the bamboo one.

"I saw this in the Notch and thought it looked familiar," he says, handing it back to me. I take it and hold it tight, this stick that has become my old friend. I'll cherish it forever as a reminder of this trip: all the mountains, all the people, everything I've learned.

"Did you see any other sticks?" I ask. "Like a bamboo one?" I don't want it back, but I'm curious. I have the feeling it's disappeared forever, dropped into a black hole, irretrievable.

"I didn't see anything except this one. It's really nice. If you didn't want it, I would have kept it."

I'm so happy to have it back, this reminder of all I've gained from the Trail. And I can use it on the hike out and down to a road.

I've decided to hike five miles over Old Speck Mountain, then down to Route 26, where I can hitchhike back to Gorham. I need a place to go for a few days, a transition zone between the Trail and civilization so I don't get culture shock. I'll go to Gorham and rest in the Hiker's Paradise for a few days.

That night the others light their lanterns, look at maps, and talk about Katahdin. It's cold and a wet mist is blowing, so I hang my tarp over the entrance, and we're all sealed in, quiet and thoughtful. I'm happy they're all going to Katahdin, but it seems so removed from me now. I ask the German guy, whose name is Frank, how the reunification of East and West Germany has affected him.

"Ah," he says, "reunification. That is why I am here. I lost my job. I used to guard the border, but now there is no border, so I am here, walking and thinking of what to do next."

It's a beautiful walk the next day, despite the screaming pain in my knees. I hike slowly, looking at everything, knowing I have all day to go five miles, mostly downhill. There are rocks filled with big facets of mica all along the Trail, and I pick up the most perfect ones and put them in my pack: an unimaginable luxury during the rest of the hike, when I couldn't justify carrying such useless weight. I pick up a mica pebble from Old Speck Mountain and put it in my pack with the pebble I got on Springer Mountain, way back in Georgia. I'll keep both of them as a reminder of how far I've come.

I stop and sit and look at mountain views with no pressure to get anywhere, and I have a long conversation with a red squirrel who's sitting on a log nearby, neatly eating seeds out of pine cones one by one. This is hiking!

When I come to the valley, I stand on the shoulder of Route 26 at the place where the Trail crosses the road, for the rest of the afternoon, as the sun moves from its noon position toward its late-afternoon one behind the mountains.

Traffic on this road is almost nonexistent, but the wait is peaceful. If there's one thing I've learned on the Trail, it's how to wait. I have everything I need to be comfortable except food, and I'm not terribly concerned about that; after all, I don't have to hike anymore.

I play a rousing game of road hockey (no score), scour the nearby woods for fallen sheets of birch paper to take home, and write in my journal. I peel a mica rock apart, and when all the facets are as big and shiny as they can get, I set it up on a stone where hikers will pass and see it, a legacy to those still walking.

Whenever I hear the hum of an oncoming vehicle, there's plenty of time to get to the road and stand hopefully with my thumb out.

Traffic is light, mostly logging trucks and cars full of old people. The trucks barrel along at 60 miles an hour, the ground shakes, and with a jingle and a clatter they're gone. The drivers aren't allowed to stop for hitchhikers, and even if they were, it would be dangerous to try to stop on such a small, curving road.

The old people, mostly Canadians looking at the fall leaves, as if they don't have them at home, stare out at me with the surprised, bemused expression tourists get when they see a moose beside the road: *What's that? Oh, too late for the camera*. I've learned from experience that elderly tourists never pick you up and neither do Canadians—maybe they've seen too many movies about American hitchhiking killers—and old Canadians are the worst prospect for a ride that I can think of. I try to look friendly and harmless, but just in case there are any maniacs out today, I also try not to look like someone who'd be easy to pick up and carry off into the woods and kill.

The Canadians wave brightly and speed on.

A couple in a car with a Quebec license plate slow down and turn into the parking lot. I run over to their car, assuming they've stopped to give me a ride.

"Gee, thanks for stopping! I really appreciate it! Would you mind giving a tired hiker a ride to town?" I ask breathlessly.

They glance at each other, taken aback. It's obvious they had no intention of giving me a ride and hadn't even seen me until I ran up to their window. I babble something about how I've been living in the woods for six months and am trying to get back to civilization now. They've never heard of the Trail and don't know what I'm talking about.

"Uh, we're going to go hiking up here." They tell me the name of the side trail. It's a short one, a loop up to a view and back. They're clearly reluctant to give me a ride, but I'm desperate. I say if I don't get another ride, I'll wait for them to come back after their hike. Politely, they nod.

They disappear into the woods. No cars go by for a very long time. The sun is touching the top of the mountain; I'm standing in shade, and it's getting colder. I take some more layers of clothes out of my pack and put them on.

A park ranger comes by and says he's on official business and can't take me now, but at the end of his shift he'll pass this way again and if I'm still there he'll take me.

The Canadians should have been back long ago, but they're not. I wonder if I should go looking for them. They're old, they don't seem like woodspeople, and they didn't take any food or water. I imagine they're hiding in the woods, watching me from behind a spruce tree, muttering, "Isn't she gone yet?"

I scuff patterns in the dust with my feet, sing "Wabash Cannonball" about a hundred times, wash my face and hands with a wet towelette I found back in Gorham, clean my nails with my Swiss Army knife, listen to ravens spreading the raven news, caw news of my own back to them, and let them spread it farther on down the Trail. I can almost see a tree down the road turning colors; it seems to be getting redder as the day wears on and night approaches. More logging trucks. No more old Canadians—they're probably all in nearby towns, eating supper. Which I would love to do. I'm all out of food and have one snack left, a single granola bar, which I'm saving for a dire emergency. This isn't dire yet. There's always the ranger, always the people from Quebec whose car I'm effectively holding hostage. If no one returns, I'll just camp nearby and get up and hitch again in the morning. Eventually some of the weekenders whose cars are parked here will have to come back.

Ages pass. I consult the map and look at the trail the people from Quebec said they were taking. Even allowing time for a picnic, which it's too cold for, it shouldn't have taken them more than an hour or two. They're probably lurking up there watching the road, watching me scuff around in the dirt and peel bark and polish stones, listening to my thin songs floating up to them. I imagine them cursing in French: *Merde,* she's still there!

I take out the granola bar and hold it in my hand. It's so light. I toss it in the air and catch it, over and over again. I catch it delicately, as if it's a butterfly or a rare bird. I can feel the bumpy, crunchy little oats through the wrapper. I imagine that I can smell the peanut butter flavor. The bar has broken in half in my pack, and I can flex it back and forth. The two ends grind crisply together inside the package. It's crunchy, all right.

Maybe I could just eat half.

I unwrap the bar, and before I know what I'm doing, it's gone.

A man in a pickup stops. He's an unlikely angel. We talk as we drive nine miles to Bethel, the nearest town. Gorham is too far away, in the other direction, and this is great for now.

The man has the classic Maine accent—"pizzer" for "pizza," "cah" for "car"—and is a type I love: a ranter. He's an American classic—an ornery, independent, outdoorsy type who thinks Maine is being ruined by people moving in from New York and other Eastern cities. He has big plans to move to Alaska, live in the bush, then agitate to have Alaska secede from the United States. He's happy to hear that I've been living in the woods for six months; it gives him hope for humanity, and he admires it even more because it's such an odd and tough-seeming thing for a woman to do. He asks my political views. I'm not interested in debate. I already know my views; I want to hear more of his. I make noncommittal noises and ask him about his work, which leads into an entertaining monologue. We are allied in our distaste for bosses and managers, insurance agents, landlords, and other parasites. He's a self-employed contractor and handyman, perfectly equipped to build his own cabin in the tundra. He's divorced and told his teenage son, who apparently is just like him, that he'll take him too. It'll only take a few years for them to save the rest of the money they need, and then they'll kiss those New Yorkers and suburbanites and goddamned developers goodbye.

I wish him well. In the same way he's pleased to see a woman who's not afraid to live in the woods, I'm pleased to see someone who has strong, almost crackpot views. This has always been a quirk of mine: Even if I disagree with someone, I'm gratified by the fact that they have a strong opinion. A strong opinion about anything is better than a weak opinion about nothing. Religious zealots, political extremists, ranters, and tract-passers always entertain me, and I never argue; the stranger their views, the more gratified I am to find them, like someone collecting rare butterflies. The exotics, the kooks, the rare visitors to my mental ecosystem.

I wish this guy had a tract to hand out. This Alaskan secession plot is new, not the usual religious stuff. It's fresh, at least to me. And it has a certain attraction—the frontier, the new place, the escape. It mirrors the last 10 years of my life: Looking for something? Keep moving, maybe you'll find it.

I stay in a B&B in Bethel, and the next day a kind, shy old man from the auto parts store gives me a ride back to Gorham, where I settle in at the Hiker's Paradise. It's good to be back. I need a place that's halfway between the hike and civilization, a place to rest and decompress before I go. The next few days, it rains a lot. I spend time in the hostel, resting and taking baths. The drain won't close, so I fill a zip-lock bag with water, suck out the remaining air and seal it, and lay it against the drain hole before filling the tub. The heaviness of the water and the suction action of the drain pull it down against the opening, making a tight seal. I feel smug. Give a hiker a zip-lock bag and some duct tape, and there's nothing she can't do.

Other hikers filter in and out. They sit in the common area, talking about Maine, sorting food, dreaming of Katahdin. We cook lobsters from the seafood store next door. I feel peaceful, removed, happy they're walking on, but I don't have much to say. They're in another stream of life, still on the Trail. I'm not sure what stream I'm in, but it feels good to be here.

I go to the thrift store and buy books, and lie on my bunk reading them. It's such a luxury. I put my empty pack on, walk two miles to the grocery store, fill it with a heavy load of food, walk home, and cook big dinners for whatever hikers show up: roasted chicken with mushroom gravy and mashed potatoes, spaghetti, chili. My knees are OK when I walk on flat ground, but going up stairs, and even getting up and down from chairs, is agony. I'm deeply tired, the kind of tired, remote feeling you get from the flu.

I go for a walk in the nearby woods. They're full of diseased trees, marked with bracket fungi and red ribbons for cutting. It rains some more. These woods feel spooky, neglected, dangerous not because of animals but because of the presence of people. I walk slowly, exhausted, and lean down to pick up birch paper without bending my knees.

I wonder why I'm walking when I'd rather be in bed at the hostel, reading, or lying in the bathtub. It's hard to get walking out of your system when it's been your job for the past six months. Also, even though I want to rest, I'm unable to. My body has forgotten what it's like to be still.

After a few days I get a ride to Boston with the city manager from a nearby town. He overhears me asking about the price of tickets at the convenience store/gas station/bus stop and offers me a free ride instead, since he's filling up on gas and is on his way there for business. I size him up and say yes.

As we drive, he talks about the need to manage loggers' needs with ecological demands, about vitamins in the diet, about his daughters from a previous marriage, running, science fiction and whether its function is to predict the future or to comment on the here and now, and a host of other topics. He turns and looks at me.

"You have a lot of energy," he says. "A real powerhouse, almost hyperactive."

By my standards I'm tired, worn out, and injured, but after spending months strenuously exercising 10 hours a day, the few days' rest has left me feeling pent-up and, by normal people's standards, incredibly energetic. My knees ache from the unchanging bent position, and I look at the mountains speeding by the window and want to get out and walk. Sitting still in the car is difficult. I feel as if I'm filled with a kind of radiant force, barely contained, as if I could move things just by looking at them. That must be what he's talking about.

We pass a moose standing in a pond, chewing, looking moodily at the passing cars. How strange to see it here. Like the moose, I feel out of place: too much concrete. What is to be done?

"You need to channel that energy," he says. True. Well, as soon as I learn to sit still again, maybe I can.

We pass through a small New Hampshire town, and my throat closes up at the sight of six-story buildings. Billboards. Strip malls. Fast-food joints. Crap. Then we get on the highway again, speeding between rock outcroppings and more mountains on fire with fall, and I almost cry at this final glimpse of the mountains that have been my home for the last six months.

He tells me about his family. He asks if I plan to have children, and I say I don't know.

"Why not?"

"I just think my temperament and personality are unsuitable. I'd make a better aunt than a mother. Actually, a better uncle."

I wonder why he's asking. People ask the strangest questions; it says more about what's on their minds than about you. I get the feeling I've come up short in his estimation because of my apparent flightiness, my history of wandering, my unchanneled energy, my refusal to fit into a neat social category. How do I know if I'll ever have children? I've just spent six months figuring out that being with a man isn't for me. *Ask me again in a few years,* I feel like saying. And if anyone ever calls me fickle again, I'll tell them to hike for six months and then come talk to me about perseverance.

Return

When a heart insists on its destiny, resisting the general blandishment, then the agony is great; so too the danger. Forces, however, have been set in motion beyond the reckoning of the senses. Sequences of events from the corners of the world will draw gradually together, and miracles of coincidence bring the inevitable to pass.

—Joseph Campbell, *The Hero With a Thousand Faces*

September 22
Grafton Notch, Maine

Chapter Eleven

On the train, on the way home. To Wisconsin. It's a night of trying to sleep in various uncomfortable positions, with my legs draped over my pack and my sleeping bag wadded up to lean against. It's a hundred kinds of knee agonies—the only time they don't hurt is when my legs are straight, and that's impossible in the coach section of the train.

I wake from a groggy haze in the night and glance outside, and the flatness of the land hits me like a slap. We're crossing Indiana. Of course I knew it would be flat—I come from a flat place and have always loved the plains—but I've forgotten, forgotten deep down, and this is like a punch in the gut. I close my eyes and pull down the window shade. Where are the mountains? Those big curves, always there, enfolding you—it's like being used to sleeping with a lover, and then one day you wake up and find her gone with no explanation, the sheets unwrinkled and empty. This land is like an abstract concept in geometry: an infinite plane, inhuman.

I wonder whether people are simply not designed to travel so quickly between such vastly different landscapes. I think about the long road trips my parents took us on when we were little, and about more recent drives and trips in airplanes and on trains, that feeling of exhaustion and unreality that overtakes you, even though you've just been sitting all day and theoretically should be rested. You never are. You get off the plane from Wisconsin after only a couple of hours, and suddenly the white snow is white sand, and the 20-below-zero weather is transformed into 90 degrees and an ocean breeze. You think back to that morning, to getting on the plane, and it seems like an impossibly remote dream, a lifetime ago.

When you walk, you know the distance you've covered in your tired bones, and it's impossible to go so far that you lose the thread of continuity between "there" and "here." Walking connects you to the land, it sews a seam between you and it that is very hard to unstitch. As I walked the Trail, every mountain I went over became a part of me; months or years from now, I believe I could go back to any section of the Trail and remember the terrain, what to expect, where the springs are.

Now, going back to Wisconsin after such a long absence—a six-month, 1,800-mile absence—I don't know what to expect, but I'd better figure it out soon, because I'll be there within a day. It's not much time to prepare.

Across the aisle, an Army guy in uniform has his light on. He's painstakingly coloring an *Aladdin* coloring book with a 64-color box of Crayolas. Neatly, never straying outside the lines, he fills in every space, softly and evenly, with delicate parallel strokes. The overhead light is gentle on his face and hands, soft. What would his sergeant say if he could see him? And I wonder, Why aren't adults encouraged to color? It looks therapeutic. If everyone in the Army spent time coloring, what would the state of our national security be? It reminds me of that bumper sticker that says something about what would happen if the school system got all the money it needed and the Army had to have a bake sale to raise money for bombs.

In the bathroom on the train I find a $100 bill on the floor, half-hidden behind the toilet. I find it because of a habit I learned on the Trail: When you leave a place, always turn and look it over as you walk away to be sure you haven't left anything behind. Obviously, the person who lost the money wasn't a hiker.

No one claims it. It's more Trail magic, a parting gift to ease the transition to civilization. Apart from this found money, I'm completely broke.

I ready myself for a shock and look out the window again. The plains are still there, still flat, but they don't look as bad this time. All those months of walking, seeing the local people so at one with their land and their regional culture, listening to their accents, I wished I had a region and a culture too. Now I know what it is: Wisconsin. It's my home, it's where I come from. Even if I eventually go elsewhere, I'll always be from there. I'll always have that Wisconsin accent that makes people in other parts of the country ask if I'm from Canada. The Great Lakes, the wide land, the rivers and forests. The people. I'm going home.

The moon, riding over the wide farmlands, is in eclipse, the full disk slowly being eaten by the shadow of the earth. There was a lunar eclipse the night I left for the Trail. I saw it from the train on the way from the Midwest to Georgia, traveling the other way on these same tracks across the plains. This is a strange coincidence, a bracketing of time. Between these two eclipses, you will travel and be protected. And you will change.

When I was a child I read books about white pioneer children who were adopted into Native American tribes but eventually were taken back by their original white families. These children, after years in the woods, were often unable to adjust to the culture that had produced them. Shoes chafed them, chairs made them squirm, and beds were strange contraptions. In the morning their parents would find them sleeping on the floor. The settlers' neat, square houses were a claustrophobic hell. Forget about sitting still in church, neatly in a pew, hands folded, listening to a preacher talk for several hours!

I've only spent six months in the woods and have had contact with civilization fairly often during that time, but the return is difficult. Other hikers have told me that when they returned they fell into a depression. They missed the Trail and its simple life, they missed their Trail buddies, and now that they were back they still weren't sure what they wanted to do with their lives; or else they had learned that they needed a change but didn't know what it was or how to make it happen.

Now that I'm back, I don't want this to happen to me. I want to move on. I'm no longer on the Trail, and I don't want to spend the rest of my life wishing I were. I do want my life after the Trail to have the same kind of flow, the same kind of openness and rightness and sense of home. I've changed, and now I'm beginning to see how.

On the Trail, your old difficulties, obsessions, and problems follow you, riding in your pack, making you tired, until you eventually outwalk them. You're not the same person, and you have a different view of your limitations. The horizon, a place that looks so far away, isn't that far. You look at it and know you've outwalked it many times. All your old limitations seem to fall away. If you put your mind to something, you can do it—if you really want to. Set a goal. You can reach it.

Knowing this, and knowing that a 9-to-5 job will only make me miserable, I decide to start my own business, to freelance. This leap, which would have seemed huge before the Trail, seems not only painless, but fun. I can keep the freedom I've found on the Trail, to choose the work I want to do, to walk for hours every day, to look at the sky, the trees, and the lake.

I send out résumés and get steady freelance work almost immediately. I'm grateful for this good fortune, which is a gift: Trail magic continuing onward.

The physical transition, the change in routine, is more difficult. For the winter after I return to civilization, I can't go to the movies. I can't sit still, enclosed in a room, for any length of time. Rooms make me restless; closed windows make me feel like I'm suffocating. Like the pioneer children brought back from the wilderness, I sleep on the floor. I go for several days without taking a shower, wearing the same clothes, because my concept of cleanliness has changed. If I haven't sweated in my clothes, they don't seem dirty. I go on walks that last all day; 20 miles on flat land, with no pack, is effortless compared to hiking on the Trail. One day I walk to a friend's house to say hello. She lives 22 miles away.

Soon after returning from the Trail I meet friends at a three-day writers' conference, and instead of actually attending the panels, discussions, and readings, I end up spending the entire weekend in the hotel pool and gym because I'm unable to sit still in rows of chairs in an enclosed room, listening to people talk. The discussion seems inbred and irrelevant: people talking about reading, reading about writing, writing about talking. Words on words, and nothing concrete and real, just this fog of talk in stuffy rooms without windows. I feel like Spooky Joe, the man who scared so many hikers on the Trail. It's all I can do not to throw a shirt over my face and mutter, "You *writers,* all you ever talk about is your *words* and your *books* and other *writers,* and then more writers come, and you talk about your *words* and your *books,* over and over again..."

Instead I run and swim, happy to be alive. My friends, who are mostly sedentary, as writers often are, all end up in the pool and exercise room too, horsing around, running on the treadmill for as long as possible, playing games, seeing who can swim the farthest and hold their breath the longest. The conference is a lot more fun now that we're all in motion.

I stay for a while with my friends Rob and Troy in Madison, and then move to a cooperative household—some would call it a commune—of 40 adults, four children, and four cats, in a four-story brick house, originally built to be a sorority house, on the shore of Lake Mendota. Although there's heat in the bedrooms, the only heating in the communal rooms of the house comes from a wood stove and the ovens in the kitchen. This suits me fine; even on subzero days, in my bedroom I leave the window open and don't turn on the heat. I'm used to the cold, the fresh air, and I love the continued necessity and ritual of making a fire in the stove downstairs. The frozen lake outside, ideal for cross-country skiing, is a refuge, and so are the nearby state parks. The casual, shared-space, shared-chores, we're-all-in-this-together, tribal feeling of the household is as close to the Trail as you can get and still stay in one place. In addition, everyone in the house is "moving" in the spiritual sense, looking for something, reflecting on their lives and values. I like this sense of motion and shared destination, but even in the midst of this, I know the house and its community is only a transitional place for me and that eventually I'll leave it. I don't know how soon this will be, but I'll keep my options open.

Nomad and I get in touch again and talk on the phone. Like me, she's going to freelance. "Look," she says, "I don't know what all that crazy shit was all about at the end when we went our separate ways, but I'm sorry."

"Yeah, me too," I say. "I think we were all just too worn out and malnourished and tired. Everyone was getting cranky. I'm still proud to be your friend. You were the best traveling buddy anyone could have."

"You too," she says. "I would have quit in Virginia if I hadn't met you. Thanks for a great trip."

In October, two weeks after I get back from the Trail, I get a letter from Gladys. She writes:

> ...I wanted to tell you how much of an inspiration you were that day and for many to

> follow...when you get a chance, please drop a line. I would like to know that you have made it back safely...

I write back. Then she writes back: "I had so many questions and things to say to you, but just didn't quite know how to say them." We talk on the phone, and feel again that deep kinship we felt on the Trail, the deep connection, the mysterious coincidence that brought us together. We are shy with each other, both overwhelmed by the intensity of the connection we feel and by the opposing fact that, logically speaking, we don't know each other at all.

We get to know each other through daily letters and phone calls. I tell her about my life, my family, the trip, and she tells me about the war in Lebanon, about living on the Green Line between the two warring halves of Beirut, about the shells that flew over her house and exploded nearby, about the sniper who targeted her family's kitchen—whenever anyone opened the refrigerator door and the little light went on, he'd fire at them through the window, so for two weeks they stayed out of the kitchen, crawled around on the floor out of sight, and starved, until someone else finally picked him off. She tells me how they had to shoot out the streetlights and run, zigzag, up the street in the dark, when they fled the war in Beirut and headed for the mountains.

"We lived on a mountaintop in a stone house with no running water for a year," she says. "I loved it. That was the best time of my life. I love camping because it feels the same way: free."

I'm impressed. Other refugees I've known who lived in similar conditions hate camping because it reminds them of the hell they've been through. She's resilient and positive; I admire the way she found the best in that experience.

When she came to the United States she spoke French and Arabic but no English, but immediately went to college anyway, at age 16, to study biochemistry. But she's not a one-sided scientist. She's warm, human, and funny, full of contradictions: rides a motorcycle but loves the opera; reads French literature but her favorite TV show is *I Love Lucy*; loves to travel but also loves being home; is perfectly at ease in New York City and also in the woods. You'd never know she's a doctor; she's modest, not interested in material things, and down-to-earth.

Now, that's my kind of woman, I think. *She's worth walking all those miles for.*

In April, a year after I began walking the Trail, I pack everything I own into my little blue car and head east. My job, unlike hers, is portable, so it's logical that I should be the one to move.

It's a leap of faith. After all, the last time I did this, I got burned. My friends are skeptical. They've seen me being stupid before. They don't know what I've been through; don't know what I've learned, walking over the mountains. This time, I know what I'm doing.

Gladys and I live together in a rented flat, and it's like we've known each other all our lives and been together forever.

In August our landlady dies, and instead of renting again and throwing our money away, we buy a house. It's a cottage surrounded by oak trees, on the beach in a small fishing village on the ocean, only an hour and a half from New York City. We find the house almost by accident, on the day our old landlady, who was like a grandmother to us, would have turned 95. She was concerned about us, and worried about what we would do and where we would go after she died, and it's almost like she's still looking out for us.

"Thanks, Meama," we say, and put her picture on the mantel. We transplant irises from her old garden to our new home, a reminder of our first place together, a reminder of our happiness, our rootedness together. For the first time in both our adult lives we feel grounded, at home. We paint a white blaze on our gate: The Trail led us both here, an unlikely ending to a trek through the mountains.

A few weeks after we move into the house, we go for a walk on the beach. The water is calm, the waves so soft we can barely hear them. The stars are all spread out overhead. Farther down the beach, one light shines over the water, and a heron is hunting there where the fish are drawn to the light.

I think about the Trail: how much it meant and how far it led me—to such unexpected happiness. I think about Katahdin, how I never got there, and how someday I'd like to go there and truly finish the trip.

We hold hands and walk. "We have a trip to do next summer," Gladys says, reading my mind.

"Oh? Where are we going?"

"To Maine."

"Maine? How did you know?"

She grins; I see her teeth flash in the reflected light. "We're going to finish the Trail. We're going to do the part you missed. We'll do the 100-Mile Wilderness and hike up Katahdin. Only this time, it will be different."

"You bet it will," I say. "Because this time, we'll do it together."

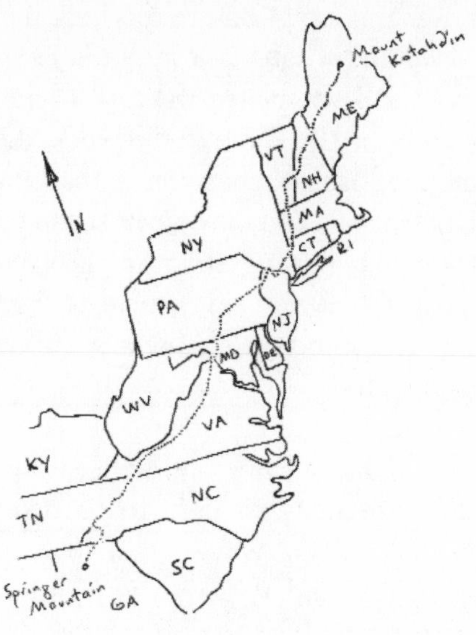

Epilogue: Passing It On

On the Trail my name was Amazin' Grace, a name given to me in a dream. The name says a lot about the experience; the trip *was* grace in the spiritual sense, a gift handed to me when I was lost and confused and needed help.

Out there hiking, or standing at the edge of the road looking for rides, I felt what the writer Natalie Goldberg describes as "Great Determination." She quotes her Zen Buddhist mentor, Katagiri Roshi, who told her, "Your little will can't do anything. It takes Great Determination. Great Determination doesn't mean just you making an effort. It means the whole universe is behind you and with you—the birds, trees, sky, moon, and ten directions." This is how I felt on the trip, and it was a gift, something I had not earned, a journey given to me for reasons I didn't understand but that I trusted. I believed in the absolute necessity of what I was doing; if I quit before reaching the place I needed to get to, wherever and whatever it might be, I would have to keep coming back until I completed the task I had been given. I felt, simply, blessed to be there, doing the work, doing the walk.

One thing the Trail teaches you is that when you get a gift, you have to pass it on. You may never see the people who helped you again—you may never even know their names—so you can't pay them back. What you do instead is "pay forward": Help some other hiker, someone else who's looking for something, who's struggling along.

This is what I want to pass on:

I realize now that all my wandering came from not having found the life I needed. It's easy to be dedicated, stable, and grounded if you're doing what's right for you. Or if, as in too many cases, you're afraid, if secretly you know you haven't found your true life but can't bear to take the risk of losing the half-life you have. Fear keeps more people in one place than happiness does, because sometimes finding happiness requires taking risks.

If you're someone like that, I want to encourage you to take that risk. Whatever it is. It may not be a hike on the Trail; in fact, it probably won't. It may not involve a physical journey at all. Maybe you're unhappy in love; take a risk and be alone for a while. Maybe you want to start your own business. Do it. Maybe you've always wanted to be an artist but keep telling yourself you don't have time, it doesn't pay the bills. You pass an art store and see the bright rainbow of paints in the window, and something in you aches. Go inside. Buy a set, even a small one, and try it. Be patient. Be open to the process. Listen. Talk to other people in the same situation.

Give your heart to the path, and beauty will come.

Works Cited

Attar, Farid ud-Din, *The Conference of the Birds*, translated by C.S. Nott. Copyright © 1954 by C.S. Nott. Reprinted by permission of Pir Publications, Inc., Accord, NY.

Campbell, Joseph, *The Hero With a Thousand Faces,* copyright © 1949 by Princeton University Press. Reprinted by permission of Princeton University Press.

Chah, Achaan, edited by Jack Kornfeld and Paul Breiter, *A Still Forest Pool: The Insight Meditation of Achaan Chah*, copyright © 1985 by Theosophical Publishing House. Used by permission of Theosophical Publishing House.

Goldberg, Natalie, *Writing Down the Bones,* copyright © 1986 by Natalie Goldberg. Reprinted by arrangement with Shambhala Publications, Inc., Boston, www.shambhala.com.

Niebuhr, Richard R. "Pilgrims and Pioneers," reprinted from *Parabola: The Magazine of Myth and Tradition,* Vol. IX, No. 3 (Fall, 1980).

Snyder, Gary. *The Practice of the Wild,* copyright © 1990 by Gary Snyder. Reprinted by permission of North Point Press, a division of Farrar, Straus and Giroux LLC.

For more information on hiking the Appalachian Trail, please contact the Appalachian Trail Conference, P.O. Box 807, Harpers Ferry, WV 25425. They provide hikers with books, maps, advice, volunteer trail-maintaining opportunities, and connections to other folks who are interested in the Trail.